Life
a Loaded Gun

My Life a Loaded Gun

. . . .
. . . .
. . . .

Dickinson, Plath, Rich, and Female Creativity

PAULA BENNETT

UNIVERSITY OF ILLINOIS PRESS

Urbana and Chicago

Illini Books edition, 1990

© 1986 by Paula Bennett. Reprinted by arrangement with Beacon Press.
Manufactured in the United States of America
P   5   4   3   2   1

This book is printed on acid-free paper.

Library of Congress Cataloging-in-Publication Data

Bennett, Paula.
    My life, a loaded gun : Dickinson, Plath, Rich, and female
creativity / Paula Bennett.
        p.   cm.
    Includes bibliographical references.
    ISBN 0-252-06117-9 (alk. paper)
    1. American poetry—Women authors—History and criticism.
2. Dickinson, Emily, 1830-1886—Criticism and interpretation.
3. Rich, Adrienne Cecile—Criticism and interpretation.   4. Plath,
Sylvia—Criticism and interpretation.   5. Feminism and literature—
United States.   6. Women and literature—United States.
7. Creation (Literary, artistic, etc.)   8. Women authors—
Psychology.   I. Title.
PS147.B46   1990
811.009'9287—dc20   89-28909
                                                          CIP

To Marta and Erin

It is from the knowledge of the
genuine conditions of our lives that
we must draw our strength to live and our
reasons for acting.
—Simone de Beauvoir

Contents

Acknowledgments

In order to be faithful to the circumstances of this book's creation, I would have to acknowledge the contribution of virtually every person I have known and every book I have read. Since this is manifestly impossible, I would like to thank the following individuals whose advice, encouragement, and support had a direct effect on the writing of *My Life:* Sally Bolger Bobbitt, Margaret Cruikshank, Joe De Roche, Jim Doan, Rachel Blau DuPlessis, Marcia Folsom, Lillian Faderman, Linda Gardiner, Jonathan Goldberg, Marilyn Hacker, Jane Lilienfeld, Judith McDaniel, Roslyn Reed, Ellen Cronan Rose (*My Life*'s official godmother), Rochelle Ruthchild, Judith Saunders, Mary Sharkey, David Tutein, Dean Marilyn Wiener, Bonnie Zimmerman, and the anonymous gentleman from Chicago who wrote "crap" all over the margins of the original introduction. I would also like to thank the following groups and organizations that intersected my life during the period in which this book was written and that contributed to it one way or another: the editorial collective of *Focus: A Journal for Lesbians*, the Gay and Lesbian Caucus for the Modern Language Association, the WOBBLES book club, the staffs of the Dartmouth College Library and the Schlesinger Library at Radcliffe College, my students at University College, Northeastern University, the participants in the parent/child workshops held at the DeSisto School, West Stockbridge, Massachusetts, and the central office staff of the Lincoln Public Schools and the Lincoln School Board, past and present, which has put up with me and my book since 1980.

For their thorough readings of the entire manuscript and crucial editorial assistance, I would like to thank Kate Dunn, Joanna Hopkins, Estella Lauter and, above all, Susan Riley Solberg: "Do not cease, Sister. Should I turn in my long night I should murmur 'Sue'." Without their critiques at key junctures in its composition, this book would not have the shape it does. My errors are my own.

I would like to thank Beacon Press for holding the manuscript for so many years and for having faith in its ultimate completion, given all the deadlines I set and passed.

Finally, I would like to thank three persons whose influence upon me and my thought has been profound: Edward W. Tayler of Columbia University, who first taught me how to read a poem, and Donna O'Connell Blatt, L.I.C.S.W., and Michael DeSisto, director of the DeSisto School, who over the past two years have helped me live *My Life* at last. It's so much easier to know than it is to do.

Abbreviations

Citations to all primary sources appear directly in the text together with page numbers. In the case of Dickinson, poems have also been numbered according to the Johnson system for ease of recognition. The following abbreviations have been used:

EMILY DICKINSON

L   *The Letters of Emily Dickinson.* Edited by Thomas H. Johnson and Theodora Ward. 3 vols. Cambridge, Mass.: Belknap Press of Harvard University Press, 1958.

MS   *The Manuscript Books of Emily Dickinson.* Edited by R. W. Franklin. 2 vols. Cambridge, Mass.: Belknap Press of Harvard University Press, 1981.

P   *The Poems of Emily Dickinson* Edited by Thomas H. Johnson. 3 vols. Cambridge, Mass.: Belknap Press of Harvard University Press, 1955.

SYLVIA PLATH

BJ   *The Bell Jar.* New York: Harper and Row, 1971.

CP   *The Collected Poems of Sylvia Plath.* Edited by Ted Hughes. New York: Harper and Row, 1981.

LH   *Letters Home: Correspondence 1950–1963.* Selected and edited with commentary by Aurelia Schober Plath. New York: Harper and Row, 1975.

JP   *Johnny Panic and the Bible of Dreams: Short Stories, Prose and Diary Excerpts.* Edited by Ted Hughes. New York: Harper and Row, 1979.

J   *The Journals of Sylvia Plath*. Foreword by Ted Hughes. Edited by Ted Hughes and Frances McCullough. New York: The Dial Press, 1982.

ADRIENNE RICH

CW   *A Change of World*. New Haven: Yale University Press, 1951.

DC   *The Diamond Cutters and Other Poems*. New York: Harper and Brothers, 1955.

DW   *Diving into the Wreck: Poems 1971–1972*. New York: W. W. Norton, 1973.

DCL   *The Dream of a Common Language: Poems 1974–1977*. New York: W. W. Norton, 1978.

FD   *The Fact of a Doorframe: Poems Selected and New 1950–1984*. New York: W. W. Norton, 1984.

Lf   *Leaflets: Poems 1965–1968*. New York: W. W. Norton, 1969.

NL   *Necessities of Life: Poems 1962–1965*. New York: W. W. Norton, 1966.

OWB   *Of Woman Born: Motherhood as Experience and Institution*. New York: W. W. Norton, 1976.

OL   *On Lies, Secrets and Silence: Selected Prose 1966–1978*. New York: W. W. Norton, 1979.

PSN   *Poems Selected and New: Poems 1950–1974*. New York. W. W. Norton, 1975.

SDL   *Snapshots of a Daughter-in-Law: Poems 1954–1962*. New York: W. W. Norton, 1969.

S   *Sources*. Woodside, Calif.: The Heyeck Press, 1983.

NJG   "Split at the Root," in *Nice Jewish Girls: A Lesbian Anthology*. Edited by Evelyn Torton Beck. Watertown, Mass.: Persephone Press, 1982, pp. 67–84.

WP   *A Wild Patience Has Taken Me This Far: Poems 1978–1981*. New York: W. W. Norton, 1981.

WC   *The Will to Change: Poems 1968–1970*. New York: W. W. Norton, 1971.

Credits

Grateful acknowledgment is made for permission to reprint the following: lines from "Medussa" from *The Blue Estuaries: Poems 1923–68* by Louise Bogan, copyright 1922, copyright © renewed 1949, 1968 by Louise Bogan, by permission of Farrar, Straus, & Giroux;

"Give Me Back" by Chrystos from *This Bridge Called My Back*, edited by Cherrie Moraga and Gloria Anzaldua, by permission of Kitchen Table Press;

poems from *The Complete Poems of Emily Dickinson* edited by Thomas H. Johnson, Copyright 1914, 1929, 1935, 1942 by Martha Dickinson Bianchi, copyright renewed 1957, 1963 by Mary L. Hampson, by permission of Little, Brown and Company;

poems from *The Poems of Emily Dickinson* edited by Thomas H. Johnson, Cambridge, Mass.: The Belknap Press of Harvard University Press, copyright 1951, © 1955, 1979, 1983 by the President and Fellows of Harvard College, reprinted by permission of the publishers and Trustees of Amherst College;

lines from "I have a Bird in Spring" from *Emily Dickinson Face to Face* by Martha Dickinson Bianchi, copyright 1932 by Martha Dickinson Bianchi, copyright © renewed 1960 by Alfred Leete Hampson, by permission of Houghton Mifflin Company;

"Title divine is mine" from *Life and Letters of Emily Dickinson* by Martha Dickinson Bianchi, copyright 1924, copyright renewed 1952 by Alfred Leete Hampson, reprinted by permission of Houghton Mifflin Company;

"Medusa" from *Wells* by Rachel Blau DuPlessis, copyright © 1980, reprinted by permission of the author;

"A Woman Is Talking to Death" from *The Work of a Common Woman, the Collected Poetry of Judy Grahn, 1964–1977* by Judy Grahn, copyright © 1978 Judy Grahn, by permission of The Crossing Press;

"In Mind" from *Poems, 1960–67* by Denise Levertov, copyright © 1963 by

and History," "Transcendental Etude," and "Sibling Mysteries" from *The Dream of a Common Language: Poems 1974–1977* by Adrienne Rich, W. W. Norton, 1978;

"Mother-in-Law," "Rift," "Images," and "Turning the Wheel" from *A Wild Patience Has Carried Me This Far: Poems 1978–1981* by Adrienne Rich, W. W. Norton, 1981;

and "North American Time" and the excerpts from *Sources* from *The Fact of a Doorframe: Poems Selected and New 1950–1984* by Adrienne Rich, W. W. Norton, 1978, all selections reprinted by permission of the author and W. W. Norton & Company, Inc.;

"Witch" by Jean Tepperman from *No More Masks* edited by Florence Howe and Ellen Bass, reprinted by permission of the author.

Introduction

. . . .
. . . .
. . . .

Ah, but what is "herself"? I mean, what is a woman? I
assure you, I do not know. I do not believe that you know. I
do not believe that anybody can know until she has expressed herself in all the arts and professions open to human
skill.
—Virginia Woolf

Like every artist, the woman poet is gifted. And
her gift, her creative power, carries with it, as such gifts so often do, a curse.
For insofar as she seeks to exercise her power, the woman poet qua woman is
an anomaly, unable to fit our society's definition of what a woman is. What
she does with this paradoxical blessing, how she learns to live with it or not,
and how her struggles relate to female creativity and to women's lives in
general is what this book is about.

. . .

When asked by the Women's Service League to speak on the employment of
women, the British novelist Virginia Woolf responded by describing what
she called two adventures of her professional life. The first occurred when as
a novice reviewer she found that she could not speak her mind unless she
first did "battle with a certain phantom." The phantom was a woman and
Woolf called her after the heroine of a phenomenally popular nineteenth-

century poem by Coventry Patmore, "The Angel in the House." "Had I not killed her," Woolf reports,

> she would have killed me. She would have plucked the heart out of my writing. For, as I found, directly I put pen to paper, you cannot review even a novel without having a mind of your own, without expressing what you think to be the truth about human relations, morality, sex. And all these questions, according to the Angel of the House, cannot be dealt with freely and openly by women; they must charm, they must conciliate, they must—to put it bluntly—tell lies if they are to succeed.[1]

To Woolf, the Angel represented everything a woman was supposed to be: sympathetic, charming, utterly unselfish, domestic, self-sacrificing, and, above all, pure. Her nature was, of course, fictitious but therein lay the roots of her immense appeal. It was, Woolf discovered, "far harder to kill a phantom than a reality." Yet kill her she must if she wished to be an effective writer. Indeed, "Killing the Angel in the House," Woolf decided, "was part of the occupation of a woman writer" and necessary to pursuit of her craft.[2]

Woolf was less sure of how successful she was in her second adventure. Having turned to the writing of novels, she found that though she might kill the Angel, learning to tell "the truth about [her] own experiences as a body" was a very different matter, for here the artist's imagination ran foul of the censor within.[3] Exploring "the depths, the dark places" of the self, she discovered "something about the body, about the passions which it was unfitting for her as a woman to say," and, quite involuntarily, she was "roused from her dream," the imaginative dream that made art possible. Aware that she had come in contact with feelings and needs that were unacceptable in women, she was "left in a state of the most acute and difficult distress," the full promise of her creativity thwarted by inhibitions deriving from her sex.[4]

If Woolf is speaking accurately in these passages of the difficulties that confront the woman reviewer and the woman novelist, she is speaking even more poignantly of the conflicts that beset the woman poet. To adopt Woolf's terms, poetry, or more precisely lyric poetry, is "the freest of all professions for women."[5] All it requires is paper and pen and, unlike writing novels, relatively brief periods of concentrated time. Of the literary genres, poetry should therefore be the easiest for women to pursue. Yet in striking contrast to women novelists, until the second half of this century significant women lyricists in our culture have been few and far between. To Woolf, writing in the first half of this century, there were—or seemed to be—none.

In *A Room of One's Own,* written before her speech to the Women's Service League, Woolf attributed the dearth of women poets largely to social factors. But it is the psychological issues that she raises in the speech that have proved the most serious impediments to women's successful pursuit of this particular genre or career. As the voice of her poem, the lyric poet must be willing to put herself on the line and stand at the center of her verse. These are *her* feelings, *her* thoughts. As Woolf observes, however, there are many feelings and thoughts that women in our culture, whether or not they are poets, simply are not supposed to have. And conspicuous among them are the very self-empowering ones (pride, anger, self-centeredness, daring, the need to assert oneself not just emotionally but intellectually) that are not only fundamental to the creative process but are absolutely indispensable to the creation of a convincing poetic persona or lyric self. For women, raised in a culture that denies them such feelings and thoughts by definition, the creation of lyric poetry must inevitably therefore be a self-alienating and even dangerous business in a way that other forms of writing are not. "If the novelist," Sandra Gilbert and Susan Gubar write of this problem,

> . . . inevitably sees herself from the *outside,* as an object, a character, a small figure in a large pattern, the lyric poet must be continually aware of herself from the *inside,* as a subject, a speaker: she must be, that is, assertive, authoritative, radiant with powerful feelings while at the same time absorbed in her own consciousness—and hence, by definition, profoundly "unwomanly," even freakish.

"For the woman poet," they conclude, alluding ominously—and somewhat misleadingly—to Woolf's unhappy tale of "Judith Shakespeare" in *A Room of One's Own,*

> the contradictions between her vocation and her gender might well become insupportable, impelling her to deny one or the other, even . . . driving her to suicide. For, as Woolf puts it, "who shall measure the heat and violence of the poet's heart when caught and tangled in a woman's body?"[6]

Most women poets have, of course, avoided the self-destruction that Woolf invents for Shakespeare's fictitious sister in her famous essay. With a few notable exceptions (Sylvia Plath prominent among them), they have not committed suicide. But the response of many, if not most, to the dilemma posed by their genre has in some ways been suicidal nonetheless. For unable or unwilling to kill "the Angel in the House" or to confront fully the truth of their own experience and feelings as women, poets from Anne Bradstreet and Christina Rossetti to Marianne Moore and Elizabeth Bishop have tended to suppress in their verse unacceptable elements within themselves instead. In flight from conventional notions of what a woman poet was supposed to be, some, Albert Gelpi writes, such as Moore, Bishop, and, I would add, the young Adrienne Rich

> tended to obscure or deflect passion and sexuality in favor of fine discriminations of perceptions and ideas. Others, such as Edna St. Vincent Millay and Elinor Wylie, took as their woman's strain precisely the thrill of emotion and tremor of sensibility which rendered them susceptible to the threats of the masculine "other."[7]

In either case, it was their poetry that lost. Where one in an effort to legitimize her power sought to transcend the perceived limitations of her gender by neutralizing her speaking voice, the other accepted the limitations and gave up her claim to everything else. Only a few women poets writing prior to the early 1960s (among the best known, Elizabeth Barrett Browning in *Aurora Leigh,* Emily Dickinson, Amy Lowell, and H. D., particularly in her later poems) actually made a serious and concerted effort to broaden their concept of womanhood and what was "fitting for . . . a woman to say" to express what they refused to "obscure or deflect" in themselves.

Lacking the male poet's long-established tradition of self-exploration and self-validation, women poets in our culture have been torn between restrictive definitions of what a woman is and their own fears of being or seeming unwomanly. As a result, they have been unable to allow the full truth of their experience to empower their speaking voice. Without predecessors to whom they might appeal or upon whom they might model themselves, they have either fit into the existing masculinist tradition, or they have worked within a subcultural tradition of their own—the literature of the "poetess." In either case, they have inevitably been led *to dissociate the concept of creative power from their woman selves.* Though often possessed, as in Bishop's case, of extraordinary gifts, they have rarely felt these gifts as inherently theirs.

For the woman poet to exercise her creativity to its fullest, she must first be able to heal the internal divisions that have historically distorted and controlled her relationship to her craft. The acceptance of the self, whatever that self is, is the base upon which the woman poet must work, the source of her greatest authority and strength. But for her to arrive at this self-acceptance, she must possess a definition of her womanhood that is broad enough, flexible enough, to encompass all that she actually is. Without such a definition, she can never fully own her powers or achieve in her poetry the depth and scope of which her experience might otherwise make her capable. Burdened with ambivalence and self-doubt, like too many creative women in every field, she will remain a stranger to herself and to other women.

·   ·   ·

No poem written by a woman poet more perfectly captures the nature, the difficulties, and the risks involved in this task of self-redefinition and self-empowerment than the poem that stands at the center of this book, Emily Dickinson's brilliant and enigmatic "My Life had stood—a Loaded Gun":[8]

My Life had stood—a Loaded Gun—
In Corners—till a Day
The Owner passed—identified—
And carried Me away—

And now We roam in Sovreign Woods—
And now We hunt the Doe—
And every time I speak for Him—
The Mountains straight reply—

And do I smile, such cordial light
Upon the Valley glow—
It is as a Vesuvian face
Had let it's pleasure through—

And when at Night—Our good Day done—
I guard My Master's Head—
'Tis better than the Eider-Duck's
Deep Pillow—to have shared—

To foe of His—I'm deadly foe—
None stir the second time—
On whom I lay a Yellow Eye—
Or an emphatic Thumb—

Though I than He—may longer live
He longer must—than I—
For I have but the power to kill,
Without—the power to die—
(no. 754; P, 574)*

Composed during the period when Dickinson had reached the height of
her poetic prowess, "My Life had stood" represents the poet's most extreme
attempt to characterize the Vesuvian nature of the power or art which she
believed was hers.⁹ Speaking through the voice of a gun, Dickinson presents
herself in this poem as everything "woman" is not: cruel not pleasant, hard
not soft, emphatic not weak, one who kills not one who nurtures. Just as
significant, she is proud of it, so proud that the temptation is to echo Robert
Lowell's notorious description of Sylvia Plath, and say that in "My Life had
stood," Emily Dickinson is "hardly a person at all, or a woman, certainly
not another 'poetess.'"¹⁰

Like the persona in Plath's *Ariel* poems, in "My Life had stood,"
Dickinson's speaker has deliberately shed the self-protective layers of conventional femininity, symbolized in the poem by the doe and the deep
pillow of the "masochistic" eider duck.¹¹ In the process the poet uncovers
the true self within, in all its hardness and rage, in its desire for revenge and
aggressive, even masculine, sexuality (for this is, after all, one interpretation of the gun in the poem). The picture of Dickinson that emerges, like
the picture of Plath that emerges from the "big strip tease" of "Lady
Lazarus" (CP245) and other *Ariel* poems, is not an attractive one. But,
again like Plath, Dickinson is prepared to embrace it nevertheless—together with all other aspects of her unacceptable self. Indeed, embracing
the true or unacceptable self appears to be the poem's raison d'etre, just as it
is the raison d'etre of Plath's last poems.

In writing "My Life had stood," Dickinson clearly transgresses limits no
woman, indeed no human being, could lightly afford to break. And to

---

*All quotations from Dickinson's *Poems* and *Letters* have been reprinted as they appear in the
Johnson variorum editions. No attempt has been made to regularize spelling, punctuation,
or grammar.

judge by the poem's final riddling stanza, a conundrum that critics have yet to solve satisfactorily, she knew this better than anyone. As Adrienne Rich has observed, Dickinson's underlying ambivalence toward the powers her speaker claims to exercise through her art (the powers to "hunt," "speak," "smile," "guard," and "kill") appears to be extreme. Of this ambivalence and its effect on women poets, Rich has written most poignantly, perhaps, because of her own position as poet. For Rich there is no easy way to resolve the conflict entangling Dickinson in the poem. "If there is a female consciousness in this poem," she writes,

> it is buried deeper than the images: it exists in the ambivalence toward power, which is extreme. Active willing and creation in women are forms of aggression, and aggression is both "the power to kill" and punishable by death. The union of gun with hunter embodies the danger of identifying and taking hold of her forces, not least that in so doing she risks defining herself—and being defined—as aggressive, as unwomanly ("and now We hunt the Doe"), and as potentially lethal. (OL, 174)

Yet despite these dangers and despite her recognition of the apparent dehumanization her persona courts, in "My Life had stood" Emily Dickinson does take precisely the risks that Rich describes. In the poem's terms, she is murderous. She is a gun. Her rage is part of her being. Indeed, insofar as it permits her to explode and hence to speak, rage defines her, unwomanly and inhuman though it is. Whatever constraints existed in her daily life (the breathless and excessive femininity so well described by her preceptor, Thomas Wentworth Higginson), inwardly it would seem Emily Dickinson was not to be denied. In her art she was master of herself, whatever that self was, however aggressive, unwomanly, or even inhuman society might judge it to be.

Given Dickinson's time and upbringing, it would, of course, have been unlikely that she, any more than we today, would have been comfortable with the high degree of anger and alienation which she exhibits in this extraordinary poem. But the anger and the alienation are there and, whether we are comfortable or not, like Dickinson we must deal with them. If, as Adrienne Rich asserts, "My Life had stood—a Loaded Gun" is a "central poem in understanding Emily Dickinson, and ourselves, and the condition of the woman artist, particularly in the nineteenth century" (OL, 174), it is so precisely because Dickinson was prepared to grapple in it with so many unacceptable feelings within herself. Whatever else "My Life had stood" may be about, it is about the woman as artist, the woman who must deny her femininity, even perhaps her humanity, if she is to achieve the fullness of her self and the fullness of her power in her verse.

•   •   •

To a degree unique among women writers whose poetic identities were formed prior to 1960, the three women to whom I have devoted this book, Emily Dickinson, Sylvia Plath, and Adrienne Rich, are all poets who were prepared to engage in the task of self-redefinition and self-empowerment which Dickinson describes in "My Life had stood."

Dickinson, Plath, and Rich are all specifically woman poets. That is, their gender is central to their poetic development, not only yielding much of their thematic substance but, more importantly, comprising their lyric identity, or voice. They do not just write poems about women; they are women in their poems and their identity as women is what they write about. In them, or rather, in their most significant and characteristic work, no separation exists between gender and genre. Their womanhood enables their verse and gives them their poetic power just as, traditionally, manhood and the masculine point of view have provided the focus, themes, and substance of the male poet's verse.

No less important, however, all three poets are prepared to challenge and successfully transcend conventional notions of what women are supposed to be: how women should think, feel, and act, and how women poets in particular should write. Their best poetry tends to be experimental, and in their poems their views of self are equally nonconformist and frank. If all three are poets of rage, anger, and alienation, as "My Life had stood—a Loaded Gun" demonstrates, they are poets of liberation as well. As such, they represent three key moments in the history of women's poetry, moments when specific women writers chose to reject the definitions controlling them in order to assume without shame or reservation the crown or lyric "I" they knew was theirs. In many ways, the course of women's poetry in America over the last twenty years has been a recapitulation on a large scale of what happened individually in these three poets' lives, as women have finally come to grips with the power they innately possess but which social, literary, and psychological attitudes, including their own inhibitions, have historically denied them.

For all three poets, this act of redefinition involved both pain and a price. For Dickinson, imprisoned in what Carroll Smith-Rosenberg has aptly called the nineteenth century's "female world of love and ritual,"[12] the price came in the form of acute sexual and social deprivation. Unwilling either to marry or to devote her days to "useful" service, she lived out her life in virtual isolation, expending her tremendous energies almost entirely on her art. If, as Allen Tate has written, "her life was one of the richest and deepest ever lived on this continent,"[13] this richness and depth were achieved only after years of severe depression in which she struggled to arrive at a concept of womanhood that would allow her both to mature and to create; that is, to be both a woman and an artist at once.

Unlike Emily Dickinson, Sylvia Plath was never able to give up entirely her desire for the sexual and social rewards that come in our culture with being a good girl and a loving wife and mother. By the end of her life she clearly understood how terribly destructive conventional definitions of these roles were to her both as a woman and as an artist. Nevertheless, her sense of having failed to be the woman she thought she was supposed to be, was a primary factor leading to her tragic death in 1963. Although it helped her produce her greatest poetry, her transition to a new, more powerful concept of womanhood came too late to save her life.

Of the three poets, only Adrienne Rich has managed, despite periods of intense personal pain, to negotiate successfully a complete transition from dutiful daughter to woman poet. Supported by the women's movement and, in particular, by the presence of an articulate lesbian-feminist community within it, Rich has been able to put aside her early devotion to male literary traditions and to patriarchal values, and in recent years has emerged as the spokeswoman for an entire new generation of women poets. Forced to sacrifice neither her self nor the sexual and social rewards to which we should all be entitled, she has become the model for innumerable women writers—both lesbian and heterosexual—who now feel that they can safely talk about their lives, their feelings, and their sexuality as never before.

The concept of self as woman is essential to the development of these three poets, profoundly affecting not only their themes but their style and, most important, their voice. Since their changing concepts of womanhood—and hence their poetic power—flow from the pressures, contradictions, and needs of their lives I have found it impossible not to dwell at some length upon the biographical circumstances surrounding their poetic development. While this book describes the emergence of a feminist poetic, it is, even more, a study of the psychological circumstances of female creativity. My aim has been to illuminate as specifically as possible just what in the lives and personalities of these three writers allowed them (or in Plath's case, forced her) to transcend the conventions of their time and culture, to redefine themselves as women, and release their energies fully and unequivocally in their art.

A great deal of critical attention has been paid in recent years to the implications for creativity of the charged relationship between the poet and his or her literary precursors. In the oedipal conflict between the poet father and poet son, which Harold Bloom has elaborated in a series of books, the roots of the male writer's struggle for self-definition and self-empowerment have, presumably, been laid bare. And, many feminist scholars have argued, so have the origins of the woman poet's ambiguous and difficult relationship to both the literary tradition and her own creative drives. [14]

But the highly poeticized and extremely limited Freudian romance that Bloom depicts in books like *The Anxiety of Influence*—while clearly parallel-ing the woman poet's struggle for separation and individuation—is at best only indirectly relevant to that struggle. The woman writer's principal antagonists are not the strong male or female poets who may have preceded her within the tradition, but the inhibiting voices that live within herself. The chief source of her anxiety is not that she will be insufficiently distinguished from her literary predecessors but that in fulfilling her destiny as poet, she will be forced to hurt or fail those whom she loves— whether they be mother, father, husband, lover, friends, or children—and thus bring society's opprobrium upon herself. Her struggles are, in short, not literary but part of life. It is to her life, therefore, that we must turn to understand the process by which she comes both to define and to accept herself as woman and poet.

For a good part of this century, advocates of the "new criticism" encouraged students of literature to ignore or diminish biographical and gender elements in art. Literature, we were told, should strive for the universal, and great art should transcend both the author's life and such ultimately temporal concerns as "he" and "she." The major writer spoke not for his or her sex but for all people as well as for all time. As an explanation of literature's meaning and appeal this theory was very pure.

But like the angel image that distorted our knowledge of what women actually are, this theory also idealized and distorted art's true nature. We do not read Homer and Sappho, John Milton and Jane Austen because they speak to us of universal truths—allowing that the apprehension of such truths is possible—but because they possess in abundance the capacity to speak for and interpret the truths of their cultural milieus, including the truths of their sex. Nor can we ask of writers, anymore than we ask of ourselves, that they transcend the perspective to which flesh falls heir. People, not angels, create art, though we long to attribute art to angels. And people, whether male or female, can write only what their lives enable them to say.

This book is written, accordingly, in the belief that the gender as well as individual identity and life of the particular writer are necessary components of her work and cannot be separated from our understanding of it. Just as important, it is written in the conviction that Dickinson, Plath, and Rich have a special place in the history of women's poetry in our culture precisely because they were willing to grapple with the issues of gender and identity directly in their work. Not only is much of their finest poetry drawn from the raw material of their lives, but their readiness to look unflinchingly at themselves as women is the reason they were able to release their power fully and base their craft upon their sex.

Whatever their original intentions, by founding their genre upon their gender, these three poets helped establish an entirely new poetic for women, a new way for women writers to re-create themselves in art. They showed that women qua women can present themselves as figures of power in their poetry, that they need not hide behind the mask of the universal or accept the limitations that culturally established gender roles prescribe. Finally they proved that the woman poet can find in her womanhood not only the source of her poetic strength but the lineaments of her own personal yet generic vision.

While there were women poets prior to the early 1960s who attempted to make their lives and womanhood a source of power central to their art — I think particularly of Elizabeth Barrett Browning and H.D. — none were so wholly committed or so devastatingly honest in their approach. This commitment and honesty sets the work of Dickinson, Plath, and Rich apart and makes them the true foremothers of women poets writing today. They did not hide from themselves or others the extent of their rage, the extent of their unacceptability, or "the passions which it was unfitting for . . . [women] to say." And because they did not, they found in their "depths, [their] dark places," the power that made them whole.

It is true that all three poets oscillate between verse that is more or less public and verse that is private or confessional. And all three tended at one point or another in their careers to wear self-alienating masks, Dickinson and Rich early on, Plath throughout much of her brief life. But all finally learned how to discard the mask and speak directly from the unacceptable core of their beings, to claim their loaded guns. In so doing, together they helped create the foundation for the woman-centered or feminist poetic whose fruits we now see all around us — in the ubiquitous poetry readings, the small women's magazines and presses, the dropped masks, and the freedom women now feel to express their lives, their selves, their emotions in their verse. Unlike Virginia Woolf, we need no longer wonder where the women poets are. They are all around us. Their power finally their own.

EMILY DICKINSON

Autonomy and Creativity

1. A New England Adolescence

For centuries women have felt their active, creative impulses as a kind of demonic possession.
—Adrienne Rich, 1976

There is nothing in the universe that I fear but that I shall not know all my duty, or shall fail to do it.
—Mary Lyon's epitaph, 1849

Sometime in late 1850, toward the end of her nineteenth year, Emily Dickinson wrote Abiah Root, closest of her "circle of five" childhood friends, a long, sentimental letter dealing with her growing sense of alienation from her peers. As far as can be proved, Dickinson had not yet begun to write poetry seriously. But her awareness of the active, creative impulses stirring within her permeates the letter, along with her ambivalence over the differences now dividing her from her former friends.

> You are growing wiser than I am, and nipping in the bud fancies which I let blossom—perchance to bear no fruit, or if plucked, I may find it bitter. The shore is safer, Abiah, but I love to buffet the sea—I can count the bitter wrecks here in these pleasant waters, and hear the murmuring winds, but oh, I love the danger! You are learning control and firmness. Christ Jesus will love you more. I'm afraid he don't love me *any*! (L, 104)

Dickinson does not specify exactly what she means by "control and firmness" in this passage. But in a second section of the letter, when she speaks of a similar distance that has developed between herself and Abby Wood, another member of the once inseparable circle of five, her meaning becomes clear and with it, the true nature of the problem confronting her.

> I see but little of Abby; she cannot come to see me, and I walk so far not often, and perhaps it's all right and best. Our lots fall in different places; mayhap we might disagree. We take different views of life, our thoughts would not dwell together as they used to when we were young—how long ago that seems! *She is more of a woman than I am, for I love so to be a child*—Abby is holier than me—she does more good in her lifetime than ever I shall in mine—she goes among the poor, she shuts the eye of the dying—she will be had in memorial when I am gone and forgotten. (L, 104–5; italics added)

However important their acceptance of Christ, it is Abiah's and Abby's acceptance of mature womanhood and "doing good" that is the real cause for Dickinson's alienation from her former friends. Abiah and Abby have chosen to stay on the safe shore of nineteenth-century Christian life and assume the adult responsibilities prescribed to them as women. These responsibilities Dickinson, on the other hand, has no wish to fulfill, preferring, if need be, to remain a child instead. Although she clearly recognizes the dangers of her course—failure to mature, alienation from her peers—she is overwhelmingly drawn to it not only by her romantic temperament ("I love to buffet the sea"), but also by the inner forces urging her to create ("bear fruit").

No life choice could in fact have made Emily Dickinson more of an anomaly in her society than her desire, however nascent, to be a poet. While pious and conventional women writers abounded in nineteenth-century evangelical New England, women who refused to do their Christian duty and work for the good and happiness of others did not.[1] In wanting to remain a child and let her fancies bloom—that is, in wanting to write simply for the pleasure of writing—Dickinson was not just being sentimental or coyly rebellious. She was violating the basic prescriptions of her time and the entire thrust of the education she received both at home and at school. In the process, she was also redefining herself as a poet and woman.

Any understanding of the particular course Dickinson's career took must, consequently, start here, in the poet's adolescent rebellion against the lot to which she, as a nineteenth-century woman living in rural New

England, was assigned by the "laws of God, made known by nature and by providence and also by the Bible."² As a poet, Dickinson began writing seriously only fairly late, after her twenty-sixth year. But the roots of her vocation and power were sunk deep into her past: in her sense of herself as a woman; in her romantic attachments to other women, especially her sister-in-law, Susan Gilbert; and in the rage she felt, living in a society that demanded that she take up the conventional duties of a woman whether these duties fit her gifts or not.

• • •

Abby Wood was "more of a woman" than Emily Dickinson not because she was older or sexually more mature but, simply enough, because she was willing to do her duty. It was duty, particularly as embodied in the evangelical doctrine of usefulness or doing good, that defined a man's or woman's adult role and mature identity during this period. In an article entitled "How to be Useful," which appeared in *The Mothers' Journal and Family Visitant* in 1856, one writer, signed S.M.B., put the doctrine of usefulness and its rationale, the imitation of Christ, in their simplest terms:

> Children should be taught from infancy that one great object of human life is to make others good and happy, and that it is their duty to imitate our GREAT PATTERN, who, while here on earth, ever sought to do good, and though now exalted, is yet interceding for poor sinners.³

For a child to become a "useful" adult, he or she must learn early to imitate Christ and do good for others. To live a life of self-indulgence and self-gratification such as Dickinson contemplates in her 1850 letter to Abiah Root was not just to devote oneself to worldly and therefore damnable ends. It was also to show an immature lack of "control and firmness." In the adult world, true happiness and fulfillment, let alone salvation, lay in bringing happiness to others. Only thus could the dangerous waters of childhood's selfish pleasures be escaped.

As the presence of S.M.B.'s article in *The Mothers' Journal* (a sort of nineteenth-century *Ladies' Home Journal*) attests, this doctrine exerted a powerful influence over child-rearing practices in Dickinson's lifetime. It was inculcated in handbooks for mothers and in women's magazines. It was preached from pulpits and taught in schools. Most important for our purposes, it molded the principles, approach, and expectations of the educational institutions — Amherst Academy and Mount Holyoke Female

Seminary—Dickinson attended, affecting, indeed controlling, not only the curriculum of these schools but also their view of students' personal growth and development.

When applied to the course of studies offered women, the doctrine of usefulness meant that women were instructed in what were called the useful sciences: disciplines designed to help them function efficiently in the domestic and social spheres to which they were called. The result, interestingly enough, was a rigorous, science-oriented education in many ways admirable in itself, but singularly poor fodder for a mind like Dickinson's which was romantically or poetically inclined. Remarks made by Samuel Fowler Dickinson, the poet's grandfather and one of the founders of Amherst Academy, typify evangelical thought on the curriculum appropriate for the instruction of young women.

> A good husbandman will also *educate well his daughters*. I distinguish the education of daughters from that of sons; because, Nature had designed them to occupy places, in family, and in society, altogether dissimilar.
> Daughters should be *well instructed,* in the useful sciences; comprising a *good* English education: including a thorough knowledge of our own language, geography, history, mathematics and natural philosophy. The female mind, so sensitive, so susceptible of improvement, should not be neglected. . . . God designed nothing in vain.[4]

If we remember that natural philosophy was a broad term for science during this period, then the curriculum recommendations made by Dickinson's grandfather match almost point for point the curriculum his poet granddaughter later followed. History, geography, botany, algebra, geometry, physiology, anatomy, geology, logic, natural theology, and in English only such "safe" authors as Milton, Young, Watts, and Cowper— this was the basic list of her studies at both Amherst Academy and Mount Holyoke, where she spent her single college year. While one could receive instruction in art, music, and modern languages at both institutions, in some cases for a special fee, such exposure was hardly enough to offset the heavy emphasis on science. Nor was it intended to do so. For the evangelical educators of Dickinson's day, like the minister's wife who wrote "Letters to Young Ladies" in *The Mothers' Journal,* the goal of education was the cultivation of life, not the cultivation of pleasure or the imagination. The reading of novels along with other profitless exercises that encouraged daydreaming were deemed "fatal to happiness and future usefulness."[5] "Life," one writer fulminated in a diatribe against George Sand, "is too much of a reality to be trifled away in the perusal of fiction, or in the chase of dreams."[6]

Rather than supplement their rigid academic curriculum with worldly or frivolous activities, these ardent evangelists subjected their young charges to a pervasive form of religious and moral instruction. In her commemorative biography, *The Power of Christian Benevolence,* Mary Lyon, founder and first president of Mount Holyoke, receives high praise for taking the young women sent to her "thoughtless and bent on pleasure" and returning them home "serious, and bent on doing good."[7] Similarly, Lavinia Dickinson and her roommate, Jane Hitchcock, were told by their instructor, Mr. Cowles, at Ipswich Academy that they were "not placed in this world to *have a good time.*" Nor did their parents send them "to this Seminary to enjoy [them]selves." They were there "to improve [their] immortal minds, to strengthen & make better the part *that never dies.*"[8]

To accomplish these goals, educators paid obsessive attention to their students' religious and moral development. The Bible and Christian doctrine formed the basis for learning in every area. Even textbooks in botany and geology were designed to instill wonder at God's creating hand as well as respect for the scientific truth of revelation. Teachers had to be "firmly established in the faith of the Christian religion."[9] And students were soundly and frequently enjoined to profess Christ. Indeed, at Mount Holyoke, Mary Lyon made it her yearly mission to convert as many students as possible. For young women, the primary aim of this education was to help them accommodate themselves spiritually and psychologically to a role that was deemed, by nature's and God's law, service-oriented, domestic and subordinate to the male. "The excellence of the female character," Lyon wrote,

> . . . consists principally in a preparation to be happy herself in her social and domestic relations, and to make all others happy around her. All her duties, of whatever kind, are in an important sense social and domestic. They are retired and private, and not public, like those of the other sex.[10]

If a young woman wishes to be an "important teacher," Lyon explains, "her most vigorous labors should be modest and unobtrusive." If she is a missionary, she must find "a retired spot, where, away from the public gaze, she may wear out or lay down a valuable life."[11] The happiness of others, not her own glory, was to be her only concern.

Along with correct reasoning, industry, and perseverance, "patience, meekness and gentleness," were, therefore, qualities that Mary Lyon felt it essential for her students to acquire.[12] To encourage the growth of these qualities, opportunities to practice self-denial were carefully structured into their days. Of her experience at Mount Holyoke under Lyon, one college alumna glowingly recalls:

> One great principle which she inculcated was the subordination of individual inclinations to the welfare of the community. It made it easy to observe rules. Minor inconveniences were more than balanced by the habit of exalting the general good above our private preferences. But beyond this was that noblest of all lessons, self-sacrifice. By precept, by example, and by occasions for their practice, *the Christian duty and the value of self-sacrifice* were impressed upon us. (italics added).[13]

Mary Lyon knew that she had to impress "the Christian duty and the value of self-sacrifice" upon her students because she knew what fate lay in store for most of them. If they were not to be teachers or missionaries, her first hope for them, they most assuredly would be wives and mothers. Education in learning how to put "the general good" above their "private preferences" was, therefore, essential if they were to reach useful womanhood.

For Mary Lyon as for Emily Dickinson, it was precisely a young woman's willingness to assume her self-sacrificing duties at home and in the world which marked childhood's end and the beginning of an adult Christian life: the life of middle-class, nineteenth-century woman lived not only in willing subordination to the male but in subordination to the demands of a society and a religion that beginning in childhood taught her that doing good for others should be her chief, if not her only, concern.

•   •   •

Emily Dickinson's temperamental incompatibility with the doctrine of usefulness and its psychological sequelae: self-denial, a willingness to serve others, an obliging and grateful disposition, and so on, is evident from the first letters we have from her hand. At age eleven, writing to a close friend, Jane Humphrey, she speaks with unbecoming immodesty of an interaction between herself and a fellow student.

> There was one young man who read a Composition the Subject was think twice before you speak—he was describing the reasons why any one should do so . . . he is the sillyest creature that ever lived I think. I told him that I thought he had better think twice before he spoke. (L, 7)

At fourteen, she is even more sure of herself, frankly revealing to Abiah Root not only her arrogance but her selfishness, as she explains to her friend why she delayed writing to her.

> I received your note by Sabra for which you have my hearty thanks. I intended to write you by Sabra, but . . . I thought as all the other girls wrote you, my letter if I wrote one, would seem no smarter than any body else, and you know how I hate to be common.   (L, 10)

To be self-effacing and self-denying were not part of Dickinson's repertoire in early adolescence. Nor were these qualities evident three years later when she wrote to her brother, Austin, still at the time her fellow-spirit, from Mount Holyoke. In an extraordinary letter, dated February 17, 1848, Dickinson not only refers to herself gaily as Austin's *"highly accomplished & gifted elder sister"* (L, 63)—the poet's italics—but with savage wit satirizes the ideals of "female propriety & sedate deportment" which the seminary was determined, and designed, to instill.

> I deliberated for a few moments after [your letter's] reception on the propriety of carrying it to Miss Whitman [Mary Lyon's second-in-command]. . . . The result of my deliberation was a conclusion to open it with moderation, peruse it's contents with sobriety becoming my station, & if after a close investigation of it's contents I found nothing which savored of rebellion or an unsubdued will, I would lay it away in my folio & forget I had ever received it.   (L, 62)

However more sober or more tractable students may have felt, Dickinson obviously had other concerns on her mind besides the "good of the whole," her own good being chief among them.

If Dickinson was arrogant, she was also rebellious. At Amherst Academy, which, as befits a lower school, was considerably more lenient than Mount Holyoke, she was one of the school's two wits, a reputation she seems to have maintained by writing mock sermons parodying the rhetorical efforts of the local clergy.[14] On a deeper level, even at the reasonably liberal academy, she recognized that one of the primary functions of such institutions was the socialization of the young into their adult roles and she defended herself against it. At fourteen she wrote to Abiah Root, then away at school:

> I expect you have a great many prim, starched up young ladies there, who, I doubt not, are perfect models of propriety and good behavior. If

they are, don't let your free spirit be chained by them. I don't know as there [are] any in school of this stamp. But there 'most always are a few, whom the teachers look up to and regard as their satellites.   (L, 13)

Academically gifted though she was, Dickinson was not cut out to be a teacher's satellite, an academic dutiful daughter, not if it meant putting her free spirit or her imagination in chains.

Nor was Dickinson any more tractable at home, that sacred altar where mothers were supposed to set before their daughters lifetime examples of obedience, gratitude, and selfless service. Possibly in accordance with the apprenticeship system of the period, at fourteen Dickinson was kept from school for a term so that her mother could instruct her in the domestic arts, best taught, Mary Lyon asserted, in the home.[15] Her response to her situation was frankly and mordantly bitter. To Abiah Root she wrote:

You asked me if I was attending school now. I am not. Mother thinks me not able to confine myself to school this term. She had rather I would exercise, and I can assure you I get plenty of that article by staying at home. I am going to learn to make bread to-morrow. . . . I advise you if you don't know how to make the staff of life to learn with dispatch. I think I could keep house very comfortably if I knew how to cook. But as long as I don't, my knowledge of housekeeping is about of as much use as faith without works, which you know we are told is dead.   (L, 20)

Contrary to the expectations expressed in this letter, however, her attitude toward housekeeping did not improve with the passage of time or the acquisition of new skills. Her letters, early and late, testify to the fact that she never learned to tolerate—let alone enjoy—general housekeeping duties like cleaning and polishing. As for cooking, with the notable exception of bread making, which she may have liked because of the punching-down involved, she confined herself as much as possible to the manufacture of exquisite and superfluous desserts. "Aunt Emily stood for *indulgence,*" her niece, Martha Dickinson Bianchi, reports.[16] No Mary Lyon, she.

Far more important, the poet's relationship with her mother, a pious, unassuming woman, was profoundly, even irreparably, damaged by the latter's total commitment to the social and domestic duties which devolved upon her as Edward Dickinson's wife. In an age when, according to Carroll Smith-Rosenberg, mother-daughter relationships were typified by "close-ness and mutual emotional dependency," Dickinson's condescending, frequently hostile attitude toward her mother is anomalous to say the least and may strike the reader as altogether too modern.

Where Smith-Rosenberg found that "daughters routinely [in their letters] discussed their mother's health and activities with their own friends, expressed anxiety in cases of their mother's ill health and concern for her cares," Dickinson's comments on such topics almost invariably center on herself and the impositions her mother's indispositions created for her. In contrast to the "sympathy and understanding" toward mothers which Smith-Rosenberg found in the thousands of letters she drew on in writing "The Female World of Love and Ritual: Relations Between Women in Nineteenth-Century America,"[17] Dickinson's attitude, particularly as she reached late adolescence, is typically self-pitying and often close to downright ugly. At nineteen Dickinson wrote to Abiah Root complaining of her situation when her mother was struck down by an acute bout of neuralgia.

> I have been at work, providing the "food that perisheth," scaring the timorous dust, and being obedient, and kind. *I* call it kind obedience in the books the Shadows write in, it may have another name. I am yet the Queen of the court, if regalia be dust, and dirt, have three loyal subjects, whom I'd rather relieve from service. Mother is still an invalid tho' a partially restored one — Father and Austin still clamor for food, and I, like a martyr am feeding them. Wouldn't you love to see me in these bonds of great despair, looking around my kitchen, and praying for kind deliverance. . . . *My* kitchen I think I called it, God forbid that it was, or shall be my own — God keep me from what they call *households*, except that bright one of "faith"! (L, 99)

In no mood to be either obedient or kind, Dickinson, like a perverse Cinderella, blames her mother for the intolerable dust-and-cinders position to which she has been consigned. Nor, one may note, would the arrival of a Prince Charming save this sad queen from her hated fate. On the contrary, to marry would simply confirm her in it, giving her a household of her own to which she would be forever chained in "bonds of great despair." Better that her mother should simply recover and carry on, so that her much put-upon daughter could return to her private — selfish, childlike — existence and the "timorous dust" need fear her no more.

Whatever Mrs. Dickinson may actually have been like, it is clear that to her daughter she was the epitome of everything Dickinson detested in the lives of the adult women who surrounded her. In a formidably angry letter to Jane Humphrey, written in January of 1850 (about the same time as the letter to Abiah), Dickinson let loose more pointedly than she ever would again, the contempt she harbored for the duties which society imposed on her and for the women, including her mother, who carried them out.

> The Sewing Society has commenced again—and held its first meeting last week—now all the poor will be helped—the cold warmed—the warm cooled—the hungry fed—the thirsty attended to—the ragged clothed—and this suffering—tumbled down world will be helped to it's feet again—which will be quite pleasant to all. I don't attend—notwithstanding my high approbation—which must puzzle the public exceedingly. I am already set down as one of those brands almost consumed—and my hardheartedness gets me many prayers.   (L, 84)

Rightly or wrongly, Dickinson believed that her mother was trying to force a similar way of life on her, to the detriment of all that she considered most precious and real in herself. And just as she hated these duties, she appears to have hated her mother as well.

> I *do* love—and remember you Jane—and have tried to convince you of it ocularly—but it is not easy to try just as we *are* at home—Vinnie away—and my hands but *two*—not four, or five as they ought to be—and so *many* wants—and me so *very* handy—and my time of so *little* account—and my writing so *very* needless—and really I came to the conclusion that I should be a villain unparralleled if I took but an inch of time for so unholy a purpose as writing a friendly letter—for what need had *I* of sympathy—or very much less of affection—or less than they all—of friends—mind the house—and the food—*sweep* if the spirits were low—nothing like exercise to strengthen—and invigorate—and help away such foolishness—work makes one strong, and cheerful—and as for society what neighborhood so full as my own? The halt—the lame—and the blind—the old—the infirm—the bedridden—and superannuated—the ugly, and disagreeable—the perfectly hateful to me—all *these* to see—and be seen by—an opportunity rare for cultivating meekness—and patience—and submission—and for turning my back to this very sinful, and wicked world. . . . The path of duty looks very ugly indeed—and the place where *I* want to go more amiable—a great deal. . . . I dont wonder that good angels weep—and bad ones sing songs. (L, 82)

With her sister, Lavinia, away at school and temporarily unable to act as her buffer, Dickinson found herself fully encumbered with work she loathed, and her rage and sense of entrapment knew, it seems, no bounds.

But while Dickinson's lashing out in this letter may strike some readers as singularly unattractive, her concerns were real enough. However much she might mock her mother's bromides (*"sweep* if the spirits were low"), this was the social and domestic niche into which she, like Abiah and Abby, was supposed to fit. And had it not been for her father's money and her sister Vinnie's, compliance, her choices would in fact have been a good deal more limited than they finally were.

Yet it is also evident that one need not view Emily Norcross Dickinson as a totally inadequate or withholding mother in order to understand the enormity of the poet's anger at her.[18] On the contrary, there is a good deal of evidence, much of it from Dickinson herself, to suggest that, as a mother Mrs. Dickinson behaved in ways that were entirely consonant with her culture's expectations. She was obedient, kind, patient, and gentle. "Mother," Lavinia Dickinson said, when summing up the principal attributes of each member of her family, "loved."[19] She adored birds and flowers—two tastes her daughter Emily adopted fully. And when not debilitated by one of her frequent illnesses, she ran an efficient and congenial home. In a family of exigent personalities, she fulfilled her role as Angel in the House. But by that very token, she could not give her oldest daughter the two things that Dickinson needed most: support for the active, creative impulses latent within her and permission through her mother's example to assert her own autonomy in the world. Like so many "good" mothers, Mrs. Dickinson seems to have hoped and expected that her children would fit the pattern society deemed normal, even as she herself had. For Emily Dickinson, however, this meant that she "never had a mother" (L, 475), and that she was "Homeless at home" (no. 1573; P, 1084).

For Dickinson, the consequences of her inability to conform were personally devastating. Neither at home, where she was expected to do housekeeping and to feel cheerful sweeping, nor in society, where the sewing circle lay in wait, could she hope to find the encouragement she needed to pursue the solitary and selfish pleasures of her nascent craft. In her own eyes as well as the eyes of others, her rejection of "the path of duty" made her one of the devil's party. Writing to Jane Humphrey in 1850, she joined her voice in her own condemnation:

> They say you are teaching in Warren—and happy—then I know you are good—for none *but* the good are happy—you are out of the way of temptation—and out of the way of the tempter—I did'nt mean to make you wicked—but I was—and am—and shall be—and I was with you so much that I could'nt help contaminate. (L, 83)

If she was not happy, and clearly she was not, how could she possibly be good.

Dickinson's estrangement from her childhood friends peaked in the early 1850s, when Amherst was swept by waves of evangelical fervor. For the young women of Dickinson's period, conversion was not just an emotional outlet.[20] It was a rite of passage leading them into psychological reconciliation with their adult fates. The tear-filled gentleness and kindness that followed conversion were the necessary emotional preludes to their acceptance of subordinate domestic roles. For Dickinson, however, it rendered her erstwhile companions—not surprisingly—as alien as if they had stepped from another planet. To Jane, she wrote:

> How lonely this world is growing, something so desolate creeps over the spirit and we dont know it's name, and it wont go away, either Heaven is seeming greater, or Earth a great deal more small. . . . Christ is calling everyone here, all my companions have answered, even my darling Vinnie believes she loves, and trusts him, and I am standing alone in rebellion, and growing very careless. Abby, Mary, Jane, and farthest of all my Vinnie have been seeking, and they all believe they have found; I cant tell you *what* they have found, but *they* think it is something precious. I wonder if it *is*? How strange is this sanctification, that works such a marvellous change. . . . They seem so very tranquil, and their voices are kind, and gentle, and the tears fill their eyes so often, I really think I envy them.   (L, 94)

Though she claimed to envy her friends' tranquility and happiness, she could not emulate their obedience to Christ's and society's call. Nor at bottom could she comprehend it.

Although Dickinson recognized that the maturation of her former companions was inevitable, there was in fact no way in which they could mature that did not meet with resistance from her. Indeed, nothing moved her more quickly to self-pity than the mere idea that one of them might be showing signs of growing up. Thus she wrote to Abiah Root in 1850:

> Where are you now, Abiah, where are your thoughts, and aspirings, where are your young affections, not with the *boots* and *whiskers*; any with *me* ungrateful, *any* tho' drooping, dying? I presume you are loving your mother, and loving the stranger, and wanderer, visiting the poor, and afflicted, and reaping whole fields of blessings. Save me a *little* sheaf— only a very little one! Remember, and care for me sometimes, and scatter a fragrant flower in this wilderness life of mine.   (L, 99)

The prospect that Abiah might be interested in men and marriage was, clearly, no more appealing to the poet than the idea that her friend might be reaping "whole fields of blessings" by "visiting the poor, and afflicted" or, significantly, by "loving {her} mother," since in all these cases, it meant that Dickinson would be left behind.

Nor was Dickinson any less wayward in her attitude when one of her friends, Emily Fowler Ford, actually did marry three years later. Even in its most charitable construction, the note of congratulations which the poet sent the new Mrs. Ford seems designed to make the young bride feel nothing but guilt:

> I knew you would go away, for I know the roses are gathered, but I guessed not yet, not till by expectation we had become resigned. . . .
> . . . There's a verse in the Bible, Emily, I don't know where it is, nor just how it goes can I remember, but it's a little like this—"I can go to her, but she cannot come back to me." I guess that isn't right, but my eyes are full of tears, and I'm sure I do not care if I make mistakes or not.   (L, 277)

The intense emotional dependence which these letters exhibit suggests, however, that Dickinson was not devastated by the loss of her friends simply because they had once provided support for her recalcitrant positions on religion, womanhood, and domesticity. She also seems to have viewed these young women, albeit inchoately, as so many lovers, and their desertion left her, as she was to be left so often in her life, feeling martyred and alone.

Abiah, Abby, Emily, and others were walking a path she could not follow and her attitude toward them is one of hostility for their implicit judgment of her ("I presume you are loving your mother") mingled with coy jealousy at their unfaithfulness to her ("Save me a *little* sheaf"). After the extended period of childhood, they were deserting her as potential fellows in rebellion and as fellow spirits with whom she could share tender moments and romantic dreams. Although she recognized on one level the inevitability of this desertion, on another, she insisted on looking back nostalgically to the time when two had been as one and the "golden links" that bound them had not yet been "dimmed." Thus to Abiah she wrote in one of the most telling passages from the 1850 letters:

> Do not think we are aught than friends—though the "silver cord *be* loosed" the "golden bowl" is *not* broken. I have talked thus freely of Abby because we three were friends . . . because the golden links, though dimmed, are no less golden. . . .

Won't you say what you think of Abby—I mean of her heart and
mind—when you write me. . . . And tell me of *some one else*—what *she* is
thinking and doing, and whether she still remembers the loves of "long
ago," and sighs as she remembers, lest there be no more as true—"sad
time, sweet times, two bairns at school, but a' one heart"—*three* bairns,
and the tale had been truer.   (L, 105)

In being loved by her friends and loving them in return, Dickinson had,
in fact, been given a taste of the kind of life, filled with emotion and
imagination, romance and danger, she wished to experience, the pleasant
but unsafe sea she wished to buffet. In obedience to the behest of society and
the call of their religion, one by one her friends had abandoned her, together
with their own childhood dreams, taking up lives of active usefulness
instead; but not before they gave the poet a priceless gift: the knowledge
that for her, the love and freedom they shared as children were a "silver
cord" and "golden bowl" worth the price of Mary Lyon's heaven. It was a
gift Dickinson did not relinquish or forget.

•   •   •

The tensions that permeated Dickinson's adolescence—her rebellion
against duty, her sense of alienation and abandonment, her need for
romance and intense imaginative experience—came to a head during the
poet's early twenties in her romantic friendship with her sister-in-law,
Susan Gilbert. It was this relationship that prolonged and then decisively
terminated Dickinson's adolescence.[21]

The basis for the strong emotional attachment between Gilbert and
Emily Dickinson appears to have lain in a sympathy of mind that Dickinson
was unable to achieve with her other girlhood friends. Abiah Root, Abby
Wood, Jane Humphrey, and others had fulfilled Dickinson's affectional
needs from childhood. But though she treated their burgeoning interest in
men with consistent jealousy, she also knew that their understanding and
appreciation of her was limited at best. Even Jane Humphrey, by far the
closest of these friends as they entered their twenties, would, Dickinson
feared, "tremble" if she knew all that was going on in her heart (L, 95).
With women like Abiah Root and Emily Fowler Ford, in whom religion
and convention increasingly dominated, she made no attempt at all after
her nineteenth year to share her deepest self.

Nor, contrary to many biographers' opinions, does Dickinson appear to
have shared this self with the various young men who visited her and her

sister, Vinnie, in their father's house during the early fifties. Where the letters she wrote to women overflow with emotion and exhibit complex tensions and restraints, the notes she sent off to Henry Emmons, George Gould, and her cousin, John Graves, in this period are singularly free of ambivalence. They are brief, witty, direct, and comradely. They deal almost exclusively with the sharing of ideas, poetry, and, above all, books.[22] A letter written to Henry Emmons, probably the closest of these young male friends, in the spring of 1853 is typical of her style at its wittiest.

> Since receiving your beautiful writing I have often desired to thank you thro' a few of my flowers [poems?], and arranged the fairest for you a little while ago, but heard you were away—
> I have very few today, and they compare but slightly with the immortal blossoms you kindly gathered me, but will you please accept them—the "Lily of the Field" for the blossoms of Paradise, and if 'tis ever mine to gather those which fade not, from the garden we have not seen, you shall have a brighter one than I can find today.   (L, 246)

If Dickinson is actually referring to her own poems here, and not simply to flowers, then this letter speaks very well indeed of her relationship with Emmons. But in no way does it suggest that she had a deep personal attachment to him. On the contrary, when Emmons became engaged a year later, Dickinson's note of congratulations, in striking contrast to the letter of congratulations she sent Emily Fowler Ford upon her wedding, could hardly be more straightforward and sincere. "My heart is full of joy, Friend—Were not my parlor full, I'd bid you come this morning, but the hour must be *stiller* in which we speak of *her*" (L, 301). There is nothing in this sentence, or in any comments Dickinson made thereafter regarding the engagement, to suggest that she was the slightest bit jealous or dismayed at Emmons's decision to marry another, although she told Susan she would "miss Emmons very much" (L, 305) and clearly cared for him a good deal. Her statements contain only simple, unaffected warmth, the warmth of someone who always thought of herself as nothing more or less than a good friend.

All the available evidence suggests that Dickinson's relationships with young men were in fact intellectual rather than affectional. She thirsted to share books, ideas, and poetry with them in ways that after mid-adolescence she no longer comfortably could with her women friends. But beyond that, as Joseph Lyman, a suitor of Vinnie's, observed, she held men at arm's length, assuming a nunlike posture too "pure, rare, fine," and "delicate," for any mere mortal man to breach.[23] "Emily you see," Lyman explained to his fiancée, when comparing Dickinson to her considerably more compliant sister, Vinnie, "is platonic—she never stood 'tranced in long Embraces mixed with kisses sweeter, sweeter than anything on Earth.'"[24]

But Lyman was wrong. Dickinson had stood "tranced in long Embraces," only not with a man.

In June of 1852 Dickinson wrote the absent Susan Gilbert a letter that puts the erotic basis of their relationship or, at any rate, the depth of the poet's physical response to her brother Austin's future wife beyond doubt.

> Susie, will you indeed come home next Saturday, and be my own again, and kiss me as you used to? Shall I indeed behold you, not "darkly, but face to face" or am I *fancying* so, and dreaming blessed dreams from which the day will wake me? I hope for you so much, and feel so eager for you . . . that the expectation once more to see your face again, makes me feel hot and feverish, and my heart beats so fast—I go to sleep at night, and the first thing I know, I am sitting there wide awake, and clasping my hands tightly, and thinking of next Saturday, and "never a bit" of you. (L, 215)

Dickinson must have realized the implication of her physical symptoms because she concludes this section of the letter by saying:

> Why, Susie, it seems to me as if my absent Lover was coming home so soon—and my heart must be so busy, making ready for him. (L, 215–16)

Yet important as it seems to us today, it was not simply Susan's erotic appeal to Dickinson that gave her such significance in the poet's life at this time. Far more important, Susan was the "blessed dream" itself, the bright romance, for which Dickinson had yearned throughout adolescence, finally materialized in the flesh. And Dickinson loved her with all the pent-up intensity of her being, with all the as yet unexpressed "poetry" in her heart.

> I mourn this morning, Susie, that I have no sweet sunset to gild a page for *you,* nor any bay so blue. . . . You know how I must write you, down, down, in the terrestrial; no sunset here, no stars; not even a bit of *twilight* which I may poetize—and send you! Yet Susie, there will be romance in the letter's ride to you. . . . Oh Susie, I often think that I will try to tell you how very dear you are . . . but the words wont come, tho' the *tears* will, and I sit down disappointed—yet darling, you know it all—then

why do I seek to tell you? I do not know; in thinking of those I love, my reason is all gone from me, and I do fear sometimes that I must make a hospital for the hopelessly insane, and chain me up there such times, so I wont injure you.   (L, 181, 182)

In Susan Gilbert, the orphaned daughter of a local tavern-keeper, Emily Dickinson believed that she had found at last not just a "Lover," but her true soul mate, one who was uniquely capable of meeting her deepest intellectual and affectional needs. And in most respects she appears to have been right. For, whatever her limitations, Susan was unquestionably a brilliant and challenging young woman and the two friends shared a number of qualities and attitudes in common.

In contrast to other women friends, with Susan, Dickinson was free to voice her unorthodox opinions. (Martha Dickinson Bianchi, Susan's daughter, reports that her father, Austin, always found it "queer that Sue was never shocked by sacrilege in Emily.")[25] And she could indulge in the heights of her "land of Canaan" style. For Sue, unlike the rest of the Dickinson family, appears to have enjoyed the poet's youthful rhetorical flights. Indeed, if her two surviving letters to Dickinson mean anything, she may have tried to match them with flights of her own.[26] They traded and discussed books throughout their lives. And, most important at this point in Dickinson's career, they partook together in the same romantic dreams and reveries, the very kind of "useless," poem-inducing reveries Dickinson knew the rest of her family and society condemned.

Not surprisingly then, Dickinson believed she had found in Susan Gilbert a fellow poet, whatever Sue's actual qualifications for that exalted title might have been.

It is such an evening Susie, as you and I would walk and have such pleasant musings, if you were only here — perhaps we would have a "Reverie" after the form of "Ik Marvel," indeed I do not know why it would'nt be just as charming as of that lonely Bachelor, smoking his cigar — and it would be far more profitable as "Marvel" *only* marvelled, and you and I would *try* to make a little destiny to have for our own. . . .

Longfellow's "golden Legend" has come to town I hear — and may be seen *in state* on Mr. Adams' bookshelves. It always makes me think of "Pegasus in the pound" — when I find a gracious author sitting side by side with "Murray" and "Wells" and "Walker" [three compilers of "useful" language texts] in that renowned store — and like *him* I half expect to hear that they have *"flown"* some morning . . . ; but for our sakes dear Susie, who please ourselves with the fancy that we are the only poets, and everyone else is *prose,* let us hope they will yet be willing to share our humble world.   (L, 144)

Admittedly it is disconcerting to find a poet of Dickinson's stature turning for sustenance to such second-rate romancers as Longfellow and "Ik Marvel" (Donald G. Mitchell, author of *Reveries of a Bachelor,* a syrupy collection of poetical essays on life and love, published in 1850). Nevertheless, these writers, and Susan with them were vital to her at this time. Together they validated the view of life—emotional, intense, sensual, vibrant with ecstasy and imagination—on which her vocation as poet was based. They nourished the poet in her, first by exalting the power of the imagination over reality. Marvel, for example, claims he will not marry because daily living might reduce the woman he loves to "the dull standard of the actual."[27] Second, such poets provided Dickinson with the possibility of an alternate definition of self: not as woman, duty-bound and devoted to service, but as woman-poet, a winged horse indeed. Only later would she turn to such writers as Shakespeare to justify these same ideals.

The problem for Dickinson lay, of course, in the fact that the "little destiny" she dreamed for herself and Susan was not the same destiny that Gilbert had in mind for herself. Susan was more dependent on social approval than Dickinson. She was also financially strapped. If she enjoyed being the poet's "bright romance," she nevertheless wanted and needed to get married. Dickinson knew perfectly well that her brother was courting her best friend. Indeed, in keeping with the customs of the time, she assisted their courtship by addressing his envelopes for him so that the relationship could maintain some privacy in the small town in which they lived. But although she knew that some day "he" would take her away "to live in his new home" (L, 203), she nevertheless persisted in fantasizing a future menage à trois in which Austin, not she, played the shadowy third.

You wont cry any more, will you, Susie, for my father will be your father, and my home will be your home, and where you go, I will go, and we will lie side by side in the kirkyard.   (L, 201)

And rightly or wrongly (the future course of Austin's marriage suggests she was correct), Dickinson seems to have believed that at some level Susan did share her own deeply held reservations concerning marriage.

In the often-quoted "man of noon" passage from a letter written about June of 1852, Dickinson poured forth in intense symbolic language the dread she felt when contemplating the loss of self marriage would entail.

For the bride or fiancée, Dickinson writes, life is a bright romance, for her "days are fed with gold . . . [she] gathers pearls every evening." But "to the *wife*," the "dull" life led by romantic friends such as herself and Sue may "seem dearer than all others in the world";

> you have seen flowers at morning, *satisfied* with the dew [apparently, romantic friendship], and those same sweet flowers at noon with their heads bowed in anguish before the mighty sun; think you these thirsty blossoms will *now* need naught but—*dew?* No, they will cry for sunlight, and pine for the burning noon, tho' it scorches them, scathes them; they have got through with peace—they know that the man of noon, is *mightier* than the morning and their life is henceforth to him. Oh, Susie, it is dangerous, and it is all too dear, these simple trusting spirits, and the spirits mightier, which we cannot resist! It does so rend me, Susie, the thought of it when it comes, that I tremble lest at sometime I, too, am yielded up. (I., 210)

In one of their favorite books at this time, *Kavanagh*, Longfellow had called romantic friendships such as Dickinson and Gilbert enjoyed the "rehearsal in girlhood" for "the great drama of woman's life." But for Dickinson, at least, it was precisely the fact that such friendships led to the *transmutation of erotic passion into romantic devotion* that made these relationships seem a safer and preferable course to the "great drama" itself. While she recognized the power of heterosexual passion, its consequences for her as a woman, including, most particularly, loss of will and subordination to the dominant male, were too frightening to contemplate. If the girlhood dew she shared with Susan could never satisfy either of them sexually in the way that a heterosexual relationship presumably would, their love lacked heterosexuality's debilitating social and psychological dangers as well.

Whether Dickinson thought that by such writing she could dissuade Susan from marrying Austin cannot be known, but surely it is a curious letter for the poet to have sent the woman she knew her brother had picked out for his wife. It seems probable that part of her at least hoped that Susan would heed her warning. To Dickinson, marriage was a sun that could only consume the woman, and she feared it enough to want no part of it. Unhappily, however, her anxieties had no effect on Susan's plans. Less than a year after the "man of noon" letter, Austin announced his engagement and the die was cast for all three lives.

Dickinson's reaction to her brother's engagement is, not surprisingly, a masterpiece of ambivalence, a letter so filled with barely suppressed rage that it boggles the mind to find a scholar as sensitive as Richard Sewall claiming the writing shows the relationship between brother and sister "at its sprightliest."[28] The letter opens with a double-edged salutation to "Oliver," and goes on from there.

> Oh my dear "Oliver," how chipper you must be since any of us have seen you? How thankful we should be that you have been brought to Green-ville, and a suitable frame of mind! I really had my doubts about your reaching Canaan, but you relieve my mind.

In Shakespeare's romantic comedy *As You Like It,* Oliver is the successful suitor of Celia, Rosalind's cousin and romantic friend. Overtly it is to Oliver's success as a wooer that Dickinson is referring here. But, as she well knew, Oliver begins the play in a much less attractive role as vicious brother of the play's hero, Orlando. Driven by insane jealousy of his superior younger sibling, he attempts to defraud Orlando of his birthright along with his life. Since much of the rest of Dickinson's letter has to do with Austin's encroachment on areas she felt rightfully belonged to her (Susan, poetry), the sobriquet had an appropriateness that would not have been lost on the poet even if, as some biographers believe, the nickname originated with Austin himself.

Dickinson's tone in the passage is, in any case, obviously sarcastic, particularly in respect to the thankfulness she feels now that Austin has finally reached Canaan. In a number of letters she had already identified Susan with Canaan or heaven, going so far in one passage as to parody Saint Paul: "'Eye hath not seen, nor ear heard, nor can the heart conceive' *my* Susie, whom I love" (L, 208). Now heaven or Canaan has been snatched from her and the poet's voice becomes bitter and cynical as she contemplates the joy her brother savors at her expense.

> Trust you enjoy your closet, and meditate profoundly upon the Daily Food! I shall send you Village Hymns, by earliest opportunity.
> I was just this moment thinking of a favorite stanza of your's, "where congregations ne'er break up, and Sabbaths have no end."
> That must be a delightful situation, certainly, quite worth the scrambling for!

From the loss of Canaan, Dickinson then turns to the question of poetry. Here she is on considerably surer ground. Austin had, apparently, included a poem in his letter to her announcing his engagement. Her lack of enthusiasm for his effort is obvious. But her real concern seems to be that

Austin has entered the lists in competition with her and she is notably anxious to give his winged horse a fall.

> And Austin is a Poet, Austin writes a psalm. Out of the way Pegasus, Olympus enough "to him," and just say to those "nine muses" that we have done with them!
> Raised a living muse ourselves, worth the whole nine of them. Up, off, tramp!
> Now Brother Pegasus, I'll tell you what it is — I've been in the habit *myself* of writing some few things, and it rather appears to me that you're getting away my patent, so you'd better be somewhat careful, or I'll call the police!

One calls the police to catch a thief. Austin had stolen her patent and her beloved muse as well ("dear Susie . . . we are the only poets . . . everyone else is *prose*").

Dickinson must have realized that her hostility was coming too close to the surface because at this point she stops the letter in full career and tenders an apology.

> Well Austin, if you've stumbled through these two pages of folly, without losing your hat or getting lost in the mud, I will try to be sensible, as suddenly as I can, before you are quite disgusted.

The good resolution does not last, however. She knows that she is speaking mud and that he will get disgusted; but within a few lines she is recommending "hot irons, and Chinese Tartary" as suitable punishments for entrapping "a young woman's 'phelinks' in such an awful way."

Only at the end of the letter does she come as near as she can to an open, undisguised admission of the rivalry between them and her own terrible defeat.

> Dear Austin, I am keen, but you are a good deal keener, I am *something* of a fox, but you are more of a hound! I guess we are very good friends tho', and I guess we both love Sue just as well as we can. (L, 234–36)

At this point little else was left to say.

Increasingly alienated from others throughout her late adolescence, Dickinson was now cut off from the two people with whom, emotionally and intellectually, she had the most in common. Although she claimed that a "golden link" bound them "all together" (L, 238), she now knew for certain that Susan would go to live in her brother's house and not, as she seems to have fantasized, in her own. And inevitably, perhaps, she came to recognize that no matter how much she and Susan loved each other, their feet were unalterably set on different paths.

> Sue—you can go or stay—There is but one alternative—We differ often lately, and this must be the last.
>
> You need not fear to leave me lest I should be alone, for I often part with things I fancy I have loved, —sometimes to the grave, and sometimes to an oblivion rather bitterer that death. . . .
>
> Sue—I have lived by this. It is the lingering emblem of the Heaven I once dreamed, and though if this is taken, I shall remain alone, and though in that last day, the Jesus Christ you love, remark he does not know me—there is a darker spirit will not disown it's child.
>
> Few have been given me, and if I love them so, that for *idolatry,* they are removed from me—I simply murmur *gone,* and the billow dies. . . . We have walked very pleasantly—Perhaps this is the point at which our paths diverge—then pass on singing Sue, and up the distant hill I journey on.   (L, 305–6)

Like Abby Wood and Abiah Root before her, Sue had accepted Jesus Christ and with him, her womanly duty. She would marry and live a life of active usefulness such as her society and religion said she should, albeit, as it proved, with a difference. But Dickinson would not give up her "idolatry"—her passionate commitment to earthly romance in all its intensity, all its poetry—even though it meant that a "darker spirit" would own "his child" and even if friend after friend was removed from her because of it.

In the end, Dickinson's intuitions proved correct. The taproot of her poetry and her future sense of identity as a woman and a woman poet lay in her rejection of duty and the Christian path that Susan and the others chose to tread. If the martyr's pose in this letter was a pose and a sentimentalized one at that, it was also the same pose from which the "Queen of Calvary," idolatrous, rebellious, sacrilegious, would someday spring.

At the end of the "go or stay" letter, Dickinson included a poem. Other than valentines, it is her third extant poem. To our knowledge she was not to write another for four years. As a poem, it is not particularly memorable in itself. But in the contrast it draws between the love that is unrequited here and that same love compensated for in the "Bright Melody" of eternity, where poetry and love are one, "I have a Bird in spring" is a clear

omen of things to come and an earnest given by the poet against her own
maturation:

> I have a Bird in spring
> Which for myself doth sing—
> The spring decoys.
> And as the summer nears—
> And as the Rose appears,
> Robin is gone.
>
> Yet do I not repine
> Knowing that Bird of mine
> Though flown—
> Learneth beyond the sea
> Melody new for me
> And will return.
>
> Fast in a safer hand
> Held in a truer Land
> Are mine—
> And though they now depart,
> Tell I my doubting heart
> They're thine.
>
> In a serener Bright,
> In a more golden light
> I see
> Each little doubt and fear,
> Each little discord here
> Removed.
>
> Then will I not repine,
> Knowing that Bird of mine
> Though flown
> Shall in a distant tree
> Bright melody for me
> Return.
>
> (no. 5; P, 7–8)

2. The Tangled Road
Children Walk: 1858–61

. . . .

. . . .

. . . .

You ask of my Companions Hills—Sir—and the
Sundown—and a Dog—large as myself, that my Father
bought me—They are better than Beings—because they
know—but do not tell—
—Dickinson to T. W. Higginson, 1862

After 1853 Dickinson's letters travel a steady
downward path toward suicidal depression. With the loss of Susan to
Austin, part of the dream had died. And with it went not only Dickinson's
enthusiasm for life but even, it seems, her clear sense of vocation as a poet.
The letters that she wrote to friends and family alike in this period are filled
with major and minor complaints. Many are morbid and reeking of
nostalgia for a lost, better past. She sees herself increasingly as old
fashioned, that is, not out-of-date but out-of-touch, an anomaly in her
society at whom people will stare (L, 299). She avoids old friends, refusing
invitations. She recalls and dwells on those who passed away years before,
particularly Benjamin Newton, and mourns insistently the passing of those
who have left her orbit either because, like Henry Emmons and John
Graves, they have moved from Amherst or because, like Emily Fowler
Ford, they have married. She develops a "box of Phantoms" in which she
places the lost ghosts of the past, "blossoms" she "will . . . gather in

Paradise" when "on the shores of the sea of Light" she seeks her "missing sands" (L, 330). She sends one friend, Mary Warner (Crowell), a sentimental poem by John Pierpont on the death of a young child. To another, Elizabeth Holland, she writes that she wishes she were "a grass, or a toddling daisy, whom all these problems of the dust might not terrify" (L, 324). In April of 1856 she sends her cousin John Graves a strange, surrealistic letter in which she describes her garden as steeped in death even as it comes to life. It is filled with "crumbling things": "crumbling elms and evergreens" and "*wings* half gone to dust" (L, 327). By August, a month after Austin's wedding to Sue, she is frankly suicidal.

> Don't tell, dear Mrs. Holland, but wicked as I am, I read my Bible sometimes, and in it as I read today, I found a verse like this, where friends should "go no more out"; and there were "no tears," and wished as I sat down tonight that we were *there*— not *here*—and that wonderful world had commenced, which makes such promises. . . . And I'm half tempted to take my seat in that Paradise of which the good man writes, and begin forever and ever *now*, so wondrous does it seem.   (L, 329).

In his ground-breaking psychoanalytical biography of the poet, *After Great Pain*, John Cody argues that Dickinson was not only suicidal in 1856 but that she had a psychotic breakdown as a result of the internal conflicts generated by Austin's marriage to Susan.[1] Without further data Cody's assertion, based almost entirely on his reading of the poems, cannot be proved, but what does seem clear is that for a year and a half after the wedding, Dickinson went into a depression, perhaps better called a retreat, so complete that she all but died to the world. From August 1856, when she wrote Mrs. Holland, to the beginning of 1858, only three small facts are known of her. In October of 1856 her bread won second prize at the local agricultural fair. On December 12, two days after her twenty-sixth birthday, she cut an advertisement for tombstones out of the *Express*. On August 26 of the following year she was listed as one of the judges of rye and Indian bread at the forthcoming cattle show; we do not know if she actually served in this capacity. Otherwise nothing remains: no letters, no poems, not even references to her by other persons. If she wasn't "dead," she might as well have been. And given her predilection for symbolic acting out, it may well be that this is precisely how she thought of herself during this period. If so, however, then "death" by withdrawal turned out to be an excellent counterploy to suicide itself.

For Dickinson did not die in 1856 nor in all likelihood did she go insane, although she certainly feared, and possibly believed, that she would. Rather, she seems to have gone underground, to have pulled herself in for however long it took until she was ready to start living again. In 1858 she reemerged, still morbid, still depressed, still, apparently, very much in love with Susan, but ready at last to take those first tentative steps toward poetry and toward loving other people which would eventually allow her to live, as she chose to define living, in the world again.

The story of Dickinson's recovery from the depression of 1853 – 57 is not one of immediate success but of slow and often stumbling progress against difficult and painful odds. Adolescence had left her beached like a whale. Her love for Sue was stymied. Her own sense of gender identity was not clearly defined. Even her vocation as poet seems to have become unclear, for there is no evidence that she wrote poetry between 1854 ("I have a Bird in spring") and 1858, when, according to Johnson's dating, she began writing again.[2] The major tasks of adolescence — the consolidation of the ego in respect to gender identity and the acceptance of one's adult role in life — had not occurred in her. Like her body, which she said at fourteen would "always remain the same old sixpence" (L, 21), her personality, too, appears to have been suspended in the middle world of preadolescent androgyny. At twenty-six she could still describe herself to Mrs. Holland as a "simple child" living at home, unable, or more accurately perhaps, unwilling to take up the clarifying (and ultimately, stultifying) responsibilities that in her society went with bodily change.

Susan's marriage had such severe psychological repercussions for Dickinson not just because of the internal conflicts it generated but because it spelled out, at least for a while, the end of any hope she had for herself. As long as she thought she possessed Sue, Dickinson's own values and sense of identity had been justified. She and Susan were lovers and poets together, children perhaps, but able to survive with gratifications of their own. With Susan's loss, however, Dickinson was thrust back into an isolation even more severe than "when love," as she told Susan in 1855, "first began, on the step at the front door, and under the Evergreens" (L, 315) back in 1850. For Dickinson in 1856, only the past contained the seeds of an identity, a life, she could believe in. In the future lay nothing at all.

"I play the old, odd tunes yet," she wrote at the conclusion of her April letter to John Graves, "which used to flit about your head after honest hours — and wake dear Sue, and madden me, with their grief and fun — How far from us, that spring seems — and those triumphant days — our April got to Heaven *first* — Grant we may meet her there — at the 'right hand of the Father'" (L, 328). If, as seems most probable, April stands for Susan in this passage, then Susan's loss, that special friend who went to heaven or marriage before her, meant the end of the poet's spring as well. No wonder that she saw her garden as steeped in death. Like herself, it was an empty, crumbling place where once "a bird resided."

In coming out of the depression of 1853–57, the task that confronted Dickinson was more than anything else the formation of her long-postponed adult identity, an identity that would allow her to have a future by permitting her to be both a poet and a woman. Dickinson had refused the path to maturation which her society held out to her, the life of active usefulness which she despised. But in identifying her desire to be a poet so totally with her childhood, she had also, however inadvertently, closed the future on herself. For all the seeming freedoms it allowed—freedom from responsibility, freedom to dream, freedom to write and to be what she wanted to be—childhood, as she appears to have discovered forcibly in the mid-fifties, was a dead-end option. Permitting neither growth nor, ultimately, love, it doomed her to a life of nostalgia and, as her letters suggest, a hollow, suicidal self.

If Dickinson was to have a future, the identification that she had made as an adolescent between child and poet had to break down. In the years between 1858 and 1861—a period in which Dickinson actively struggled to find reasons to survive—I believe that she was able to break it down. By the end of this period, a new identification had taken its place. In this identification, as the following letter to the Norcross sisters, written in 1861, makes clear, the poet is no longer a child. She is a queen, a mature, empowered woman.

Your letters are all real, just the tangled road children walked before you, some of them to the end, and others but a little way, even as far as the fork in the road. That Mrs. Browning fainted, we need not read *Aurora Leigh* to know, when she lived with her English aunt; and George Sand "must make no noise in her grandmother's bedroom." Poor children! Women, now, queens, now! And one in the Eden of God. . . . Take Heart, little sister, twilight is but the short bridge, and the moon (morn) stands at the end. If we can only get to her! Yet, if she sees us fainting, she will put out her yellow hands. (L, 376)

In the titanic struggles of George Sand and Elizabeth Barrett Browning, whose biographies fortuitously appeared a few months apart in the 1861 *Atlantic Monthly*,[3] Dickinson had found the models she sought so long. The miseries of isolation and silencing that these great writers had endured as children were kin to her own. And the writers' later triumphant maturity provided the inspiration for the American poet's own eventual escape from childhood's tangled road. She, too, might someday be a "queen," a woman writer, if she did not faint: if she did not lose confidence and give in again to her own weakness and perhaps (the moon/morn passage is ambiguous) to her longing to die.

It would be naive to assert that the path that Dickinson eventually worked out for herself as an adult was normal, just as it would be unreasonable to pretend that she lived her life without a tremendous amount of pain. As Sandra Gilbert and Susan Gubar have noted, in maturity Dickinson resolved the conflict between her gender and her genre by becoming a poser.[4] And the poses she struck—loving but troublesome daughter to her parents, "myth" to Amherst at large, "cracked poetess" to Thomas Wentworth Higginson,. fellow child and conspirator to her niece and nephews, occasionally childish confidante to her women friends, "sufferer polite" to Samuel Bowles and, possibly, Charles Wadsworth—do not always ring true.

But this does not mean, as Gilbert and Gubar seem to suggest, that Dickinson's behavior as an adult was necessarily pathological or even that all of her poses were insincere. Some, like her withdrawal from society, were understandable responses to the inhospitality of the world in which she lived. Powerful, willful, and romantic, she had no place in that world. Why should she join it, especially at such cost? "I have been in a savage, turbulent state for some time—," Samuel Bowles wrote revealingly to her brother, Austin, in 1863, "indulging in a sort of [   ] disgust at everything & everybody—I guess a good deal as Emily feels."[5] Bowles knew Dickinson better than most and I think we can take his word for it that Dickinson's disgust at everything and everybody sprang a good deal less from disabling fear than it did from the more savage but positive and active emotions, distaste and rage.

Other poses, such as the little girl role she played for her preceptor, Higginson—a preceptor who had nothing to teach and everything to learn—were, on the other hand, clearly reactive and feigned. At best they were strategies for survival. But underneath these guises, none of which was her sum, there lay a whole and integrated, if admittedly very angry woman.

When Gilbert and Gubar ask, "How did Dickinson, who seemed to Thomas Wentworth Higginson so timid, even so neurotically withdrawn, manage such spectacular poetic self-achievement" in "the most Satanically assertive, daring, and therefore precarious of literary modes for women:

lyric poetry?"[6] they appear sincerely bemused by their own question. Like Higginson's wife, who could only express her total dismay at the poet's 1873 comment, "there is always one thing to be grateful for—that one is one's self & not somebody else" (L, 519), the contemporary critics see Dickinson largely through Mr. Higginson's nineteenth-century male eyes: as a little, timid, childlike woman, dressed in white, and behaving very much like a moth. For such a person to have written "Satanic" poetry makes no more sense than that she should be relieved to be herself and not someone else. But despite Dickinson's all too disingenuous disclaimer, "When I state myself, as the Representative of the Verse—it does not mean— me—," it was the woman Higginson thought he saw, not the speaker of her poems, who was Dickinson's true "supposed person" (L, 412).[7] In a period when women were not supposed to possess power, Dickinson possessed power in abundance but she confined it to the speaker of her verse. The seemingly pathetic creature others saw was the mask the poet wore, even after she had matured inwardly, in order to maintain the freedom she needed to explore within the confines of her art the "Finite Infinity" (no. 1695; P, 1149) of what she called with such magnificent arrogance, her "Columnar Self" (no. 789; P, 595).

Much of the mystery that surrounds Dickinson's "spectacular poetic self-achievement" and that makes her seem, in Mary Higginson's blunt terminology, "insane" (L, 519), disappears once we recognize that the author of the poems was not the person about whom the myths have grown. The myths, or masks (or, as Austin acutely said, the pose), were a shell behind which the real woman, Dickinson's poet–queen, came to live out her "Satanically assertive" life. It was, Martha Dickinson Bianchi reports, their own immature pity that led Bianchi and her brother, Ned to feel sorry for their aunt's "straitened" life. After they came to understand her better, "The perspective had changed. We were those hemmed in. Aunt Emily was free to her chosen horizon."[8]

•   •   •

When after a four-year break Dickinson began to write poetry again in 1858, she had three principal themes: nature, to which she returned constantly for imagery; death, about which she obsessed; and Susan, to whom or about whom she wrote at least ten of the fifty-odd poems attributed to this year. The majority of the poems on nature were written to accompany gifts of flowers or fruit and they tend to be occasional as well as conventional. Whatever faults they possess, the poems on Susan and death, on the other hand, speak directly to Dickinson's later development as woman and poet. These poems are, moreover, intimately connected with each other.

With only one exception, "One sister have I," the poems Dickinson wrote to her sister-in-law in 1858 are morbid and confused. Like most women in our culture who have experienced the loss of a lover, whether that lover is male or female, Dickinson was left feeling empty or hollow following Susan's marriage to Austin, and in the poetry she wrote two years later on the subject, she equates this empty feeling with death. Where in the 1856 letter to John Graves she depicted her garden as crumbling and abandoned, in 1858 she describes her heart as a coffin, an empty, crumbling, forgotten nest:

> It did not surprise me—
> So I said—or thought—
> She will stir her pinions
> And the nest forgot,
>
> Traverse broader forests—
> Build in gayer boughs,
> Breathe in Ear more modern
> God's old fashioned vows—
>
> This was but a Birdling—
> What and if it be
> One within my bosom
> Had departed me?
>
> This was but a story—
> What and if indeed
> There were just such coffin
> In the heart instead?
>   (no. 39; P, 33)

With its coy references to "Birdlings" and "boughs," "It did not surprise me" is not a good poem. The imagery and language are flat. The theme is sentimentalized. The poet's failure to state clearly either her anger or her loss gives the poem an arch quality that is distasteful. At the conclusion of the poem the reader is left with a set of questions that suggest but do not confirm the experience that the speaker describes. Nevertheless, the poem does help establish how closely Dickinson's feelings for Susan were tied into the initial stages of her poetic development. In 1858 she still felt childlike, helpless, wounded, and abandoned. From these feelings the majority of her poems spring.

Dickinson had, in fact, linked the loss of Susan with the idea of death, or a deathlike state, from the very beginning. In a letter Johnson dates 1854, she describes herself as "cold," a "block" or "stone," after not hearing from Susan for an unusually long time.

> I do not miss you Susie — of course I do not miss you — I only sit and stare at nothing from my window, and know that all is gone — Dont *feel* it — no — any more than the stone feels, that it is very cold, or the block, that it is silent, where once 'twas warm and green, and birds danced in it's branches.   (L, 304)

And at the conclusion of the 1854 letter in which she told Susan to either go or stay, she consoled herself over Susan's loss with the idea that after death,

> . . . that Bird of mine
> Though flown
> Shall in a distant tree
> Bright melody for me
> Return.
>   (no.5; P, 8)

That is, some day, doubt, fear, and discord would be resolved as the two women were joined together in eternity.

In 1858 she returns to this same idea in what is undoubtedly one of her most bizarre and macabre, but developmentally speaking, most important efforts.

> I often passed the village
> When going home from school —
> And wondered what they did there —
> And why it was so still —
>
> I did not know the year then —
> In which my call would come —
> Earlier, by the Dial,
> Than the rest have gone.

It's stiller than the sundown.
It's cooler than the dawn—
The Daisies dare to come here—
And birds can flutter down—

So when you are tired—
Or perplexed—or cold—
Trust the loving promise
Underneath the mould,
Cry "it's I", "take Dollie",
And I will enfold!
                              (no. 51; P, 39–40)

Like "It did not surprise," "I often passed the village," is not a good poem. But the many similarities it possesses to the far finer "Because I could not stop for Death," written in 1862, when Dickinson reached maturity as an artist, make it an important benchmark for her poetic and psychological development. By putting the two poems side by side, their differences can be quickly noted.

Because I could not stop for Death—
He kindly stopped for me—
The Carriage held but just Ourselves—
And Immortality.

We slowly drove—He knew no haste
And I had put away
My labor and my leisure too,
For His Civility—

We passed the School, where Children strove
At Recess—in the Ring—
We passed the Fields of Gazing Grain—
We passed the Setting Sun—

Or rather—He passed Us—
The Dews drew quivering and chill—
For only Gossamer, my Gown—
My Tippet—only Tulle—

We paused before a House that seemed
A Swelling of the Ground—

The Roof was scarcely visible—
The Cornice—in the ground—

Since then—'tis Centuries—and yet
Feels shorter than the Day
I first surmised the Horses Heads
Were toward Eternity.

(no. 712; P, 546)

Despite the remarkable refinement in Dickinson's poetic technique, "Because I could not stop for Death" and "I often passed the village" have a great deal in common. Both poems draw a sharp distinction between life's noisy schoolyard and the still, cool habitation of eternal rest. Both describe death in terms of a call and a journey or passage which the speaker must make alone. In both, death is associated with sundown and the end of work and leisure. And finally, in both poems, the poet clearly identifies the speaker with herself, assuming an air of feminine ingenuousness as she describes her new home beneath the ground.

But here the resemblance between the two poems ends. "Because I could not stop for Death" may draw much of its strength from Dickinson's personal death-obsession but it is not a personal poem. Rather it uses the speaker's situation as the basis for a generalized rumination on the affective quality of eternity, an eternity that virtually opens up for the reader as it does for the poet in the poem's final lines. "I often passed the village," on the other hand, is a morbid, self-centered appeal to a concrete and specific person, "Dollie" or Sue, to "Trust the loving promise / Underneath the mould" and join Dickinson in death.

"Because I could not stop for Death" expands the limits of the poet's biographical situation as well as her pain, dignifying both and giving both wider significance. "I often passed the village" does not extend beyond itself and appears, therefore, maudlin, outrageous, and absurd. Neither poem was intended for publication. The difference between the two poems lay not in the author's conception of her audience, but in Dickinson's conception of her self and the vision this self could encompass in her verse.

"I often passed the village" is a bad poem not because it is unprofessional—in the sense in which that term is usually taken, all Dickinson's poetry is unprofessional—but because it lacks what we think of as professional authority. It is bad not because it is biographical—some of Dickinson's finest poetry is biographical—but because it fails to enlarge biography and give it more general appeal. While Dickinson was able to achieve a number of remarkable successes between 1858 and 1861, the bulk of what she wrote during this period, especially in the early years, suffers from basically the same limitations. Although usually not so personal and bizarre as "I often passed the village," it is poetry of little weight and narrow dimension. Simply enough, Dickinson had not yet arrived at a concept of self as woman-poet that would allow her to speak with full authority in her verse. Rather, the poetry that she wrote tends to be narrow, flat, and weak, even as her sense of self—abandoned, wounded, helpless, and childlike—was similarly restricted during much of this time.

Viewing Dickinson's development in this way, it is easy to understand why, particularly in the first few years of her career, she wrote so many poems in the "poetic nursery jargon"[9] Ivor Winters justifiably finds so offensive. As her letters make clear, she continued to see herself as a weak, helpless child well into 1861 and this same view of self all too often controls her poetic speaking voice as well. Thus in her letters she speaks of her night fears (L, 351), her childish hopes (L, 358), how she cannot be alone because "children fear the dark" (L, 354). She talks of misbehaving (L, 366) and how she "done wrong" (L, 348) as if she were indeed a little child. Even her room is "little" (L, 348) when, in fact, it was not. Her garden, too, is "a little knoll" (L, 357) and she herself, naturally, is a "little Bob O'Lincoln" in it (L, 366).

In her poetry, this sense of littleness or childishness results directly in some of her very worst verse, particularly when she chooses to combine it with the more sentimental poetic conventions of the day. Thus in "Poor little Heart!" (1860) the unhappy conflation of her own personal experience of feeling deserted and the language of "Robbie" Burns results in a poem that is so impoverished in imagination that it approaches the pathetic.

Poor little Heart!
Did they forget thee?
Then dinna care! Then dinna care!

Proud little Heart!
Did they forsake thee?
Be debonnaire! Be debonnaire!

Frail little Heart!
I would not break thee—
Could'st credit *me*? Could'st credit me?

Gay little Heart—
Like Morning Glory!
Wind and Sun—wilt thee array!
(no. 192; P, 138)

Nor, unhappily, is this the worst that she could do. In "'Twas such a little—little boat" (1859) a "greedy, greedy wave" devours her (no. 107; P, 81) and in "If *He dissolve*—then—there is *nothing—more*" (1861) she is "*His little Spaniel*" "*leaking—red—*" (no. 236; P 170–71). These are silly poems, poems written without dignity and totally lacking power, let alone the "Satanic self-assertiveness" of which Gilbert and Gubar speak. And in keeping with the contemporary critics' thesis, they do indeed suggest that the author is a woman whose core of self is dismally hollow.

But even as early as 1859, there is also evidence that Dickinson was trying to gain control over the childlike element in her poetry and, very probably, in herself. If in "Poor little Heart!" she is swamped with self-pity at the ease with which she has been forgotten, in poems such as "Papa above!" and "'Arcturus' is his other name—," as in the somewhat later "I'm Nobody! Who are you?" (1861), on which Gilbert and Gubar largely seem to base their case for the poet's fatally low self-esteem, she uses her smallness and insignificance ironically as a source of power. And the result is poetry that, while still limited, is nonetheless of quite a different order.

Thus, for example, in "Papa above!" she creates an impudent mouse that snugly ensconces itself in the "seraphic Cupboards" of the universe "While unsuspecting Cycles / Wheel solemnly away!" (no. 61; P, 46). And in "'Arcturus'" she presents a little girl whose knowledge is obviously superior to that of the savants who purport to instruct her (no. 70; P, 55–56). In both cases, the smallness and insignificance of her chosen personae are part of what allows them to maintain their subversive or skeptical postures. These masks appear, therefore, to be guises that the poet has donned in order to express "at a slant" (no. 1129 P, 792) what would otherwise be a mature disenchantment with the way things are. In these poems, Dickinson's choice of persona seems, consequently, less a reflex reaction to her own childishness than a deliberately selected artistic device over which she has exercised judgment and control. While such poems certainly lack the power and depth of her later verse, they can hardly be taken as simple reflections of a self that is not there.

Nevertheless, it is also true that in continuing to write poems from the perspective of a child, Dickinson automatically limited the scope and feeling available to her as an artist. If the self in "Papa above!" and "I'm Nobody!" is not hollow, it is certainly diminished even when, covertly, as in the latter poem, its claims are very large.

> How dreary—to be—Somebody!
> How public—like a Frog—
> To tell your name—the livelong June—
> To an admiring Bog!
>
> > (no. 288; P, 206–7)

Reading such lines, one can hardly miss Dickinson's contempt for the ordinary mass of humanity. But at the same time, by casting herself as the childlike "Nobody," she has managed to escape taking full responsibility for the unacceptable impulses she wishes to express. With relatively few exceptions, such as "Success is counted sweetest" and "How many times these low feet staggered," this disguised or indirect form of statement was, I believe, the best that Dickinson could do through most of this period. But when we compare the child-persona poems to the rich, full poems she wrote from late 1861 on, the difference is too great not to be marked. Even at their finest ("I'm Nobody!", "I taste a liquor never brewed"), these poems lack the weight and scope, the self, of Dickinson's most directly assertive poetry and, therefore, lack its authority as well. They are the poems of a woman who has not yet claimed full possession of the powers within herself.

•   •   •

Dickinson's inability to achieve a firm sense of woman self in her poetry prior to 1862 is inextricably tied to her situation. Through most of the "tangled road" of 1858 to 1861, her strongest feelings, those most capable of assuming power, were the very ones that she was forced to suppress, namely her feelings for Susan. And this effort at suppression must inevitably have had an impact on her ability to integrate her sense of self in her verse. While she did allow herself to love other people during this period, her deepest emotions and needs were precisely those that, for the time being, she worked hardest to close off in herself. And shut off from direct access to them, she remained in many ways hollow at her core.

Dickinson's inability to be direct about her feelings for Susan, particularly with respect to the rage she felt at her loss, is nowhere more apparent than in the few poems she wrote explicitly on the marriage itself. In "I never told the buried gold," for example, written in 1858 and sent to Sue,

Dickinson creates a strained analogy between her brother and the pirate captain Kidd, suggesting in a quite unpardonable submerged pun, that he kidnapped Susan.

> I never told the buried gold
> Upon the hill—that lies—
> I saw the sun—his plunder done
> Crouch low to guard his prize.
>
> He stood as near
> As stood you here—
> A pace had been between
> Did but a snake bisect the brake
> My life had forfeit been.
>
> That was a wondrous booty—
> I hope twas honest gained.
> Those were the fairest ingots
> That ever kissed the spade!
>
> Whether to keep the secret—
> Whether to reveal—
> Whether as I ponder
> "Kidd" will sudden sail—
>
> Could a shrewd advise me
> We might e'en divide—
> Should a shrewd betray me—
> Atropos decide!
>
> (no. 11; P, 14)

In a later, considerably more forthright and generalized poem about marriage, "She rose to His Requirement" (1863), Dickinson bluntly reasserts her adolescent conviction, expressed in the "man of noon" letter, that marriage destroys the wife. Her gold is worn away and she herself is buried fathoms down by the husband who claims her treasures (no. 732; P, 558–9). In "I never told the buried gold," the poet deals with precisely the same ideas but under cover of allegory. The husband is depicted as a pirate-sun or sun-pirate who crouches over his prize, not just guarding it but, as in the later poem, hoarding it as well. It is a prize that, Dickinson hints, he neither has honestly won nor richly deserves. Only the speaker, it would seem, appreciates the gold or woman at her true value—the sex and sexuality of the gold are presumably established in the poem's third stanza. But the speaker does not dare reveal her knowledge, first, we learn, because she is "too close" to the "sun" (pun intended).

> He stood as near
> As stood you here—
> A pace had been between—

And second, because she fears his phallic or snake-like power.

> Did but a snake bisect the brake
> My life had forfeit been.

Having shown herself as unable to resolve her situation, the speaker-poet is also unable to come to a resolution in the final stanza of the poem, a truly dreadful piece of writing. The poet, the persona, and the poem are all left divided between conflicted and conflicting possibilities: to keep the secret or tell it, to delay while Kidd sails, to divide the wealth, or to risk betrayal and death by revealing her desire. The poem leaves us, in short, in a total muddle. We know something is going on here but we are never told exactly what, let alone why.

That Dickinson believed Austin had stolen Susan from her was manifest in her "Pegasus" letter. If my reading of the poem is correct, "I never told the buried gold" confirms that six years later this conviction had not softened. Despite the marriage, despite her own long period of depression and retreat, Dickinson was still in love with Susan and outraged at her loss. But even as late as 1862, she could deal with her feelings about the circumstances of this loss only in veiled and strikingly indirect ways.

> The Malay—took the Pearl—
> Not—I—the Earl—
> I—feared the Sea—too much
> Unsanctified—to touch—
>
> Praying that I might be
> Worthy—the Destiny—
> The Swarthy fellow swam—
> And bore my Jewel—Home—
>
> Home to the Hut! What lot
> Had I—the Jewel—got

Borne on a Dusky Breast—
I had not deemed a Vest
Of Amber—fit—

The Negro never knew
I—wooed it—too—
To gain, or be undone—
Alike to Him—One
                    (no. 452; P, 349)

Beneath the superficial differences, the similarities between "The Malay—took the Pearl—" and "I never told the buried gold" are readily apparent. In both poems, a treasure, here a "Pearl," "Richer," one suspects, "than all his tribe," has been carried off by a swarthy, sunburned fellow who could not possibly appreciate it. In both, the speaker's own fears and inhibitions, ironically, prevent her from interfering as the unworthy rival carries off his prize. She fears "the Sea . . . Unsanctified—to touch—" Unable to compete openly, she never lets him know she "wooed it—too."

But the irony of this poem is mulitplied endlessly when one realizes that even here, in a poem privately written at a time when Dickinson had reached the height of her creative prowess, the inhibition is still operating. While "The Malay—took the Pearl" is on a small scale a very fine poem—tight, beautifully managed, free of both sentimentality and romantic exaggeration—it is also an exceedingly arch and disguised one. In only one poem expressly and explicitly dedicated to Sue, "Your Riches—taught me—Poverty," does Dickinson ever achieve anything like the sweep and tragic import of her finest love poems to the master. And, ironically, this poem, which so clearly seeks to evoke the wealth and exotic beauty Dickinson believed Susan possessed, has been consistently attributed by critics to the memory of another.

Your Riches—taught me—Poverty.
Myself—A Millionaire
In little Wealths, as Girls could boast
Till broad as Buenos Ayre—

You drifted your Dominions—
A Different Peru—
And I esteemed All Poverty
For Life's Estate with you—

Of Mines, I little know—myself—
But just the names, of Gems—
The Colors of the Commonest—
And scarce of Diadems

So much, that did I meet the Queen—
Her Glory I should know—
But this, must be a different Wealth—
To miss it—beggars so—

I'm sure 'tis India—all Day—
To those who look on You—
Without a stint—without a blame,
Might I—but be the Jew—

I'm sure it is Golconda—
Beyond my power to deem—
To have a smile for Mine—each Day,
How better, than a Gem!

At least, it solaces to know
That there exists—a Gold—
Altho' I prove it, just in time
It's distance—to behold—

It's far—far Treasure to surmise—
And estimate the Pearl—
That slipped my simple fingers through—
While just a Girl at School.
                    (no. 299; P, 218–19)

Ever since 1938, when George Whicher first made the suggestion in his
highly influential study, *This was a Poet*, critics have largely accepted the
idea that "Your Riches—taught me—Poverty" was written to commemo-
rate the ninth anniversary of Benjamin Franklin Newton's death.[10] Newton, who spent two years as a law clerk in Edward Dickinson's office in the
mid 1840s, was one of the earliest of Dickinson's male friends to encourage
her writing and her gratitude was undoubtedly sincere and long-lasting.
But the dedication which she provides for the poem, "Dear Sue—/ You see
I remember—/ Emily" (L, 401), hardly requires such an involuted gloss.
Nor does the pattern of the poem's imagery fit Whicher's attribution. For
the "Riches" of which the poet speaks—gems, diadems, the glory of

queens, the wealth of dominions, the Golconda smile, India, gold, and pearls—are the riches of "scintillation," with which, Dickinson once remarked in a sour moment, Susan was "overcharged" (L, 575). Quintessentially feminine in nature, they do little to express the gentle, scholarly wealth of the poet's long-dead male friend nor do they fit the way Dickinson habitually described men as Masters, Malays, and pirates in her poetry.

The great misfortune of Whicher's misattribution lies in the fact that it helped so long obscure the only poem in which Dickinson ever felt totally free to express in direct and undisguised form the love she felt for this extraordinary and very much underrated woman. However destructive Susan's relationship with Austin may have been—and however well-deserved some aspects of her reputation—her significance for Emily Dickinson's poetic development cannot be gainsaid. Nor can it be said that Dickinson's passion for Susan diminished over the course of time, although it certainly underwent profound changes. "The World hath not known her," Dickinson wrote to Susan in late 1885, not long before the poet died, "but *I* have known her, was the sweet Boast of Jesus. . . . The tie between us is very fine, but a Hair never dissolves" (L, 893). Pulled fine though it may have been, their love did not dissolve. But it was a love of which Dickinson, unlike Jesus, could not boast and, as a result, it is a love whose pervasive importance has until recent years largely been overlooked.

•　　•　　•

While Dickinson wrote to Sue in 1864, "There is no first, or last, in Forever—It is Centre, there, all the time—" (L, 430), it is true that Susan was displaced from "Centre" twice from 1858 to 1861, first by one of Susan's own best friends, Kate Scott Anthon, and then by the man known to us only as the Master. Since the poet's attachment to the Master only had a decisive influence on her writing after he rejected her, probably in late 1861, discussion of their relationship will be reserved until the next chapter. But here something must be said of the brief phenomenon of Kate Scott Anthon in Dickinson's life, if only because this affair has been so assiduously ignored by every Dickinson critic except Rebecca Patterson who, in her turn, managed to give it a significance beyond any justification in fact.[11]

According to Patterson, Kate Scott Anthon was the Master, only Dickinson disguised her homosexual passion by switching pronouns and "pasting on" a beard and mustache to make her illicit love acceptable. Like John Cody's thesis concerning Dickinson's psychotic breakdown, Patterson's argument involves a good deal of imaginary reconstruction of missing events and as a result, it is not convincing. Only four of the letters Dickinson wrote to Anthon during the height of their involvement, from 1859 to 1860, survive, along with one nostalgic note written in 1866. These letters establish that Dickinson was passionately in love with her sister-in-law's good friend for at least a brief period of time. But beyond that nothing is clear except, perhaps, that Anthon was the one to break off the relationship for reasons neither specify.

The importance of Dickinson's relationship with Anthon lies not in the light it sheds on the Master's identity, but in the fact that it complicates the poet's relationship with that unknown individual still further. If, as is usually assumed, Dickinson fell in love with the Master in 1858, the year when her correspondence with him appears to have commenced, then what was the poet doing also falling in love with a woman at the same time, indeed just at the point when her affair with the Master was supposedly reaching its peak, between 1860 and 1861? Unlike the letters Dickinson wrote to Sue when she was nineteen, the sentimental letters to Kate Scott Anthon were written when the poet was almost thirty. Since they cannot be dismissed as the extravagant effusions of a somewhat aged schoolgirl, they tell us more about Dickinson's real feelings for women and the role women played in her life than, perhaps, many of her modern critics have been willing to learn. By the same token, however, they will also help us understand why the Master played the unique role in the development of her poetic vocation that he did.

In February of 1859 Kate Scott Anthon, a former school friend of Susan Gilbert's, visited her in Amherst for the first time. At twenty-eight, Kate was a painfully young widow whose first husband, Campbell Turner, had died in 1857. Nothing much is known about the visit except the curious "culprit mice" episode, related by Dickinson to Elizabeth Holland in a letter dated February 20, 1859. According to Dickinson, Kate and Sue had been spending the evening with her at the Homestead when they heard the front bell ring. As was her custom when visitors came, Dickinson fled. Kate, perhaps caught up in the spirit of the thing, fled with her, putting them both in an awkward situation since they had clearly been overheard. "Clinging fast like culprit mice, we opened consultation" Dickinson writes. She was for asking forgiveness of the bell-ringers, but "K[ate] was impenitent and demurred. While [we] were . . . deliberating, S[ue] opened the door, announced that [we] were detected, and invited [us] in." Dickinson claims to have been deeply chagrined over the incident. Not only did Austin, the burgeoning patriarch, reprimand her severely for rudeness but, as it turned out, one of the bell-ringers was a gentleman for whom she truly cared, a friend and neighbor of Mrs. Holland and, more to the point perhaps, a man who was willing to talk "of [her] books with [her]" (L, 348).

Yet it is also clear from the liveliness with which Dickinson records the incident that in some ways she enjoyed the little escapade mightily. As she told Mrs. Holland, in Kate she had found a confederate, one who like herself would flee when company arrived. For Dickinson, who was becoming increasingly reclusive at this time, such companionship and sympathy must have felt very good, however briefly she possessed them. And perhaps because of this, she admitted Kate into her charmed inner circle. Not only did she repay Kate's visit by joining the evening merriment at Sue's, but, according to Anthon, she would entertain them with "weird & beautiful melodies, all from her own inspiration" on the piano.[12]

Sometime in March not long after Kate left Amherst, Dickinson wrote her the first of three passionate letters which, aside from one bit of doggerel, are all that remain from their correspondence in this period. (Since the original Dickinson manuscripts are lost, the dating, based on notes made by Anthon, is more than usually conjectural.) In the letter, Dickinson asks Kate rather specifically how much she is prepared to sacrifice for a love that may never be entirely fulfilled. The letter is encoded and heavily laden with erotic suggestiveness.

> I never missed a Kate before, — Two Sues — Eliza and a Martha, comprehend my girls.
> Sweet at my door this March night another Candidate — Go Home! We don't like Katies here! — Stay! My heart votes for you, and what am I indeed to dispute her ballot — ? — What are your qualifications? Dare you dwell in the *East* where we dwell? Are you afraid of the Sun? — When you hear the new violet sucking her way among the sods, shall you be *resolute*? All *we* are *strangers* — dear — The world is not acquainted with us, because we are not acquainted with her. And Pilgrims! — Do you hesitate? and *Soldiers* oft — some of us victors, but those I do not *see* tonight owing to the smoke. — We are hungry, and thirsty, sometimes — We are barefoot — and cold —
> Will you still come? *Then* bright I record you! *Kate* gathered in March! (L, 349)

Dickinson's topic in this letter is almost certainly romantic friendship. Her concern is that Kate understand just how difficult such friendships are to maintain. Thus she asks if Kate is prepared to live in the "East," the location of woman-to-woman love on Dickinson's poetic compass. And she wants to know if Kate is "afraid of the Sun," the sun being Dickinson's preferred symbol for male power and sexual potency from the "man of noon" letter of 1852 on. Above all, will Kate prove *"resolute"* when she hears "the new violet sucking her way among the sods"? That is, leaving the obvious sexual innuendo aside, is she ready to accept the fact that sustaining such a relationship will require courage and determination on both their parts? In a world not "acquainted" with them, romantic friends, the poet warns, meet with mixed fates at best: some pilgrims, some soldiers, some victors, some barefoot, hungry, and cold. If Kate is willing to take such risks, she should "still come." But the poet is not in the business of illusions. It is up to the other woman to decide.

This letter is important because it suggests that unlike the vast majority of the women whom Carroll Smith-Rosenberg and Lillian Faderman discuss in their studies of romantic friendship, Dickinson did not believe her romantic attachments to women were in accord with her society, even apart from the complications of her relationship with Sue: "All *we* are *strangers —* dear — The world is not acquainted with us, because we are not acquainted with her."

Two reasons, beside the anachronistic one of sexual guilt which Patterson and Cody cite,[13] might account for her attitude. The first was the simple but irrefutable fact that in the course of maturation, Dickinson had experienced not once but many times the loss of women she loved: two Sues, an Eliza, a Martha,[14] not to mention an Abiah, a Jane, a Harriet, a Sarah, and an Abby, either to religion or, often shortly thereafter, to men for whom she did not care (the *"enemy's* Land," she called it in an 1855 letter to Jane Humphrey {L, 321}). By 1859, the idea that two women might actually maintain their exclusive love for each other probably struck her as nothing short of miraculous "owing to the smoke." The battle had simply been lost too many times before, most crucially and recently with Sue.

But given that Dickinson attended Mount Holyoke, it is also possible that she did view romantic friendship as she desired to experience it, as sinful, not because it was unnatural (*"Bliss,"* she wrote to Kate Scott Anthon in late 1859, "is unnatural" {L 355}), but because in wanting to love another woman so intensely, with such exclusivity, she was putting her desire for friendship above both God and her duty. In the 1854 "go or stay" letter to Susan Gilbert, she flatly called such love idolatry and allowed as how God might well remove her friends from her because of it. Mary Lyon, the founder of Mount Holyoke, makes the problem clear in an 1828 letter she wrote to Miss Grant, the first of four special friends in that worthy woman's life.

> You fear lest . . . my solicitude for you, should in some measure exclude divine realities. . . . I do not think, however, that my solicitude for you is so great a temptation as many other things. . . . It is true that I have an anxiety for you daily, which seems to enter more deeply into my heart than almost any thing else; but I have been saved almost altogether from a restless solicitude. It is true that I share with you in all your trials, in no common degree; but that I am thus permitted to share even in your sorrows, I consider a precious privilege. . . .
>   I hope you will never fear lest your letters should increase my solicitude; for the reverse is always the effect. The more definitely I know all about you, the less difficult I find it to avoid that restlessness which I always find so *unprofitable.* What you have written to me from week to week, been *useful as well as gratifying.* Sometimes, when I have been re-perusing your letters, sentence by sentence . . . I have thought it would be well for me to read my Bible with like care. [italics added].[15]

The key statement in this marvelously vacillating example of doublethink is the last one. Special friendship, the all-absorbing but potentially restless solicitude of one woman for another, was acceptable in Lyon's and Grant's dutiful view of things if and only if it could be proved "useful as well as gratifying." The fact that rereading her friend's letters makes Miss Lyon want to read her "Bible with like care" proves that her concern for Miss Grant, far from excluding "divine realities," is leading her to them. So much for temptation.

How Mary Lyon would have viewed the kind of romantic, determinedly exclusive love that Dickinson craved is another matter. Leaving aside biblical injunctions against sodomy along with all modern notions of sexual guilt, the fact is that the kind of love Dickinson longed for, when viewed the way she viewed it, as an end in itself, was sinful simply because it was not useful. In marriage, a woman loved in order to fulfill her duty. In special friendships, such as Miss Grant and Miss Lyon enjoyed, both women similarly subordinated their love for each other to their love of God and their useful and profitable endeavors in this world. There was, therefore, no stain. Indeed, Lyon's pious biographers exalt her friendships with women, depicting them as both rational and romantic and citing in the conventional manner, the love between David and Jonathan as biblical support for their heroine's lifestyle.[16]

But what could one do with a poet who believed, as Dickinson did, that her friends were her "estate" and that "God is not so wary as we, else he would give us no friends"? "The Charms of the Heaven in the bush," she declared to Samuel Bowles in 1858, "are superceded I fear, by the Heaven in the hand . . ." (L, 338). Not even the "occasionally" she tacked on to the end of that last sentence could remove the taint of blasphemy from it. The fact is that by the evangelical doctrines of her day, doctrines that made human love in all its forms subordinate to love of God and duty, Dickinson's notion of love was idolatrous and sinful. It was sinful not because it was sodomy or even, possibly, because it was sexual (hard evidence for Dickinson's active sexuality remains wanting), but because it was so intense, so heightened with romance, that it led her to place her love for her friends above her love for God. Like the glorified romantic passion that pervades Shakespeare's *Antony and Cleopatra* and to which she was later explicitly to compare it, Dickinson's concept of love was "new heaven [and] new earth" indeed.[17]

And it may well have been this very total absorption, this idolatrous exclusivity, in Dickinson's love that caused Kate Scott Anthon, like so many before her, to retire finally from the field of battle. At any rate, such an interpretation would help explain why in late 1859, long before their correspondence actually appears to have terminated, Dickinson sent her new-found, but distant friend a letter far more sarcastic than loving.

Do you find plenty of food at home? Famine is unpleasant. —
It is too late for "Frogs," or which pleases me better, dear — not quite early enough! The pools were full of you for a brief period, but that brief period blew away, leaving me with many stems, and but a few foliage! Gentlemen here have a way of plucking the tops of trees, and putting the fields in their cellars annually, which in point of taste is execrable, and would they please omit, I should have fine vegetation & foliage all the year round, and never a winter month. Insanity to the sane seems so unnecessary — but I am only one, and they are "four and forty," which little affair of numbers leaves me impotent. Aside from this dear Katie, inducements to visit Amherst are as they were. — I am pleasantly located in the deep sea, but love will row you out if her hands are strong, and don't wait till I land, for I'm going ashore on the other side — (L, 355–56)

Outnumbered and lacking the world's approval (deemed "insane"), Dickinson is impotent to prevent "Gentlemen" from "plucking the tops of trees and putting the fields in their cellars. . . ." That is, she cannot stop men from picking women off just as they mature (plucking their "tops," stopping their growth) and marrying them (hoarding them in "cellars"). If she could, or "would they please omit," then she would dine well "all the year round." But as it is, "Famine is unpleasant" and all too familiar. The pools once filled with Kate are now empty and only "many stems and but a few foliage" remain. Kate, on the other hand, she comments rather snidely, is probably dining well elsewhere. Nevertheless, if Kate does still want her, love will row her out to Amherst. As for the poet, she is only "going ashore on the other side," that is, she has no intention of changing her direction— or presumably her love for women.

What Kate made of this letter we do not know. She did visit Amherst at least four more times between 1859 and 1861. It is probable that she and Dickinson spent time with each other on each of these occasions, possibly even, as Patterson hypothesizes, spending a night together.[18] Indeed, a comment made in Dickinson's 1866 letter to Anthon—"Come & have tea with us again Katie! *How* it rained that night! We must take many a tea together in a Northeast storm o' Saturday nights, before Da Vinci's Supper!" (L, 452)—suggests that the famous "Wild Nights" (1861) may well derive at least in part from Dickinson's experience with Anthon. Certainly, the imagery of the poem, with its emphasis on entering rather than being entered, is, as Lilliam Faderman has argued, far more appropriate for one woman's experience of another than for a woman's experience with a man:[19]

Wild Nights—Wild Nights!
Were I with thee
Wild Nights should be
Our luxury!

Futile—the Winds—
To a Heart in port—
Done with the Compass—
Done with the Chart!

Rowing in Eden—
Ah, the Sea!
Might I but moor—Tonight—
In Thee!
             (no. 249, P, 179)

But whether this poem deals with Kate Scott Anthon or not,[20] it is clear that this young widow did arouse strong sensual feelings in Dickinson, for to her the poet sent the most eloquent prose passage she was ever to write to or about another woman.

> The prettiest of pleas, dear, but with a Lynx like me quite unavailable,—Finding is slow, facilities for losing so frequent in a world like this, I hold with extreme caution, a prudence so astute may seem unnecessary, but plenty moves those most dear, who have been in want, and Saviour tells us, Kate, "the poor are always with us"—Were you ever poor? I *have* been a Beggar, and rich tonight, as by God's leave I believe I am, The "Lazzaroni's" faces haunt, pursue me still! You do not yet "dislimn," Kate, Distinctly sweet your face stands in its phantom niche—I touch your hand—my cheek your cheek—I stroke your vanished hair, Why did you enter, sister, since you must depart? Had not its heart been torn enough but *you* must send your shred? Oh! our Condor Kate! Come from your crags again! Oh: Dew upon the bloom fall yet again a summer's night. Of such have been the friends which have vanquished faces—sown plant by plant the churchyard plats and occasioned angels. (L, 365)

That Kate Scott Anthon, who along with being beautiful appears to have been a giddy and not altogether honest woman,[21] hardly deserved such tenderness and yearning is not the point. For a brief period of time she seems to have satisfied Dickinson's enormous craving for love and intense emotional experience. And in her name, Dickinson authored one of the most sheerly beautiful passages of blank verse in prose form she was ever to write. Had this passage appeared in a play by Shakespeare—in whose rhythms it was, I believe, conceived—we would not question what it actually is. As it is, it serves to remind us how much love poetry we have lost in a world where "Finding is slow" and the "facilities for losing so frequent" for romantic lovers and their special friends.

By the end of 1860, Dickinson was able to attain real fullness of scope in this last letter to Anthon. But as wtih the finest poems that she wrote between 1858 and late 1861, the letter's achievement represents at most a momentary success. Dickinson unquestionably produced a number of poems before 1862 that anticipate the later development of her voice and style—in particular poems such as "Success is counted Sweetest," "Safe in their Alabaster Chambers," "How many times these low feet staggered," "There came a Day—at Summer's full," and the highly regarded "There's a certain Slant of light." But these poems are the exceptions and the latter two were almost certainly written after the September "terror" that, I believe, marks the great divide in Dickinson's work. On the whole, even the best poetry Dickinson wrote prior to late 1861 is narrow in scope and limited in voice. It is a poetry of miniatures ("I taste a liquor never brewed," "Did the Harebell loose her girdle," "Come slowly—Eden," "The Flower must not blame the Bee") even when, as in these poems, Dickinson is dealing with experience that is both ecstatic and erotic. In a large number of poems, the poet's failure to fully own her feelings, to deal directly with her experience and take responsibility for it, results in verse that is muddled and unconvincing at best, conventional and sentimental at worst.

Had Dickinson died at the end of 1861, the world would never have known what it had lost, even if by some unlikely chance her poetry had made it into print. There are simply too many bad poems for every one that succeeds. Had she died a year later, on the other hand, we would all have mourned the passing of a major poet, in Yvor Winters's judgment, "one of the greatest lyric poets of all time."[22]

3. Queen of Calvary

. . . .
. . . .
. . . .

Emerging from an Abyss, and reentering it—that is Life,
is it not, Dear?
　　　　　　—Dickinson to Susan Gilbert, 1885

Between 1858 and 1861 by Johnson's dating,
Emily Dickinson wrote 298 poems, or an average of seventy-four a year. In
1862 she wrote 366 poems, an average of one a day, and in the two
subsequent years she wrote 141 and 174 poems respectively. The change in
quantity is a change in quality as well. Not only are the vast majority of
Dickinson's most frequently anthologized poems from this period, but
perhaps more important, the general level of her writing, poem to poem,
rises to a new standard below which it only occasionally falls thereafter. In
the course of three years, what Gilbert and Gubar call her "grotesquely
childlike"[1] little girl persona, responsible for some of her very worst
writing, recedes almost entirely, to be replaced by the terse, controlled
voice of a mature, often bitterly ironic woman who could call God a
"Mastiff" (no. 1317, P, 911) and Jason a "sham" (no. 870; P, 648) and
never flinch.

Dickinson seems to acknowledge obliquely the change that had taken
place in her poetry between late 1861 and early 1862 in her second letter to
Thomas Wentworth Higginson in April 1862, when she lies outright not
only about how long she has practiced her craft but about the motivations
which led her to write in the first place.

You asked how old I was? I made no verse—but one or two—until this winter—Sir—

I had a terror—since September—I could tell to none—and so I sing, as the Boy does by the Burying Ground—because I am afraid—
(L, 404)

In point of fact, Dickinson had written over two hundred poems by the start of 1861 alone, poems that were in no possible way connected with the September "terror."

Given the rapid development her poetry was then undergoing, Dickinson's need to link her writing, possibly in her own mind as well as Higginson's, with this obscure, unspecified event is understandable enough, however. For suddenly, almost violently, sometime between September 1861 and April 1862 her poetic powers had erupted, changing and expanding in ways that even she, perhaps, was not entirely prepared for. In the extraordinary "I felt a Funeral, in my Brain," written, according to Franklin's dating, in 1862, she describes figuratively the terror she had exerienced, and its explosive effect on her, in terms of a confrontation with existential dread. Forced to look life's abyss "squarely in the face"—as she says in a later companion poem, "I never hear that one is dead" (no. 1324; P, 915)—she felt her world split apart, leaving her "Wrecked, solitary, here," the numb survivor of some kind of shattering internal cataclysm, which she compares to madness, death, and loss.

I felt a Funeral, in my Brain,
And Mourners to and fro
Kept treading—treading—till it seemed
That Sense was breaking through—

And when they all were seated,
A Service, like a Drum—
Kept beating—beating—till I thought
My Mind was going numb—

And then I heard them lift a Box
And creak across my Soul
With those same Boots of Lead, again,
Then Space—began to toll,

As all the Heavens were a Bell,
And Being, but an Ear,

And I, and Silence, some strange Race
Wrecked, solitary, here—

And then a Plank in Reason, broke,
And I dropped down, and down—
And hit a World, at every plunge,
And Finished knowing—then—
(no. 280; P, 199–200)

In this poem, as in a limited number of others that seem to have been written in either late 1861 or early 1862 (not only "There's a certain Slant of light," but " 'Tis so appalling—it exhilarates," "I like a look of Agony," and "There came a Day—at Summer's full"), Dickinson's mature voice can be heard for the first time.[2] It is a voice that possesses the scope, authority, and tragic vision of one of the world's greatest lyric poets. It is the voice of a woman who emerged from and then reentered the abyss.

What happened to accelerate the process of Dickinson's poetic development so dramatically in late 1861 can never be known absolutely, but all the evidence of her letters and poems suggests that the September terror had to do with a breakdown that occurred in her relationship with a man to whom she had been writing since 1858. It is this man whom critics and biographers, following the poet's lead, have chosen to call the Master since his true identity can probably never be confirmed.[3]

The best, indeed the only information we have on the course of Dickinson's relationship with the Master comes from the poet herself. In the second of a series of three draft letters found among her papers after her death, all presumably addressed to the same man and all possibly, but not definitely, sent to him in fair copy, Dickinson rehearses the course of their love affair, concluding with the plea that she be allowed to wait for him, no matter how long it might take. Like her letters to Kate Scott Anthon, this letter is encoded. But it does make one point very clear. Despite any number of poems Dickinson wrote to the contrary, the love affair was entirely one-sided. Her love for him, not his for her, was the force that made it move.

God made me . . . Master—I didn't be—myself. I dont know how it was done. He built the heart in me—Bye and bye it outgrew me—and like the little mother—with the big child—I

God made me. I didn't make myself. He made me love the way I did. Finally, I got tired of loving that way, my heart got too big for me to carry. I wanted rest or "Redemption."

got tired holding him. I heard
of a thing called "Redemption"—which rested men and
women. You remember I asked
you for it—you gave me something else. I forgot the Redemption [in the Redeemed—I
didn't tell you for a long time,
but I knew you had altered me
. . . and was tired—no more
. . .]. I am older—tonight . . .
but the love is the same. . . . If
it had been God's will that I
might breathe where you
breathed . . . if I wish with a
might I cannot repress—that
mine were the Queen's place—
the love of the Plantagenet is
my only apology—To come
nearer than presbyteries . . . is
forbidden me—You make me
say it over—I fear you laugh—
when I do not see—[but]
"Chillon" is not funny. Have
you the Heart in your breast
Sir—is it set like mine. . . ?
. . . You say I do not tell
you all—Daisy confessed—and
denied not.

Vesuvius dont talk—Etna
dont . . . one of them—said a
syllable—a thousand years ago,
and Pompeii heard it, and hid
forever—She couldn't look the
world in the face, afterward
. . . ! "Tell you of the want"—
you know what a leech is, dont
you . . . ?

I dont know what you can do
for it—thank you. . . . I used
to think when I died—I could
see you . . . but the "Corporation" are going Heaven too so

You remember, I asked you for
it. You gave me something else
instead. You changed me. I
didn't tell you for a long time.
But now I'm not tired (I don't
need redemption?) anymore.

I'm older now and the love
hasn't changed. It's God's will
I'm not your wife (in the
"Queen's place"); but that
doesn't stop me from wanting to
be. The love of the Plantagenet
(Shakespeare's Henry the Fifth?)
is my only excuse. I know that
it is forbidden to me, but why
do you make me say it over. I
fear you are laughing at me; but
my situation isn't funny. Do you
have a heart?

You say I don't tell you everything. I did.

Volcanoes don't talk. When one
of them did, the town that
heard it disappeared forever—it
was so embarrassing. You're
acting like a leech to ask me to
say more than I've said already
about what I need.

I don't know what you can do
for my "want" but thank you for
asking. I used to think I could
join you when I died, but then I

[Eternity] wont be seques-
tered—now. . . . Say I may
wait for you—say I need go
with no stranger to the to me—
untried [country] fold—I
waited a long time . . . but I
can wait more—wait till my
hazel hair is dappled—and you
carry the cane. . . .

(L, 373–75)

realized that the "Corporation"
(his wife? his congregation?),
would go to heaven also so we
won't be alone. Say I don't have
to go with any one else to the
to-me-untried countryfold
(heaven? heterosexuality?). I've
waited a long time. I can wait
even longer, wait until we are
both old.

In providing the above translation, I have reduced this letter to virtual child's talk because beneath the thin poetic veneer that is what it is. Whoever this man was, whether, as is most probable, he was Charles Wadsworth or Samuel Bowles, or some other, less likely candidate, he obviously was not in love with Dickinson. Nor was he encouraging her although he was clearly solicitous of her well-being. The love was entirely from her, the fundamentally needy, dependent love of a woman who had found her heart too big to support and who had turned to him originally in search of comfort, help, and, possibly, if the intended recipient was Wadsworth, quite literally redemption.

From the letter it seems clear that Dickinson knew, even after she did fall in love with him, that he neither would nor could reciprocate her love. He was, among other things, married. But as with the analysand who falls in love with her analyst, real love, love with the possibility of mature mutual reciprocation, was not the desired goal in any case, no matter how much Dickinson seems to ask for it here. The love she expresses in this letter derives rather from deep but entirely one-sided psychological need.

The second Master letter suggests a story for Dickinson's great love affair that is at once considerably less romantic and considerably more probable than most of the myths that have sprung up about it. Dickinson had turned to this man at a time when she needed support for her faltering ego and a way out of the "Chillon" or prison of her adolescent self. In the years between 1858, when presumably she began writing to him, and 1861, the Master had supplied this need by maintaining a correspondence with her, reading her poems, and accepting her love. But the basic model of their relationship was not that of an adult pairing. It was the love of parent for child and child for parent, just as we see today in the intense transference relationship between therapist and patient. And like the good therapist he was trying to be, the Master had apparently done his best to help her keep her fantasies in line ("You make me say it over"; "To come nearer . . . is forbidden me") even while providing her with the opportunity to pour forth her trials (if he was Wadsworth)[4] or her desires (if he was Bowles). Dickinson's own last request, tacked on to the end of the second letter, asking that he at least visit her in Amherst, strongly suggests that she really did not expect or perhaps want anything more.

> Could you come to New England—[this summer . . .] would you come
> to Amherst—Would you like to come—Master?
>   [Would it do harm—yet we both fear God—] Would Daisy dis-
> appoint you—no—she would'nt—Sir—it were comfort forever—
> just to look in your face, while you looked in mine—then I could play in
> the woods till Dark. . . .   (L, 375)

If my reading of the second Master letter, dated 1861 by Johnson, is correct, then it helps explain two of the more pointed anomalies in Dickinson's relationship with this man. First, it clarifies how in the middle of what was supposedly her developing passion for him, she could fall in love with somebody else, namely Kate Scott Anthon. And second, it explains why his rejection of her, which appears to have occurred in late 1861 (her September terror), was ultimately so much more crucial for her poetic development than the fantasy that he loved her.

On the basis of Dickinson's opening remarks in the letter, it appears that she did not actually realize that she was in love with the Master for quite a while, possibly not until after the Kate Scott Anthon affair. She had turned to him first not for love but for counsel and support. As in transference relationships, the desire for a real love had come only later. This would also help explain why the first Master letter, dated by Johnson 1858, is very warm without being passionate and why Dickinson did not begin seriously writing love poems to him until 1861.

At the same time, however, it is clear that this love affair with him, even at its most passionate, would never have been entirely real to her. It was a fantasy relationship that she carried out, as Vivian Pollak has recently suggested, in the safety of knowing it could never be fulfilled. Given Dickinson's well-documented anxieties concerning men and marriage, it is, as Pollak argues, singularly unlikely that the poet would have chosen for a lover a man who might actually prove available for her.[5] She simply feared too much the loss of will that marriage involved for women.

The Master's rejection of her, on the other hand, was a very different matter for Dickinson. Given her past history, rejection was the stuff of life itself. And to the poetry she wrote upon this new and terrible loss, she brought all the experience she had had—two Sues, an Eliza, a Martha, and heaven knows how many others—that made her what she was, just as upon this experience she forged a new and independent sense of self.

In early 1862 Dickinson wrote a letter to the Master of such chaotic humility that it is painful and embarrassing to read even today. While she does not actually specify what went wrong between them, the opening lines of the letter suggest that, yet once more, Dickinson had driven her lover away by the very intensity of her articulated passion. She told him the truth, possibly the very truth that he asked for and she refused to disclose in the second Master letter, and now she fears that she has in her volcanic way offended him. The third and last Master letter is a desperate attempt on the poet's part to regain what she perceives to be her lost place in his affection. She becomes the "Daisy," the flower-wife, to his male sun.

Oh, did I offend it—[Did'nt it want me to tell it the truth] Daisy—Daisy—offend it—who bends her smaller life to his (it's) meeker (lower) every day—who only asks—a task—[who] something to do for love of it—some little way she cannot guess to make that master glad—

A love so big it scares her, rushing among her small heart—pushing aside the blood and leaving her faint (all) and white in the gust's arm—

Daisy—who never flinched thro' that awful parting, but held her life so tight he should not see the wound—who would have sheltered him in her childish bosom (Heart)—only it was'nt big eno' for a Guest so large—*this* Daisy—grieve her Lord—and yet it (she) often blundered—Perhaps she grieved (grazed) his taste—perhaps her odd—Backwoodsman [life] ways [troubled] teased his finer nature (sense), . . .

Low at the knee that bore her once unto [royal] wordless rest [now] Daisy [stoops a] kneels a culprit—tell her her [offence] fault . . . dont banish her—shut her in prison, Sir—only pledge that you will forgive—sometime. . . .

. . . Master—open your life wide, and take me in forever, I will never be tired—I will never be noisy when you want to be still. I will be [glad] [as the] your best little girl—nobody else will see me, but you—but that is enough—I shall not want any more—and all that Heaven only will disappoint me—will be because it's not so dear.   (L, 391–92)

Panicked apparently by the idea that she has offended him by the things she said, Dickinson pulls out all the stops, doing her best to imitate, as it were, a virtue—proper inarticulate female subservience—which by nature she did not possess. "Backwoodsman" that she is, she will bend her small life to his. She will kneel metaphorically at his feet. Against the very grain of her being, this woman who was obsessed with words and talked compulsively to those few people she thought competent enough to listen, will shut up and be his "best little girl"[6]—a singularly unlikely occurrence.

The groveling self-abasement to which Dickinson descends in this letter does not make pleasant reading. But in light of her many statements on the overwhelmingly negative effect heterosexual union had on women, her posture in this letter should come as no surprise. Prior to her attachment to the Master, she had avoided this "untried [country]fold" precisely because she feared it would entail this kind of loss of will or independent power in herself. Thus she wrote of the flower-wives to Susan in 1852:

> they will cry for sunlight, and pine for the burning noon, tho' it scorches them, scathes them . . . they know that the man of noon, is *mightier* than the morning and their life is henceforth to him. Oh, Susie, it is dangerous. . . . I tremble lest at sometime I, too, am yielded up. (L, 210)

Having finally been yielded up, that she would act in the way she feared is unfortunately all too predictable. This was, Dickinson believed, the way women were supposed to act with respect to men, granted that the poet's predilection for romantic exaggeration led her to carry her self-abasement one step further than most women would dare go.[7] Men were the masters upon whom women were supposed to lean and from whom they were supposed to draw their strength, support, and "royal" or "wordless rest." This version of male-female relationships was embedded in the law and literature of Dickinson's day and controlled the particular male-female relationship with which Dickinson was most familiar, that of her royal father and wordless, comparatively inarticulate mother. Only the extremity of Dickinson's language, and admittedly it is extreme, distinguishes her position in the third Master letter from the one a woman would normally consider it her duty to assume: "Hee for God only, shee for God in him."

But it is, therefore, all the more worth noting that even when her need and fear are the greatest, Dickinson is not actually asking the Master to reciprocate her love. Terrified though she is at the possibility of losing her "Lord," her request posed at the end of the letter is not that he love her but that she be allowed to snuggle invisibly within his great and spacious life where "nobody else will see me." Nobody will see her only if she is not there. What she wants, what she probably always wanted, was simply that he accept her love, her presence in his heart, whether he returned it or not.

It was not his refusal to love her, but his refusal to allow her to love him that was the crucial or "harrowing event" that occurred in late 1861. Once more, she had been cast off, swept away like the beloved bumblebee in "A single Clover Plank" by "A sudden Freight of Wind," from the "Plank" that kept her safe or saved her (no. 1343, P, 927–28) and prevented her world from falling apart.

Very possibly because her relationship with the Master was not as deep or real as her love for Sue, however, Dickinson did not go into another depression following this second major rejection in her life. Hurt, angry, but ironically liberated by the experience, she turned with renewed ferocity to her poetry instead and in her role as poet found the means to bring the shattered fragments of her woman self together. When Dickinson told Thomas Wentworth Higginson in 1869 that, without knowing it, he had "saved [her] Life" seven years before (L, 460), she was referring to such validation as he gave her poetry when she first sent it to him. But it was in the poetry itself, not Higginson's meager appreciation of it, that her true salvation lay.

•   •   •

What happened to Dickinson in 1862 was an explosion in form, thought, emotion, and self. With the Master's rejection all the feelings of betrayal, greed, need, rage, desire, and fear, that Dickinson had experienced from adolescence on and that, particularly in the context of her relationship with Susan, she had been forced to suppress, came flying to the surface. Just as her love for this man was unacceptable, so every unacceptable impulse she possessed found at last a vehicle by which it could be released. And in the course of this release, this explosion, the best little girl picked up the Loaded Gun that had been her life and transformed herself through its enabling power into the Queen of Calvary. Dickinson the woman-poet was born.

How does "Nobody," as Gilbert and Gubar would say, become Somebody? How, that is, does the poetic power and authority that Dickinson exhibits in her poetry after 1861 come to be acquired by the individual woman poet? In Dickinson's case it appears to have come first and foremost through the acquisition of a new, transcendent sense of self, a self that was strong enough, bold enough, to express without fear or reservation impulses, beliefs, and needs that best little girls would hardly dare murmur.

To discover this sense of self, however, Dickinson turned not to the Master, who, after all, had just rejected her, but to a fantasy marriage that she performed in her art. Baffled once more by a love that was doomed to remain unaccepted as well as unrequited, she found in her poetry and in her role as poet the fulfillment and selfhood—as queen, bride, wife, woman, empress—that she could not find in life. No understanding of the change that occurred in Dickinson's poetry between 1861 and 1862 is possible, in my opinion, without recognition of the role played in her personal and poetic development by this newly integrated, transcendent sense of self.

In early 1862 Dickinson sent Samuel Bowles "Title divine—is mine!" along with a brief note:

> Here's—what I had to "tell you"—You will tell no other? Honor—is it's own pawn—   (L, 394)

If by any chance Bowles was the Master and not, as is most probable, the poet's confidant during this troubled period, there is a wry irony in her sending him this poem. For the message that "Title divine" contains is not that she loves him, whoever he might be, but that she has learned how to be a woman without him. To use her terms, she is "Wife," that is, a mature, autonomously empowered woman, "without the Sign," without a husband.

> Title divine—is mine!
> The Wife—without the Sign!
> Acute Degree—conferred on me—
> Empress of Calvary!
> Royal—all but the Crown!
> Betrothed—without the swoon
> God sends us Women—
> When you—hold—Garnet to Garnet—
> Gold—to Gold—
> Born—Bridalled—Shrouded—
> In a Day—
> "My Husband"—women say—
> Stroking the Melody—
> Is *this*—the way?
>   (no. 1072, P, 758)

Dickinson's ecstatic response to her newly-recognized identity could not be more clear than it is in this poem. But the full importance of this response can only be appreciated when "Title divine" is set within the context of other poems Dickinson wrote on the marriage theme prior to 1862. For the basic concept of womanhood that she expresses in "Title divine" was not new to her when she wrote the poem. Rather it was the way she achieved this womanhood and her response to it that changed. The failure of scholars to distinguish between Dickinson's pre- and post-1862 marriage poems accounts, I believe, for their failure to recognize how different Dickinson's persona and voice actually are after late 1861 and how significant this difference is for the flourishing of her poetic gift.[8]

In 1860, for example, Dickinson wrote "I'm 'wife' — I've finished that," a poem that on first glance appears to be saying the same thing as "Title divine." But on closer inspection this poem proves so ambivalent in its attitude toward its theme that Gilbert and Gubar assume it must have been written ironically, as a dramatic monologue covertly critical of the "soft Eclipse" it appears to celebrate.[9]

I'm "wife" — I've finished that —
That other state —
I'm Czar — I'm "Woman" now —
It's safer so —

How odd the Girl's life looks
Behind this soft Eclipse —
I think that Earth feels so
To folks in Heaven — now —

This being comfort — then
That other kind — was pain —
But why compare?
I'm "Wife"! Stop there!
      (no. 199; P, 142–43)

Like the post-1861 marriage poems that "Title divine" represents, "I'm 'wife'" makes a clear division between Dickinson's two states: girl and woman. But where in the later poems the speaker's new status evokes an ecstatic welcome from her, in "I'm 'wife'" it is difficult to know just how she really feels about the state her speaker has assumed. On the one hand, the speaker refers to herself as a czar, suggesting that the poet was to some extent in touch with the feelings of power with which her marriage would someday fill her. But on the other hand, the speaker describes marriage itself, as Gilbert and Gubar rightly observe, as a "soft Eclipse," one which moreover she shows suspiciously little interest in exploring: "I'm 'Wife'! Stop there!"

This ambivalence lends a curiously unconvinced quality to the poem.

Although the speaker calls herself a czar, the poet leaves the impression that her persona is, in fact, imprisoned in her new, presumably safer estate. She is compared to one who is dead, looking down at her former" Girl's life" through the "soft Eclipse" of heaven. The obvious implication—that marriage equals death—is hard to escape. The speaker's former state may have been pain, but it was also filled with life. The same cannot be said with any certainty of the existence she believes she will now lead as woman, that is, as the beloved or wife of a man.

While Dickinson wrote a great many more poems to the Master in 1861 than she did in the preceding three years, most of these poems exhibit the same ambivalence that characterizes "I'm 'wife.'" She depicts the Master's power as working directly upon her, but her own status evokes a confused response. However transformed she claims to be as his beloved, she does not actually possess this transformation. It remains something alien and apart and, therefore, something easily lost. Even the well-known "A solemn thing—it was—I said" exhibits these limitations, particularly when read with Dickinson's original wording for the fifth, sixth, and twelfth lines.

A solemn thing—it was—I said—
A Woman—white—to be—
And wear—if God should count me fit—
Her blameless mystery—

A timid [*or* hallowed] thing—to drop a life
Into the mystic [*or* purple] well—
Too plummetless—that it come back—
Eternity—until—

I pondered how the bliss would look—
And would it feel as big—
When I could take it in my hand—
As hovering [*or* glimmering]—seen—through fog—

And then—the size of this "small" life—
The Sages—call it small—
Swelled—like Horizons—in my breast—
And I sneered—softly—"small"!

(no. 271; P, 193)

For a woman to achieve womanly status—equated with marriage in Dickinson's mind as well as in her culture's ethos—is not a bold but a "timid" thing. It requires the dropping of one's life into a plummetless "mystic" well that presumably "hallows" her, but as Dickinson's original word choice for the fifth line indicates, frightens her as well. She does not see or trust the "bliss" that awaits her because she knows it only through a hovering, potentially deceptive fog, a fog that, in fact, seems remarkably similar to the "soft Eclipse" of "I'm 'wife'". While she is convinced that her new status will not be as "small" as her present status, she has not yet experienced it and does not really know. The girl has not yet become a woman. The poem, therefore, ends inconclusively with a final stanza that may be read in one of two ways: as a paen of praise to the potential lying within her as she makes the transition from girl to woman or as a rejection of all that has gone before and an assertion of the validity of the "small" life to which she clings.

In other poems of 1861 in which she tries to deal with these same ideas of transcendence and transformation, Dickinson is, if anything, even more ambivalent and in no instance is the metamorphosis completely carried through. In "The Sun—*just touched* the Morning," the lover-sun deserts his bride, leaving her without her *"Crown."*

> The Morning—*fluttered*—*staggered*—
> *Felt feebly*—for Her *Crown*—
> Her *unannointed forehead*—
> *Henceforth*—Her *only* One!
>   (no. 232, P, 168)

Or, as in another poem Dickinson included in the same fascicle, the lover himself proves inadequate, a "Slave" who does not appreciate the sturdy light that he has ignited in the loving but abandoned lamp.

> The Slave—forgets—to fill—
> The Lamp—burns golden—on—
> Unconscious that the oil is out—
> As that the Slave—is gone.
>   (no. 233; P, 169)

In neither case does Dickinson manage to speak from a position of personal, autonomous womanly power. In one poem, it is the sun who gives and takes away the speaker's crown. In the other, the lamp burns on alone, to be sure, but it is still the slave who brought the oil and the lamp presumably still burns for him. The speaker remains, that is, essentially passive in respect to her fate. It is, or was, his power that filled her. To lose him, consequently, would be tantamount to death. As she explains in one of her most extreme efforts from this period, without him she is nothing.

If *He dissolve*—then—there is *nothing—more*—
Eclipse—at *Midnight*—
It was *dark—before*—

Sunset—at *Easter*—
Blindness—on the *Dawn*—
Faint Star of Bethlehem—
Gone down!

Would but some *God—inform* Him—
Or it be *too late!*
Say—that the pulse *just lisps*—
The *Chariots wait*—

Say—that a *little life*—for *His*—
Is *leaking—red*—
His little Spaniel—tell Him!
Will He heed?

(no. 236; P, 170–71)

"If *He dissolve*" is a true "Nobody" poem and, one might add, truly awful as a result. The precipitous drop from "*Sunset—at Easter*" to "*His little Spaniel*" is not only sickening, it is absurd. But by the same token, the difference in quality between this poem and one like "Title divine" makes the difference in statement that much more significant. In "If *He dissolve*" Dickinson writes from the position of a woman whose womanhood and womanly power can only be confirmed through the presence and love of a man. In "Title divine," she takes these same qualities—one is almost tempted to say, by right of eminent domain—to herself. The result is a shift from a poem in which the loss of her lover leads to the speaker's dissolution to one in which this same loss occasions her investiture at her own hands. She is transformed, empowered, as wife, empress, woman, and bride.

Read against the earlier poems, it is clear that Dickinson meant "Title divine" to be about her mature identity as woman, an identity she assumed sometime in late 1861 or early 1862 and was apparently eager to share with Samuel Bowles. While she acknowledges that she has assumed this identity at real cost, it is also, as she underscores in the 1866 version of the poem sent to Sue, a "Tri Victory." For in becoming a "Wife—without the Sign"— that is, a wife without an actual husband and therefore, also without the "swoon" or loss of self that real marriage involved—Dickinson had at last found the way out of the personal and social dilemma that had plagued her from adolescence on. In "marrying"-without-marrying the Master, she could, albeit by a sophistical twist, free herself permanently both from her social obligation to marry and from the childhood she had sought so long to escape. By becoming a bride, as it were, *in perpetua,* she remained woman on the point of transformation, a woman who had renounced both the life that had been, childhood, and the life that in her society was meant to be, marriage. And thus she achieved a new ontological status: woman-without-being-wife.

It is this definition of self as woman on the point of transformation or bride *in perpetua* which, I believe, became the basis for Dickinson's new poetic voice after 1861. It was a voice that obtained its power from the fact that the person behind it had experienced in her poetry, if not in her life, all the stages of a woman's life, from childhood through ecstasy and marriage to, finally, martyrdom and death. This person could, therefore, speak with all the authority that Dickinson's poetry had hitherto lacked. By using her poetry to become a bride *in perpetua* or "Wife—without the Sign," Dickinson was able to make her role as poet and her role as woman one. It was a piece of linguistic legerdemain to be sure, but for Dickinson it worked. If she could not be a woman in real life without marrying, then she could marry and be a real woman in her art. Symbol-maker that she was, for Dickinson this "Victory" was more than adequate. It gave her both the security and the freedom she required to explore the powers lodged within herself. She was a poet and a woman at last.

A number of different factors made becoming a "Wife—without the Sign" or bride *in perpetua* a perfect means to Dickinson's new status as woman poet or queen. To begin with, in the nineteenth century a woman's bridal was the mid-point between the two great, unalterable mysteries in her life: birth and death. Upon these three occasions, at birth (symbolized by baptism), at death, and when she got married, a woman wore white and approached most closely the "blameless mystery" of God. Insofar as a bride took a new name or "Title," she was moreover both dead and reborn during the ceremony, dying to her old life and baptized into her new one.

As the mid-point in a woman's life, the marriage ceremony was also, equally important, her apex or "Acute Degree," the moment conferred upon her by God when she experienced her greatest rapture or joy in living.

And it was the moment in which she was translated from one state of being into another, receiving not only a new name, but a new status, power, and identity. As Dickinson explains in the ecstatic rhythms of "I am ashamed — I hide" (1862), in many ways the key poem in this series, she is no longer a "Dowerless Girl." As bride, she becomes the full-fledged sister to history's greatest or, at any rate, most flamboyant women.

> I am ashamed — I hide —
> What right have I — to be a Bride —
> So late a Dowerless Girl —
> Nowhere to hide my dazzled Face —
> No one to teach me that new Grace —
> Nor introduce — my Soul —
>
> Me to adorn — How — tell —
> Trinket — to make Me beautiful —
> Fabrics of Cashmere —
> Never a Gown of Dun — more —
> Raiment instead — of Pompadour —
> For Me — My Soul — to wear —
>
> Fingers — to frame my Round Hair
> Oval — as Feudal Ladies wore —
> Far Fashions — Fair —
> Skill — to hold my Brow like an Earl —
> Plead — like a Whippowil —
> Prove — like a Pearl —
> Then, for Character —
>
> Fashion My Spirit quaint — white —
> Quick — like a Liquor —
> Gay — like Light —
> Bring Me my best Pride —
> No more ashamed —
> No more to hide —
> Meek — let it be — too proud — for Pride —
> Baptized — this Day — A Bride —
>   (no. 473, P, 363)

It is important to note, however, that in claiming she herself was *"Baptized* — this Day — a Bride" (italics added), Dickinson was pushing the symbolic function of her marriage well beyond anything her immediate culture would have allowed. Like a nun married to Christ and perpetually his bride, "Bride," not wife, was Dickinson's true identity.[10] Married and not married at once, she was suspended ontologically at the moment of her transformation and transcendence, the moment, also—and not incidentally—of her greatest rapture and fullest being. "Born— Bridalled—Shrouded— / In a Day," she contained all these possibilities, these mysteries, within herself. Love's martyr and love's saint at once, she obtained internally and in secret, the "Diadem" of a true queen precisely because her marriage itself could never, at least in this life, be fulfilled.[11]

Rearrange a "Wife's" affection!
When they dislocate my Brain!
Amputate my freckled Bosom!
Make me bearded like a man!

Blush, my spirit, in thy Fastness—
Blush, my unacknowledged clay—
Seven years of troth have taught thee
More than Wifehood ever may!

Love that never leaped its socket—
Trust entrenched in narrow pain—
Constancy thro' fire—awarded—
Anguish—bare of anodyne!

Burden—borne so far triumphant—
None suspect me of the crown,
For I wear the "Thorns" till *Sunset*—
Then—my Diadem put on.

Big my Secret but it's *bandaged*—
It will never get away
Till the Day its Weary Keeper
Leads it through the Grave to thee.
(no. 1737, P, 1168–69)

By becoming a bride without ever being a wife, Dickinson was, in short, able to have it both ways. As the betrothed of one to whom she was and was not married, the poet could prolong indefinitely her bridal moment with all its intensity and rapture—intensity and rapture which she had always considered necessary to the practice of her craft. At the same time, however, she was able to avoid the act, actual marriage, that would eventually have destroyed both the poetry and the rapture from which it sprang. Bride for Dickinson became, in other words, an identity which not only paralleled but in some ways made possible her complete identification as poet. Both identities were the product of art and both part of an inner world she carefully shrouded from others. Equally important, in and through both, she was able to achieve the autonomy that her prolonged childhood had denied her.

I'm ceded—I've stopped being Their's—
The name They dropped upon my face
With water, in the country church
Is finished using, now,
And They can put it with my Dolls,
My childhood, and the string of spools,
I've finished threading—too—

Baptized, before, without the choice,
But this time, consciously, of Grace—
Unto supremest name—
Called to my Full—The Crescent dropped—
Existence's whole Arc, filled up,
With one small Diadem.

My second Rank   too small the first
Crowned—Crowing—on my Father's breast—
A half unconscious Queen—
But this time—Adequate—Erect,
With Will to choose, or to reject,
And I choose, just a Crown—
                          (no. 508, P, 389–90)

In her first rank or state, as infant-child-girl, Dickinson had been a "half unconscious Queen," passively receiving the name "They dropped upon [her] face," the identity and being they gave her. But this time it is different; ". . . this time—Adequate—Erect, / With Will to choose, or to reject," she has chosen for herself, taking the "Crown" not of a husband's name but of her own "Title divine": poet, "Wife," "Queen of Calvary." It was an autonomous decision and, therefore, it not only allowed her to speak from a position of complete, self-authored authority, it also made her—in this second, most crucial baptism—an adult. It changed, that is, not just her name but her very being.

Dickinson's decision to base her adulthood and her identity as a *woman-poet* upon a fantasy marriage obviously had great advantages for her. It had severe disadvantages as well. On the one hand, it made her a "Queen." She could, as she declares in "I've ceded," stand "Adequate—Erect," that is, independently and autonomously on her own. Where in the pre-1862 poems she had depicted herself as totally dependent on the Master's power for her identity and being, these qualities were now entirely within her own control. And because they were, she could now use them not only to preserve and protect but to enhance her womanly power. She had not ceded to the lover-sun, the man who would stand in her father's place and give her his name along with his crown, the symbol of his power. She had "stopped being Their's" and had become her own. It was her own "Title divine" she chose. And in so choosing, she appropriated to herself, in her art at least, a degree of personal freedom and authority few women in our society enjoy even today. As a poet, she became a self-defined, self-authorized, and authenticated woman.

But by the same token, because she was "Wife—without the Sign," Dickinson's queenship was bound to go unrecognized by the world at large. It was a secret business, carried out at night, as she appears to suggest in "Rearrange a 'Wife's' affection!" in the "polar privacy" (no. 1695, P, 1149) of her own room. Life in the real world had to be sacrificed. She could be a woman only in and through her art. Outwardly, except to a select few such as Susan and Samuel Bowles, she remained to all intents and purposes a little girl since the only way in real life for her to escape childhood was to take up the responsibilities she despised, whether as wife or in some other, equally dutiful occupation. To have her rapture, her poetry, and her womanhood, Dickinson had to live a double life. This was her "Calvary," the "Thorns" she wore each day so that she might put on her "Diadem," her poetic as well as her womanly "Crown," each night.

By early 1862, when Dickinson sent Bowles "Title divine," she had clearly reached a conscious decision to lead a double life. But she did not reach this decision, which confirmed the tendencies of her adolescence, without undergoing a tremendous amount of pain. On the contrary, in poem after poem written in the three-year period between 1862 and 1864, she returns compulsively to her terrible sense of loss, frustration, and rage at having to give up so much in order to have what she wanted most: the freedom to be and choose for herself, that is, the freedom not to do her duty. She did not feel it was asking too much of either God or society, but she knew that in any case it would be denied her. So it became, more than anything else, "The Missing All" in whose name she ceased to mourn for "minor Things" (no. 985, P, 711).

In examining the Master's role in Dickinson's life, the significant point is that in rejecting her love, he provided the context within which the feelings of rage and loss she had experienced through so much of her life could be consciously released. In this relationship and in the poetry to which it gave rise, she was able to express for the first time everything she had felt as a woman because she finally had a definition of herself as woman which was sufficiently large to justify and accommodate these feelings. The result is poetry of tremendous force or, as Gilbert and Gubar remark, "Satanic assertiveness," not because, as they contend, Dickinson was playing her own madwoman, but because within the limits of her art, if not her life, she finally had achieved the freedom to be wholly sane. "Pardon my sanity, Mrs. Holland, in a world *in*sane," she wrote prophetically to Elizabeth Holland in 1856, "and love me if you will. For I had rather *be* loved than to be called a king in earth, or a lord in Heaven" (L, 329–30). Love had led Dickinson twice to the brink of insanity, once in 1856 and again in late 1861; but in loving as she did—wildly, irrationally— she had found a higher form of sanity as well and a new definition for what a woman was supposed to be.

> Seven years of troth have taught thee
> More than Wifehood ever may!
> (no. 1737, P, 1168)

And she filled this definition with the "unannointed Blaze" of her own "*White Heat*," the "Designated Light" (no. 365; P, 289–90) of her poetic mystery.

While it may seem paradoxical or perverse to say so, what appears to have happened to Dickinson in 1862 is that by redefining herself as bride-wife-queen of Calvary, within the context of a fantasy marriage, the poet was able to integrate her feelings of loss, rage, and frustration, feelings that had left her internally divided from adolescence on, and make these feelings ego-syntonic.[12] They became a necessary part of her new definition of self as poet. And as such, they reinforced rather than took from her self-esteem. Put another way, where in adolescence these feelings had led to extreme, ultimately suicidal depression because the poet had been compelled to suppress them, the reverse now occurred. As "Queen of Calvary," she could legitimately express everything she had endured. Confronted with the "abyss"—the harrowing loss of love, the death of the external self, the "Funeral" within her brain—Dickinson was free at last, free, as her niece reports, "to her chosen horizon." And like the volcanoes that dot her poetry, she exploded.

Ironically, but perhaps inevitably, Dickinson's long-suppressed feelings for Susan, particularly her rage at the loss of Susan, provided a very large part of the fuel that made this explosion possible. While Dickinson wrote very little poetry after 1858 that is unequivocally addressed to Susan, the similarity between Dickinson's position in 1862 vis-à-vis the Master and her earlier situation vis-à-vis her sister-in-law was too close for fusion not to occur. In both cases, the poet had been the pursuer while the beloved, after some initial encouragement, held himself or herself aloof. In both cases, barriers in the form of a third party and the possibility of social opprobrium prevented the relationship from reaching fruition. And finally, in both, the lovers, according to Dickinson's stated mytho-drama, were forced to go their separate ways, the beloved to head toward warm and sunny climes, the poet to turn figuratively if not literally north. Given such similarities, the relationship with the Master could not help but become a vehicle through which a lifetime of frustration could be expressed.

While it is usually assumed that all the love poetry Dickinson wrote between 1862 and 1864 is about the Master unless a female lover is actually designated, the fact is that fewer than forty of the 681 poems written in this period are specifically and unequivocally addressed to a male.[13] In the vast majority of the love poems, the poet speaks merely of "we" or to "you" or even of "it." Since the basic situation in almost all these poems is essentially the same—Dickinson abandoned, her love unrequited, her lover taking off, literally or figuratively, for other climes—it is consequently impossible to know to whom any particular poem is addressed unless the gender of the lover has been specified within the poem itself.[14] More important, it is also unclear whether Dickinson herself made an emotional distinction between those poems she was writing to the Master and those she was writing to the woman or women she had loved. The well-known, justly popular "There came a Day at Summer's full" is a case in point.

> There came a Day at Summer's full,
> Entirely for me—
> I thought that such were for the Saints,
> Where Resurrections—be—
>
> The Sun, as common, went abroad,

The flowers, accustomed, blew,
As if no soul the solstice passed
That maketh all things new—

The time was scarce profaned, by speech—
The symbol of a word
Was needless, as at Sacrament,
The Wardrobe—of our Lord—

Each was to each The Sealed Church,
Permitted to commune this—time—
Lest we too awkward show
At Supper of the Lamb.

The Hours slid fast—as Hours will,
Clutched tight, by greedy hands—
So faces on two Decks, look back,
Bound to opposing lands—

And so when all the time had leaked,
Without external sound
Each bound the Other's Crucifix—
We gave no other Bond—

Sufficient troth, that we shall rise—
Deposed—at length, the Grave—
To that new Marriage,
Justified—through Calvaries of Love—

(no. 322; P, 249–50)

In this poem Dickinson appears to be describing in a straightforward manner a moment of terrible and poignant parting between two lovers. They stand as, indeed, in the second Master letter she longed to stand, face to face, each to each a "Sealed Church." The hours slide by and finally, each having "bound the Other's Crucifix," they part, headed toward "opposing lands" but at the same time acknowledging "Sufficient troth," that someday they will be joined in Heaven, their union "Justified—through Calvaries of Love."

To my knowledge, no critic besides Rebecca Patterson, who believed that all Dickinson's love poetry was written to a woman, Kate Scott Anthon, has had the temerity to suggest that this poem was not addressed to the Master whether they view this individual as a real person or a poetic device. Given the lushness of the writing and the final emphasis on marriage, there is, in fact, little doubt that "There came a Day" is about Dickinson's relationship with him, at least on one level. But this fact may be more misleading than helpful, for the poem implies a degree of mutual reciprocation in love that, as far as can be determined, had no basis in reality. And its many verbal and situational echoes to the two poems that follow, both written specifically and unequivocally to a woman, presumably Sue, make a straightforward reading of "There came a Day" precarious at best.

> Like Eyes that looked on Wastes—
> Incredulous of Ought
> But Blank—and steady Wilderness—
> Diversified by Night—
>
> Just infinities of Nought—
> As far as it could see—
> So looked the face I looked upon—
> So looked itself—on Me—
>
> I offered it no Help—
> Because the Cause was Mine—
> The Misery a Compact
> As hopeless—as divine—
>
> Neither—would be absolved—
> Neither would be a Queen
> Without the Other—Therefore—
> We perish—tho' We reign—
>   (no. 458; P, 353)
>
> Ourselves were wed one summer—dear—
> Your Vision—was in June—
> And when Your little Lifetime failed,
> I wearied—too—of mine—
>
> And overtaken in the Dark—
> Where You had put me down—
> By Some one carrying a Light—
> I—too—received the Sign.
>
> 'Tis true—Our Futures different lay—
> Your Cottage—faced the sun—

While Oceans—and the North must be—
On every side of mine

'Tis true, Your Garden led the Bloom,
For mine—in Frosts—was sown—
And yet, one Summer, we were Queens—
But You—were crowned in June—
                    (no. 631; P, 485–86)

The point of bringing these three poems together is not to appropriate "There came a Day" for Susan. Given the poem's richness and fullness of expression—in marked contrast to the almost cryptic compression of the two poems to women—"There came a Day" surely belongs to the series of poems in which Dickinson vented her feelings for this remote, unobtainable man. But as a love poem, it is also, and just as importantly, drawing its depth and power from experiences that predated her relationship with him. The summer in which the lovers parted was not just the poetic summer of 1861 but the very real summer of 1856. And the event that sent each lover on his or her separate way was not just the tutor's departure from the land (which Dickinson cites, albeit obliquely, in her second letter to Higginson), but Susan's marriage to Austin, a crowning which, indeed, left Dickinson feeling "wearied" and "in the Dark."[15]

The fact that one poem is almost certainly "about" the Master while the other two poems are almost certainly about Susan is, consequently, of considerably less importance in the end than the fact that all three poems are about the same experience. And hence the feelings of loss, rage, and misery are basically the same in each. The "Crucifix" and "Calvary" of "There came a Day" and the "Compact / As hopeless—as divine" of "Like Eyes that looked on Wastes," the two lovers "Bound to opposing lands" and the two queens whose "Futures different lay" are all, finally, figures in a single drama. Whether Dickinson was writing to a man or a woman in these particular poems does not matter. What matters is that in each of them, the vision of love remains the same. Love is loss; "Troth" is endless, unrequited waiting. If there is union, it must lie beyond the grave. Surrounded by "Infinities of Nought" and bound to her own crucifix, the best that the poet could hope for, as she wrote to Kate Scott Anthon, was to be a beggar at the banquet of life, a forager of "crumbs."[16]

In some poems Dickinson was prepared to be satisfied with her dainty diet and to claim she wanted no more.[17]

As the Starved Maelstrom laps the Navies
As the Vulture teazed
Forces the Broods in lonely Valleys
As the Tiger eased

By but a Crumb of Blood, fasts Scarlet
Till he meet a Man
Dainty adorned with Veins and Tissues
And partakes—his Tongue

Cooled by the Morsel for a moment
Grows a fiercer thing
Till he esteem his Dates and Cocoa
A Nutrition mean

I, of a finer Famine
Deem my Supper dry
For but a Berry of Domingo
And a Torrid Eye.

(no. 872; P, 648–49)

In other poems, however, she makes no attempt whatever to mitigate her
outrage that this should be her fate.

I should have been too glad, I see—
Too lifted—for the scant degree
Of Life's penurious Round—
My little Circuit would have shamed
This new Circumference—have blamed—
The homelier time behind.

I should have been too saved—I see—
Too rescued—Fear too dim to me
That I could spell the Prayer
I knew so perfect—yesterday—
That Scalding One—Sabacthini—
Recited fluent—here—

Earth would have been too much—I see—
And Heaven—not enough for me—
I should have had the Joy
Without the Fear—to justify—

The Palm—without the Calvary—
So Savior—Crucify—

Defeat—whets Victory—they say—
The Reefs—in old Gethsemane—
Endear the Shore beyond!
'Tis Beggars—Banquets best define—
'Tis thirsting—vitalizes Wine—
Faith bleats to understand!
(no. 313; P, 236–37)

"I should have been too glad" is not just an angry poem. It is a blasphemous poem. But no poem Dickinson wrote captures more perfectly the heresy that lay at the heart of her vision of love and, therefore, her concept of self as queen of Calvary than this one. The young woman who had once refused to abandon her *"idolatry"* even though she knew that a "darker spirit" might someday possess "its child" had become the woman-poet who measured her Calvary against Christ's and her heaven against God's and found the divine dispensations lacking. Like Moses, for whom she expressed profound sympathy in three different poems, Dickinson felt she had been given a taste of paradise only to have it arbitrarily withdrawn that she might love or fear God the more. But the reverse had occurred. She did not, and would not, accept "Life's penurious Round." She wanted "new heaven," and "new earth" in the here and now. And just as her appetite for love, seasoned not just by Shakespeare but ironically by Revelation,[19] was endless, so were her rage and sense of loss at having her vision denied.

Earth would have been too much—I see—
And Heaven—not enough for me—
I should have had the Joy
Without the Fear—to justify—
The Palm—without the Calvary—
So Savior—Crucify—.

No biographical circumstance behind any particular love poem Dickinson wrote carries with it half as much weight as this single feature: Ultimately, when taken together, her love poems express a vision of human love that passes beyond human limits. As she wrote to Susan in 1871, "All" had no "codicil" (L, 490). And it was "All" she wanted. To the woman who came to identify herself with Shakespeare's Antony as well as with the

Gospels' Christ, nothing less would do. In maturity as in adolescence, the "silver cord" and "golden bowl" remained for Dickinson the unique objects of her all too human desire. The "blessed dreams" remained the blessed dream.

·   ·   ·

There is no point in trying to pretend that Dickinson's conception of love was reasonable. It was, as it had always been, far too demanding to make sense in the real world where most of us, like most of Dickinson's contemporaries, spend our days. But it does help explain some of the positions she took and the choices she made. "Your Riches," she wrote to Susan, "taught me—Poverty!" To the Master, she declared, even more suggestively:

> You left me—Sire—two Legacies—
> A Legacy of Love
> A Heavenly Father would suffice
> Had He the offer of—
>
> You left me Boundaries of Pain—
> Capacious as the Sea—
> Between Eternity and Time—
> Your Consciousness—and Me—
>   (no. 644; P, 495–96)

Caught between riches, love, and eternity on the one hand and poverty, pain, and time on the other, Dickinson became, in effect, an explorer of the "Capacious" sea between. In her poetry, as in her life, she oscillates between the acknowledgment of two separate states, two separate consciousnesses, two separate modes of being—one the "All," where appetite is infinite and the act no longer a "slave to limit;" the other the reality, where she was netted about by the adamantine strands of time, self, and society. And inevitably, perhaps, the two states merged. The "Infinities" of love, eternity, and riches became identical to the "Infinities of Nought," as the poet acknowledged that the "Compact" she sought with her lover, and with life, was "As hopeless—as divine." Love and death once again joined. The grave became the place of fulfillment: "We perish—tho' we reign."

Dickinson's identification of love with infinite appetite and, therefore, finally with death came full circle in the poetry of 1862. From "I have a Bird in spring" on, she had seen in death the one sure path to the fulfillment of her love. By 1862 she was ready to accept the fact that for her, at least, love and death were essentially one. "All" had no codicil, not simply because it was complete in itself but because nothing could follow it. In loving whomever she loved, the way she loved, infinitely, totally, the poet committed herself in the real world and in her own private drama to death. There was no way for her love to fulfill itself except in death. "Born— Bridalled—Shrouded / In a day," the ecstatic vision of love upon which her new identity as woman and poet was founded was also the shroud in which her life was wrapped.

But having said this, we must also note that the "death" which Dickinson experienced between late 1861 and early 1862 had very different consequences for her than the one she had endured five years before. Losing Susan had brought Dickinson to the edge of suicide. For almost two years she had been virtually wiped out, in her own words, "wrecked." But the loss of the Master was another matter. According to "Ourselves were wed one summer—dear," she took this second loss as a "Sign" indicating where her true direction lay.

> And overtaken in the Dark—
> Where You had put me down—
> By Some one carrying a Light—
> I—too—received the Sign.
>
> 'Tis true— Our Futures different lay—
> Your Cottage—faced the sun—
> While Oceans—and the North must be—
> On every side of mine.
> (no. 631; P, 485)

Where in 1856 Dickinson had "died to the world," in 1862 she turned "North" instead, to the capacious sea, bounded by love on the one side and pain on the other, where time and eternity joined. And in that polar air, she found "Consciousness" and self.

While in "Ourselves were wed," Dickinson appears to disparage her garden, sown in frost, comparing it negatively to Susan's, which faces the sun, she also knew that there were some flowers, like the "little Gentian," which required frost to bloom. In "God made a little Gentian," she ranked herself among them.

> God made a little Gentian—
> It tried—to be a Rose—

And failed—and all the Summer laughed—
But just before the Snows

There rose a Purple Creature—
That ravished all the Hill—
And Summer hid her Forehead—
And Mockery—was still—

The Frosts were her condition—
The Tyrian would not come
Until the North—invoke it—
Creator—Shall I—bloom?

                                    (no. 442; P, 341)

Dickinson was no "Rose" or woman as women are socially defined and by
1862 she knew it. When she tried to be one, she had failed miserably. The
grotesque posturing of the third Master letter provides sufficient evidence
on that score. "The Frosts were her condition." They invoked her purple
dye, her natural strength or royal color, as suns (multiple puns intended)
never could. In frost, in solitude, in that capacious sea of "Consciousness,"
her garden, her self, and her poetry bloomed.

There is a solitude of space
A solitude of sea
A solitude of death, but these
Society shall be
Compared with that profounder site
That polar privacy
A soul admitted to itself—
Finite infinity.

                                    (no. 1695; P, 1149)

Maturation did not mean the end of Dickinson's pain. On the contrary,
because she finally gained complete access to it, along with all her other,
largely unacceptable, feelings, Dickinson was finally able to mature. In that
"solitude of self" brought on by rage and loss, she had discovered the
consciousness from which her deepest feelings sprang. It is from these
feelings that her poetry after 1861 comes. The years between 1862 and
1864, in particular, were years of emotional catharsis for Dickinson. As her
recurrent use of the volcano image suggests, the top had finally blown off.[19]
Like the gun that stood in the corner, loaded but useless until the master

SYLVIA PLATH

Fusion and
the Divided Self

. . . .
. . . .
. . . .

4. The Mother Bond

. . . .
. . . .
. . . .

Accommodation to parental needs often (but not always) leads to the "as-if personality." . . . This person develops in such a way that he reveals only what is expected of him, and fuses so completely with what he reveals that . . . one would scarcely have guessed how much more there is to him, behind this "masked view of himself."
—Alice Miller

Sylvia was . . . wholly authentic. By which I mean that she was true to herself, or truly herself. . . . She was incapable of any sort of falsity or affection or exaggeration.
—Wendy Campbell

There are a number of striking parallels between the lives of Emily Dickinson and Sylvia Plath. Both women were gifted students who came to their vocations early and as a result suffered increasing isolation from their peers. If Dickinson could later write with the wisdom of maturity "The Difference—made me bold" (no. 454; P, 351), for her, as for Plath, this isolation and its attendant sense of deviance or unwomanliness was a chronic source of anxiety and depression, particularly in adolescence. After extremely promising childhood starts, both Dickinson and Plath ended adolescence, Dickinson at twenty-five, Plath at twenty-one, in suicidal depressions that were followed, not many years later, by second, very different breakdowns or emotional traumas that released their poetic energies. As young women, both learned to protect—or in Plath's case, to suppress—the "imminent volcano" of their inner lives by creating what Ted Hughes has called "a prickly, fastidious defence,"[1] a holier-than-thou, don't-touch-me attitude. Finally, both came from conservative, middle-class homes in which the mothers were self-sacrificing and giving to a fault and the fathers were, as Dickinson put it, figures of "Awe."

There were profound differences between Dickinson and Plath as well, most of them too obvious to mention. But of them, by far the most important was the fact that unlike Emily Dickinson, Sylvia Plath never broke the bond that tied her to her mother. As a result she was never able to abandon the dream of normalcy, including marriage and children, that both her mother and her society held out to her as the ultimate test and reward of a successful woman's life. "Everything has gone barren," Plath wrote melodramatically in her journal in June of 1959, at a time when she desperately feared that she might not be able to bear children.

> I am part of the world's ash, something from which nothing can grow, nothing can flower or come to fruit. In the lovely words of 20th century medicine, I can't ovulate . . . I have worked, bled, knocked my head on walls to break through to where I am now . . . I want a house of our children, little animals, flowers, vegetables, fruits. I want to be an Earth Mother in the deepest richest sense. I have turned from being an intellectual, a career woman: all that is ash to me. And what do I meet in myself? Ash. Ash and more ash.
> . . . Suddenly the deep foundations of my being are gnawn. *I have come, with great pain and effort, to the point where my desires and emotions and thoughts center around what the normal woman's center around,* and what do I find? Barrenness.   (J, 311–12; italics added)

In a way strikingly unlike Emily Dickinson, Sylvia Plath "worked, bled, [and] knocked [her] head on walls" to get "to the point where [her] desires and emotions and thoughts center[ed] around what the normal woman's center around" and she paid for this hard-won normalcy with her life. "You can have your career, or you can raise a family," Eddie Cohen, Plath's prescient and dedicated pen pal wrote to the poet at the beginning of her second year at Smith. "I should be extremely surprised, however, [sic] you can do both within the framework of the social structure in which you now live."[2]

The daughter of a mother who sincerely believed she could and must have both in order to be happy and fulfilled, Plath could not accept the wisdom inherent in Cohen's warning. Until the last year of her life she seems to have been sincerely convinced that no matter how hazardous a marriage and a family might be to her as a poet, to her as a woman, they offered the only possible path to success. And, therefore, although she knew that having a career and raising a family were probably incompatible goals given the conventions of the society in which she lived, she was determined to have both, even going so far as to create an elaborate intellectual fantasy, part Robert Graves, part D. H. Lawrence, in which she was Earth Mother and the fruits of her body and the fruits of her mind were inextricably intertwined.[3]

Plath's commitment to this fantasy, which linked her poetic creativity with her biological capacity to give birth and her success as a woman with her success as a wife, eventually helped kill her, but not before the poet managed to articulate more clearly than any woman poet has done before or since the painful dilemma of the woman artist. Plath, Suzanne Juhasz writes, "is the woman poet of our century who sees the problem, the situation of trying to be a woman poet with the coldest and most unredeeming clarity, and who . . . finds no solution."[4] Thoroughly enmeshed in what Juhasz appropriately calls "the double bind of the woman poet," the conflict between the needs of her gender and the requirements of her genre, Plath wrote with frightening accuracy of the internal conflicts that divided and finally destroyed her. A woman who throughout her life inordinately wanted the love and approval of her mother, her husband, and her society, she came to understand all too well the extent to which these presumably normal female desires, thoughts, and emotions imperiled her success as a poet even as they betrayed her fullness as a human being. As Juhasz observes, "try as she might," Plath never did find the solution to the "double bind,"[5] but in confronting it head on and spelling it out with such brilliant clarity, she left a body of poetry whose value and significance for women generally goes well beyond its slim scope.

•   •   •

Sylvia Plath's relationship with her mother, an extraordinary woman in her own right, was unusually, even disconcertingly, close.[6] Not only did Aurelia Plath have virtually complete charge of her daughter during most of Plath's childhood, but even after the poet had grown up, left home, and married, the two women remained tightly bonded. During the thirteen years between her admission to Smith College and her suicide in London at age thirty-one, Plath wrote her family 696 letters, an average of one a week. Many of the letters covered two to three typewritten pages and they detailed almost every aspect of the poet's life, trivial to tragic.

Reading the letters, collected and edited by Mrs. Plath in the volume *Letters Home,* is an uncomfortable, even disturbing experience. They are too much: too bright, too bouncy, too breathless, too eager. They touch on intimate and everyday areas of this young woman's life long after these areas should have been sealed off by distance and maturity.

> I have been having a pleasant day in bed, resting and reading. Ted and I are alternating, one day each a week, until we are fully recovered from the strain of the last months and the settling in. He had his day Sunday. The one in bed orders what is desired for meals, reads, writes and sleeps. Now I am dressed and up and feeling much refreshed. Ted has made a beef stew, which is simmering ready for our supper. (LH, 367)

In many of the letters the boundaries between mother and daughter seem fatally vague so that a prize for one might as well be a prize for the other.

> You no doubt wondered what that Special Delivery letter from *our* [italics added] favorite magazine was about. I can picture you feeling how thick it was and holding it up to the light. Well, don't get *too* excited, 'cause it's only third prize, but it does mean $100 . . . in cold cold cash. (LH, 65)

And even more troubling, a baby one intends to bear seems meant for the other.

> All I can say is that you better start saving for another trip [to England] another summer, and I'll make sure I can produce a new baby for you then! (LH, 409)

Again and again, not just hopes and expectations but the joy and satisfaction of actual achievements seem, to use Mrs. Plath's own word, osmotically shared (LH, 32). As the poet wrote to her brother, Warren, in 1953, their achievements were the mother's due reward for twenty years of selfless service, the "big dividends of joy" her children owed her for the "life blood and care" she expended rearing them (LH, 113). Plath at least intended to pay this debt in full.

Shared hopes and dreams between parent and child are common enough.

But Plath's obsessional need to reward her mother by fulfilling Aurelia's expectations and, even more, the poet's obvious terror at the idea that she might not be able to do so, are another matter. If Aurelia Plath was, according to her daughter, "abnormally altruistic" (LH, 112) in the self-sacrifice she exacted from herself for her children's sake, Plath was no less extreme in her relentless desire to pay back her mother for the anguish and "life blood" Aurelia had spent in her children's care. Indeed, as Adrienne Rich has observed, Plath's compulsion "to lay in her mother's lap . . . poems and prizes, books and babies" (OWB, 230) is the single most obvious theme in *Letters Home*. So compelling and omnipresent is the poet's need that the reader of the letters may well conclude that Plath's having failed her mother in the breakup of her marriage to the British poet Ted Hughes was as much a cause of the poet's final suicidal depression as the loss of Hughes himself.

> I haven't the strength to see you for some time. The horror of what you saw and what I saw you see last summer is between us and I cannot face you again until I have a new life; it would be too great a strain. I would give heaven and earth to have a visit from Aunt Dot or Warren and Margaret. (LH, 465)

At a time when, presumably, Plath should have been eager to turn to her mother for comfort and support, this woman to whom the poet had written all of her life, with whom she had shared all of her triumphs and many of her disappointments, was precisely the one person Plath could not bear to see. The ultimate prize a successful woman wins in life—a happy marriage—had escaped her and the poet's shame is simply too great to allow her mother near.

Both Plath and her mother identified success as a woman with a successful marriage because, like virtually every woman living in the United States in the mid-twentieth century, this is what they had been told. Where in Emily Dickinson's time a woman's success was, in effect, measured by her usefulness, whether she chose to marry or not, a hundred years later, changes in American society had shrunk this narrow horizon to an even more narrow goal. Of women's expectations during the 1950s, Betty Friedan declares simply enough, "Fulfillment as a woman had only one definition . . . the housewife-mother."[7] In the literature of the time, studied extensively by Friedan for *The Feminine Mystique,* psychologists, sociologists, educators, and the writers published in the slick women's magazines on which Plath and her mother so doted, all spoke with one voice. For women the road to contentment lay in "sexual passivity, male domination, and nurturing maternal love."[8] A woman who failed to marry was not simply doomed to a life of dissatisfaction or frustration. Without a husband and children, she would become little short of a freak.

The following comments made by the Freudian psychoanalyst Peter Blos in his classic study *On Adolescence* epitomize the thinking that family experts in this period foisted as truth upon women:

> In contrast to the girl, any boy who attempts to call attention to his beauty or who parades it with exhibitionistic pleasure is always considered effeminate. It is the prerogative of the female to display her physical charm — indeed, to emphasize and enhance it through the use of cosmetics, adornments, and dress. *Her need is to be loved* [italics added]. The boy is permitted only to display what he can do; he therefore focuses his pride on prowess and accomplishment. His attainments may lie in athletic, intellectual, academic, sexual, occupational, or creative endeavors. Daring, perseverance, speed, and power are the attributes considered masculine, which can be displayed publicly by the male.[9]

Where young men are encouraged to fulfill their manhood daily in a variety of institutions and activities so that they can show what they can do, to fulfill their womanhood young women need only learn how to satisfy through "physical charm . . . cosmetics, adornments, and dress," the one man who might someday occupy their restricted social and occupational sphere. Their need is to be loved. Blos's choice of the passive voice is not accidental. A woman who went to college between 1945 and 1960, Friedan concludes, "could hardly avoid learning . . . *not* to get interested, seriously interested in anything besides getting married and having children, if she wanted to be normal, happy, adjusted, feminine."[10] Education, talent, and drive, like "daring, perseverance, speed, and power," were "attributes considered masculine." A woman who wished to be considered feminine would view these qualities as the prerogatives of the male. And she would avoid cultivating them, lest, as Matina Horner has perhaps too succinctly declared, she be "unsexed by success."[11]

Despite the apparent gains women have made in the labor market over the past century, the fact is that ideologues such as Blos have helped perpetuate a distinction between men's and women's spheres in American society that is, in effect, every bit as rigid as that promulgated by Mary Lyon a century before. Thus Nancy Chodorow in *The Reproduction of Mothering* observes of social life in America today:

Women's roles are basically familial, and concerned with personal, affective ties. *Ideology about women and treatment of them in this society, particularly in the labor force, tend to derive from this familial location and the assumptions that it is or should be both exclusive and primary for women, and that this exclusivity and primacy come from biological sex differences.* By contrast, men's roles as they are defined in our society are basically not familial. Though men are interested in being husbands and fathers, and most men do occupy these roles during their lifetime, ideology about men and definitions of what is masculine come predominantly from men's nonfamilial roles [italics added].[12]

As in Dickinson's period, the role of woman qua woman remains fundamentally private and domestic. Service- and family-oriented, it is a role of feeling and relation, lived with and for an intimate circle of others whether she also chooses to move into the labor force or not. The role of the man, on the other hand, is primarily productive and belongs to the world at large. The woman who crosses these gender-defined lines abrogates the laws governing her social and psychological destiny and her biological destiny as well.

Like most women in the 1950s and, if Chodorow is correct, most women even today, Sylvia Plath appears to have accepted the basic assumptions of this doctrine or ideology even though she knew that in many respects they ran counter to the springs of her own nature. An extraordinarily ambitious, brilliant, restless woman, possessed of a highly competitive need to excel at virtually everything and exquisitely self-centered in her pursuits, the poet nevertheless eagerly reassured her mother and others who cared for her that she had no intention of becoming a career woman, that she was "*meant* to be married and have children" (LH, 208), and that, in any case, as a writer she was merely "competent" and "small time." This, she concluded in one letter, "will make me happy enough" (LH, 212–13). "I am inclined," she wrote in a moment of ecstatic reflection in 1956, not long before she met Ted Hughes,

to babies and bed and brilliant friends and a magnificent stimulating home where geniuses drink gin in the kitchen after a delectable dinner and read their own novels and tell about why the stock market is the way it will be and discuss scientific mysticism . . . this is what I was meant to make for a man, and to give him this colossal reservoir of faith and love for him to swim in daily, and to give him children; lots of them, in great pain and pride. (J, 122)

However naive such a fantasy may strike us today, particularly in light of later events, this was the dream of normalcy Plath "knocked [her] head on walls to break through to" (J, 312). It represented the success that she as a woman sought to achieve.

But could she achieve this dream and still become the poet she also wanted to be? Plath's dilemma, one ironically reinforced by the very thoroughness with which Aurelia Plath approached her child-rearing responsibilities, lay in the fact that whatever her vision of the future might be, in her the gender-determined lines were crossed. As a poet, if not as a woman, "prowess and accomplishment . . . intellectual, academic . . . occupational [and] creative" were hers. But what if success as a poet undid the success that as a woman she wished to achieve?

In an article on Plath's early poems, Marjorie Perloff suggests that Sylvia Plath was not just "a schizophrenic girl" with "a genius for poetry." "In many ways" she was "a representative case of the American Dream gone sour."[13] The statement is true, but the dream that went sour is not that of Jay Gatsby as Perloff suggests. It was the dream of a seventeen-year-old girl who "wanted to be God" (LH, 40) and still get married, who thought she could have it both ways, by becoming what her mother vainly assumed and expected she could be: a completely fulfilled creative woman, a woman who made delectable dinners with one hand while she wrote poems with the other.

The real impact of the double message delivered by the high expectations that Aurelia Plath held out for her daughter can be truly appreciated only against the background of the mother's own life. Bits and pieces of this life can be gleaned from Mrs. Plath's lengthy introduction to *Letters Home.* The introduction is meant to be exculpatory. Given the blame that critics of Plath have tended to lay on Mrs. Plath, her desire to erase the guilt of her daughter's death is as natural and understandable as it is obvious. But the material she provides makes the internal contradictions contained in the message she conveyed to Plath all too clear.

Aurelia Plath, née Schober, was born of German-Austrian parents and raised in the primarily Italian-Irish neighborhood of Winthrop, Massachusetts, during World War I, a time of pitched anti-German sentiment. Her family was never well off and Aurelia was told from an early age that she must be a "business woman." That is, she was to get a practical education, in short, learn how to type. Basically obedient in nature, Aurelia Schober did as she was told. Determined and hardworking, she also managed, however, to complement her vocational education with liberal arts courses in German and English, and in 1928 she graduated from Boston University competent to teach both languages, together with vocational subjects, at the high-school level.

An attractive, intelligent, ambitious woman, she did not rest content. In 1929 she returned to Boston University to get a masters degree in English and German concurrently. During this period she attracted the attention of her instructor in German, Otto Plath, a full professor in the university's biology department and twenty-one years her senior. After a two-year courtship, consisting, according to Mrs. Plath, of long hikes in the Blue Hills and shared dreams of co-authorship, the two married. After marriage Mrs. Plath once again yielded to the wishes of those she loved — in this case her husband — and became "a full-time homemaker" (LH, 10). Practically speaking, this meant that she spent her days either taking care of the house or typing her husband's first book, *Bumblebees and Their Ways,* for publication. Of the first year of her married life, this bright, ambitious, lively woman declares:

> Social life was almost nil for us as a married couple. My dreams of "open house" for students and the frequent entertaining of good friends among the faculty were not realized. During the first year of our married life, all had to be given up for THE BOOK. After Sylvia was born, it was THE CHAPTER [the treatise "Insect Societies," commissioned by Clark University Press for *A Handbook of Social Psychology*]. (LH, 12–13)

Even after forty-five years Mrs. Plath's hostility toward her husband for the violation of her personal dreams appears to ride as high as her capital letters. Through marriage, Otto Plath, like other men before and after him, had gained, whether with conscious intention or not, a "slave" to exploit in what his daughter was later to call his own "private, totalitarian state" (BJ, 94). "We worked together," Mrs. Plath goes on to explain,

> on [THE CHAPTER]; my husband outlined the sections, listing authors and their texts to be used as reference (there were sixty-nine authors), and I did the reading and note-taking along the lines he indicated, writing the first draft. After that he took over, rewriting and adding his own notes. Then he handed the manuscript to me to put into final form for the printer. (LH, 12)

"By this time," Otto Plath's indispensable but unacknowledged co-author meekly concludes, "I felt I had had an intensive and fascinating course in entomology," and the reader of *Letters Home* has had an intense and possibly even more fascinating look into the dynamics of female oppression as they affect the production and publication of learned books.

Although Otto Plath claimed before marriage to subscribe to the modern fifty-fifty view of that institution, he was, according to his wife, *"der Herr des Hauses"* (LH, 13) in traditional Germanic fashion. Overwhelmed by her husband's superior age, brilliance, and reputation, or by the simple fact that burdened with a new baby, she was now financially dependent on him, Aurelia Plath decided after the first year of marriage "that if [she] wanted a peaceful home . . . [she] would simply have to become more submissive, although *it was not {her} nature to be so"* (LH, 13; italics added). And thus it happened that when Otto Plath died quite needlessly of complications resulting from untreated diabetes in 1940, this woman who had worked so hard and with such creativity to keep her future open found herself in a position fundamentally indistinguishable from that of most single mothers of limited means. Without insurance, pension, or an ongoing career to support her, she was forced to give up forever her dreams of teaching literature. When Boston University's College of Practical Arts and Letters asked her to develop a course in medical secretarial procedures, she swallowed her distaste and accepted the offer as "providential" (LH, 28). The job provided her with a small salary ($1800). Even more important to Mrs. Plath's way of thinking, it permitted her to move from Winthrop, whose sea air, she believed, was bad for her children's health. Plath and her brother both suffered from chronic sinus infections.

From a practical point of view, Mrs. Plath probably made the right decision. As a woman with no resources, trained only to type and teach, how many options did she have? But the poet, who loved Winthrop and was ambivalent at best about the wisdom of practicality, never forgave her. Years later she wrote in *The Bell Jar:*

> My mother had taught shorthand and typing to support us ever since my father died, and secretly she hated it and hated him for dying and leaving no money because he didn't trust life insurance salesmen. She was always on me to learn shorthand after college, so I'd have a practical skill as well as a college degree. "Even the apostles were tentmakers," she'd say. "They had to live, just the way we do." (BJ, 42–43)

Although Mrs. Plath nowhere admits to the secret hatred her daughter attributes to her in this passage, the introduction to *Letters Home* tends to support Plath's intuitions about her mother's true feelings. However muted, resentment for lost or violated dreams seems to burn through almost every page. The fact that Mrs. Plath's story is a familiar one makes it no less painful. What makes it doubly unfortunate, however, is that in sacrificing herself, first for her husband and then for her children, and worse, in refusing directly and explicitly to share with her children her sense of outrage and loss, Mrs. Plath may have inadvertently helped lay the foundations for the tragedy that was to follow.

Because she was an obedient daughter, Aurelia Plath apparently sought to protect her family from the negative feelings self-sacrifice engenders by pretending those feelings were not there. She did not let her children—or perhaps even herself—know just how disillusioned and angry she felt at the losses she had sustained. But, of course, on one level or another, the children knew anyway. "She . . . had to work. Work, and be a mother, too, a man and a woman in one sweet ulcerous ball," Plath wrote bitterly in her journal in 1958. "She pinched. Scraped. Wore the same old coat. . . . In all honesty and with her whole unhappy heart she worked to give those innocent little children the world of joy she'd never had" (J, 267). But try as she might to give her children joy, she could not conceal her own unhappiness. As her daughter was later to observe in the extraordinary "The Disquieting Muses," witches, or bad feelings, baked into gingerbread remain witches for all that and finally no one is fooled.

> Mother, who made to order stories
> Of Mixie Blackshort the heroic bear,
> Mother, whose witches always, always,
> Got baked into gingerbread, I wonder
> Whether you saw them, whether you said
> Words to rid me of those three ladies
> Nodding by night around my bed,
> Mouthless, eyeless, with stitched bald head.
>   (CP, 75)

By refusing to vent openly her resentment, anger, and grief, Mrs. Plath had apparently hoped to teach her children strength, courage, and an optimistic or heroic attitude toward life. If she did not weaken, then they would have nothing to fear. In defense of her failure to shed tears after Otto's death, a failure Sylvia was later to log against her, Aurelia Plath writes:

> I had vividly remembered a time when I was a little child, seeing my
> mother weep in my presence and feeling that my whole personal world

was collapsing. *Mother,* the tower of strength, my one refuge, *crying!* It was this recollection that compelled me to withhold my tears until I was alone in bed at night.   (LH, 25, 28)

Presumably this same attitude led her to hide other negative feelings from her children as well: negative feelings that were the direct and legitimate result of her lack of money, her broken health, the hard life that she led, her situation as a single working mother of two.

But while Mrs. Plath may have sincerely wanted to teach her children optimism and heroic courage, according to her daughter what she really taught them was suppression and denial. Emotions that under the circumstances were entirely appropriate and justified—grief, anger, fear, dismay—were nevertheless to be banished. What the children learned was to lie instead.[14]

> In the hurricane, when father's twelve
> Study windows bellied in
> Like bubbles about to break, you fed
> My brother and me cookies and Ovaltine
> And helped the two of us to choir:
> "Thor is angry: boom boom boom!
> "Thor is angry: we don't care!"
> But those ladies broke the panes.
> . . . .
> Mother, you sent me to piano lessons
> And praised my arabesques and trills
> Although each teacher found my touch
> Oddly wooden in spite of scales
> And the hours of practicing, my ear
> Tone-deaf and, yes, unteachable.
> I learned, I learned, I learned elsewhere,
> From muses unhired by you, dear mother.
>   (CP, 75)

And Plath in particular learned to lie about what it felt like to be a woman, living and working in a world that had been set up primarily for the advancement and benefit of men.

> My mother kept telling me nobody wanted a plain English major. But an English major who knew shorthand was something else. . . . She would be in demand among all the up-and-coming young men and she would transcribe letter after thrilling letter.

The trouble was, I hated the idea of serving men in any way. I wanted to dictate my own thrilling letters.   (BJ, 83)

Had she been less "good" as a mother—or, perhaps, more authentic as a person—Mrs. Plath might have confessed an identical desire to dictate her own thrilling letters and spared both her daughter and herself a good deal of unnecessary sorrow. But she did not because she could not. The tragedy of both women was that they lived at a time when women received no cultural support for their feelings of rage and no help from society to break through their isolation and oppression. Although filled with ambition and unquestionably talented herself, Mrs. Plath suppressed her talents and ambitions, together with a large number of her other needs, in order to fit the role of the good wife and mother. And because she was a good daughter, she expected Plath to do no less should the need and occasion arise.

In attempting to deceive her children, giving so much of herself, Mrs. Plath clearly believed she was acting in their best interests if not in her own. And in trying to hide from her daughter, in particular, the resentment she felt for the oppression she had experienced as a woman, she was doing no more than most mothers have always done: for the sake of a peaceful home—and society—becoming "more submissive, although it was not [their] nature to be so." Mrs. Plath's misfortune was that Plath, who was in a far better position than her mother to realize Aurelia's deepest ambitions, nevertheless chose to model herself on her mother's lies as well. Indeed, like her mother, Plath built her life, her personality, and her dreams of the future around such lies. "My God, I'd love to cook and make a house, and surge force into a man's dreams," she wrote in her journal in 1956, "and write, if he could talk and walk and work and passionately want to do his career. I can't bear to think of this potential for loving and giving going brown and sere in me. Yet the choice is so important, it frightens me a little. A lot" (J, 109). Plath knew what marriage was really like when she wrote these lines, and she knew what a woman's giving could amount to, knew enough to be frightened "a lot." But like her mother she would not allow herself to carry such thoughts to their inevitable conclusion. They were secrets mother and daughter shared unbidden, unacknowledged, and all but entirely unknown.

Because of the large number of secrets each was in effect concealing from the other, the close relationship between Sylvia Plath and her mother was in some ways more apparent than real. True, Mrs. Plath devoted endless hours to her daughter's education and to the development of the poet's budding talent. True, she concerned herself with the most trivial aspects of Plath's daily life and career and did all within her means and power to advance both. But given Aurelia Plath's own inordinate need to suppress pain and recognition of failure—a need that must be measured against the height of her initial aspirations and determination—Mrs. Plath seemed to have no ear for her daughter's real concerns. And Sylvia learned not to bring them to her. "Many parents," Alice Miller observes, writing perspicaciously of this situation, "are like Sylvia's mother. They desperately try to *behave correctly* toward their child, and in their child's behavior they seek reassurance that they are good parents. . . . But as a result of these efforts the needs of the child go unnoticed. I cannot listen to my child with empathy if I am inwardly preoccupied with being a good mother; I cannot be open to what she is telling me."[15]

Unable to share with her mother her doubts, anxieties, griefs, and fear of failure, Plath learned to bring to Aurelia only the good instead—the prizes, awards, and achievements, the happy, optimistic thoughts. Indeed, so stalwart were Aurelia's defenses against negative experience that, as many critics have noted, Plath ended by constructing an entirely artificial personality or "false self" for her mother's sake: the "Sivvy" personality of *Letters Home,* the bright, bouncy Smith girl who could do no wrong.

In her article on Plath's early poems, Marjorie Perloff observes that Plath's Sivvy personality was designed "to confirm her mother's fondest dreams."[16] But it was also designed to conceal Plath's worst nightmares, in particular "the disquieting muses" of rage, self-hatred, and self-doubt. With its enthusiasm and artifice, the voice Plath employs to project this personality mars and invalidates virtually all the writing in *Letters Home,* writing as striking for its artistic as its emotional hollowness and immaturity. No more convincing evidence of the corruption latent within Plath's Sivvy personality could be found, however, than a letter Plath wrote one month before her suicide. As in so much of *Letters Home,* Plath uses here the glossy, trivializing, "feminine" style that she picked up from her reading in women's magazines during the 1950s, the style she exploited so successfully as guest editor at *Mademoiselle.* It is a style appropriate to the girl her mother wanted, a girl raised on tales of Mixie Blackshort the heroic bear and inspirational stories from the *Ladies' Home Journal,* a girl who could, like her mother before her, cope gallantly with any setback that came her way.

It is amazing how much my new hairdo and new clothes have done for my rather shattered morale. . . . I plan to throw myself into painting the rest of the upstairs floors this week so I can give myself the treat of applying for an au pair first thing in the new year. . . . The little nursery school just around the corner takes children from 9:30 to 12:30, and I shall try Frieda at it next week. She seems to blossom on outside experience with other children, and I think she needs this. . . .

How lucky I am to have two beautiful babies and work! . . .

Nick is wonderfully happy and strong. . . .

It is now snowing very prettily, crisp and dry, like an engraving out of Dickens. (LH, 492, 493)

A month later, choked by snow and bruised by defeat, Plath was dead.

Reading *Letters Home,* one can hardly fail to be impressed by the lengths to which Plath was prepared to go in suppressing her own needs in order to satisfy the needs of her mother. Indeed, her compulsion to present herself in the role of the good daughter is so relentless that the volume sometimes seems a parody of the ideal mother-daughter relationship as Plath ticks off success after success achieved for the hardworking, self-sacrificing mother's sake. But as Plath knew in her more candid moments, it was not love that was motivating her to lay these achievements so obsessively in her mother's lap. It was fear, fear of the loss of her mother's approval and, above all, fear of the sense of separation (of being rejected) that loss of approval would bring.

WHAT DO I EXPECT BY "LOVE" FROM HER? WHAT IS IT I DON'T GET THAT MAKES ME CRY? I think I have always felt she uses me as an extension of herself, that when I commit suicide, or try to, it is a "shame" to her, an accusation: which it was, of course. An accusation that her love was defective. . . . I felt I couldn't write because she would appropriate it. Is that all? I felt if I didn't write nobody would accept me as a human being.

. . . . . .

MY WRITING IS MY WRITING IS MY WRITING. Whatever elements there were in it of getting her approval I must no longer use it for that. I must not expect her love for it. . . . Why is telling her of a success so unsatisfying: because one success is never enough. When you love, you have an indefinite lease of it. When you approve, you only approve single acts. Thus approval has a short dateline. (J, 281)

As an extension of her mother's self, there was nothing Plath would not do for Aurelia's sake. Even her writing belonged to her mother. But behind the poet's compulsive need to maintain this bond, as this journal extract written after Plath's return to therapy in 1958 makes heartbreakingly clear,[17] lay Plath's overwhelming fear of the separation losing Aurelia's approval would bring. It was, I believe, this fear of separation—not Plath's need for love per se—that dominated the poet's psychic life, not only leading her to suppress or conceal essential elements within herself but, when projected onto her husband, ultimately helping to set the stage for her suicide at thirty-one.

In the extraordinarily beautiful sketch of her childhood in Nauset at her grandparents' home, "Ocean-1212-W," written in the last year of her life, Plath describes her first terrifying encounter with otherness or separation. It was a sensation she claims she felt for the first time when she was two and a half years old, just after her brother, Warren's, birth. The language Plath uses to describe this experience ("baby," "center," "star," "axis," "tender universe," "polar chill," "bones," "bystander," "museum mammoth," "wall," and "skin") is of a piece with the language she uses to describe birth both in *The Bell Jar* and in the poems on her children in *Ariel,* "Night Dances" and "Morning Song," with its punning title. These linguistic parallels make it clear that Plath believed the Nauset experience was central to her developing conception of the world and her place within it. Just as important, however, the parallels suggest that the emotions of rage and despair which she experienced in Nauset as a two-and-a-half-year-old were closely allied to those same emotions that were overwhelming her even as she wrote.

> A baby.
> I hated babies. I who for two and a half years had been the center of a tender universe felt the axis wrench and a polar chill immobilize my bones. I would be a bystander, a museum mammoth. Babies!
> Even my grandfather . . . couldn't woo me from my huge gloom. . . . Hugging my grudge, ugly and prickly, a sad sea urchin, I trudged off on my own. . . . As from a star I saw, coldly and soberly, the *separateness* of everything. I felt the wall of my skin: I am I. That stone is a stone. My beautiful *fusion* with the things of this world was over.   (JP, 23; italics added)

As befits a poet of Plath's intensity, her childish response to this "awful birthday of otherness," of separation from the mother, was immediate, brutal, and highly symbolic. Enraged by her own helplessness and vulnerability and by the sense of separation rage engendered in her, she deliberately goes on to destroy a creature even more helpless and dependent than herself.

I picked up, frigidly, a stiff pink starfish. It lay at the heart of my palm, a joke dummy of my own hand. Sometimes I nursed starfish alive in jam jars of seawater and watched them grow back lost arms. On this day, this awful birthday of otherness, my rival, somebody else, I flung the starfish against a stone. Let it perish. It had no wit.   (JP, 23)

Although Plath may have thought she was attacking the starfish as a representative of the other, the rival, her rage at the poor creature appears to derive far more from her identification with it than the reverse. This was a creature she had tended and cared for just as her mother had tended and cared for her. Under the impact of Warren's birth, she recoiled against the symbol of her own helplessness and dependence, taking her rage against her mother and newborn brother out in an act of destruction that through the starfish-surrogate was directed toward the self. In thus killing the starfish rather than her mother or Warren, she set the pattern for her later life, a pattern that emerged, as Nancy Hunter Steiner says, in "the final macabre threat: 'I'll die if you desert me.' "[18]

If we take "Ocean-1212-W" seriously—it is after all the adult memory of a two-and-a-half-year old's experience[19]—Warren's birth, Plath's first real experience with separation, forged in the poet's mind an equation between birth and death. Birth equaled separation from the mother equaled autonomous self (the "awful birthday of otherness," "the separateness of everything," "I am I"); but autonomy, insofar as it involved separation from the mother, was another form of death, a death produced in rage and despair. For Plath, even the birth of her own daughter was an experience of separation and, therefore, ironically an occasion for "mourning." In "Morning Song," she writes:

Love set you going like a fat gold watch.
The midwife slapped your footsoles, and your bald cry
Took its place among the elements.

Our voices echo, magnifying your arrival. New statue.
In a drafty museum, your nakedness
Shadows our safety. We stand round blankly as walls.

I'm no more your mother
Than the cloud that distills a mirror to reflect its own slow
Effacement at the wind's hand.

(CP, 156–57)

To Plath, the only way to life was through fusion and the consequent erasure of the separate self, but it was life achieved at the price of complete dependence, a precarious, incomplete life at best—just the kind of life that, according to the social norms of the time, women were supposed to draw from marriage, motherhood, and men. Blos said no less when he declared that a woman's "need is to be loved" nor did Erik Erikson when he claimed that "womanhood arrives when attractiveness and experience have succeeded in selecting what is to be admitted to the welcome of the inner space 'for keeps.' "[20] For these two experts, as for their myriad pop promulgators, the writers examined by Friedan in *The Feminine Mystique,* a fulfilled woman is a woman who has achieved a happy marriage. And conversely, the woman who fails to marry is a woman whose identity—whose womanhood and sense of being—can never be complete.

In "Ocean-1212-W," Plath claims that she finally resolved her conflict that awful day by adopting the sea, a primitive symbol of oneness or fusion, as her mother. But all the evidence of her writing suggests otherwise. Not only did birth, as in *The Bell Jar* and *Ariel,* remain a traumatic event for her, a symbol of separation and, therefore, ironically of death; but the desire to return to a state of fusion, whether with her mother or with her socially acceptable, mother-surrogate husband, became the dominant feature of her psychic life. Indeed, it is clear from her other writing that for Plath, life without fusion, without the unequivocal approval of her mother or the unconditional love of her husband, was no life at all.

Taken together with Aurelia Plath's own deep need to fuse and to see only good in everything, Sylvia Plath's fear of separation inflicted, in short, a profound wound on the poet's psyche. From this wound sprang Plath's divided self. To be one with her mother or, later, her husband, she had to suppress her otherness, her bad side. She had to be a good girl, a girl modeled out of Mixie Blackshort and Ovaltine. To be herself, separate, autonomous, gave her the freedom only to be bad. The plastic wife of *Letters Home,* the sweet, submissive, self-sacrificing, and courageous girl who clipped recipes from the *Ladies' Home Journal* and "dried plates with [her] dense hair" (CP, 214), and the considerably more exotic "bitch goddess,"[21] the red-haired lioness who "eat[s] men like air" (CP, 244), are the inevitable if contradictory consequences of one desire: the poet's overwhelming need to maintain fusion by fulfilling in every way her mother's narcissistic expectations. Insofar as she failed to meet those expectations, her sense of otherness and estrangement devoted her, as in the episode in Nauset, to rage, self-hatred, and death.

On one level or another, Plath knew even as an adolescent that the bond between herself and her mother had the potential to destroy her. In August of 1950 she wrote with eerie prescience in her journal of finding herself locked inside her mother's house.

> I twisted the lock . . . and still the door stuck, white, blank, and enigmatic. I glanced up. Through the glass square, high in the door, I saw a block of sky, pierced by the sharp black points of the pines across the street. And there was the moon, almost full, luminous and yellow, behind the trees. I felt suddenly breathless, stifled. I was trapped, with the tantalizing little square of night above me, and the warm, feminine atmosphere of the house enveloping me in its thick, feathery smothering embrace.   (J, 12)

But although she recognized dangers of this closeness—entrapment, suffocation, the ultimate death of the independent self—and struggled poignantly at times against it, she was never able to break free. More surely ever than Emily Dickinson, Sylvia Plath remained a prisoner within her home, for she took her home with her wherever she went, even three thousand miles across the sea.

In an extraordinary passage from her diary as a seventeen-year-old, a passage sadly belied by the facts of her life, Plath did dream momentarily of what it would be like to be a truly separate and autonomous woman:

> I am afraid of getting married. Spare me from cooking three meals a day—spare me from the relentless cage of routine and rote. I want to be free—free to know people . . . free to move to different parts of the world. . . . I want, I think, to be omniscient . . . I think I would like to call myself "The girl who wanted to be God." Yet if I were not in this body, where *would* I be—perhaps I am *destined* to be classified and qualified. But, oh, I cry out against it. I am I—I am powerful—but to what extent? I am I?   (LH, 40)

But Plath was not God. She was a child of the American fifties, the inhabiter not just of a body but of a woman's body, and the daughter of a mother who claimed to believe that success for a woman lay in marriage even though she knew from personal experience just how destructive marriage could be. Without direct access to real power or freedom and unable to break the bond that tied her to her mother, Plath submitted in turn to the destiny of classification and qualification that awaited her. She became, or tried to become, the good girl, the loving wife and doting mother her mother wished her to be and her society told her she had better be if she wished to be either normal or loved. Seven years after the diary entry, Plath wrote to her mother of her engagement to Hughes:

> I shall be one of the few women poets in the world who is fully a rejoicing woman, not a bitter or frustrated or warped man-imitator, which ruins most of them in the end. I am a woman and glad of it, and my songs will be of fertility of the earth and the people in it through waste, sorrow and death. I shall be a woman singer, and Ted and I shall make a fine life together.   (LH, 256)

And after Hughes's first book of poetry, *Hawk in the Rain,* was accepted for publication, she wrote:

> I am more happy than if it was my book published! I have worked so closely on these poems of Ted's and typed them so many countless times through revision after revision that I feel ecstatic about it all.
> I am so happy *his* book is accepted *first.*   (LH, 297)

In these statements and others like them, the self-empowering God fantasy of Plath's adolescent diary yields entirely before the far more socially acceptable notion that women who are autonomous are bitter, frustrated man-imitators and that she, as a woman, will only find true fulfillment married to a man, even if that marriage entails endless, personally barren hours before a typewriter and the willingness to accept second place in the market of ideas.

From an explanatory note she saw fit to include in *Letters Home,* it is clear that Mrs. Plath observed and encouraged such self-sacrificial attitudes in her daughter from an early age.[22]

> From the time Sylvia was a very little girl, she catered to the male of any age so as to bolster his sense of superiority. I recall her, when she was four years old, watching a boy of eleven demonstrating his prowess on a trapeze for her, clapping her hands, crying, "Juny [Junior], you are *wonderful!*"
> In her diary, written when she was a seventh-grader, she described coming in second in the Junior High School spelling contest—a boy came in first. "I am so glad Don won," she wrote, "It is always nice to have a boy be *first*. And I am second-best speller in the whole Junior High!"

She did not pretend the male was superior: she sought out those who were, and her confidence in her husband's genius was unshakable.   (LH, 297)

In marrying the up-and-coming Ted Hughes, Sylvia Plath had fulfilled her mother's greatest hope and expectation for her: that her very superior daughter would someday meet, marry, and cater to an even more superior male just as the mother had once done herself.

The fragile foundation on which Sylvia Plath was encouraged to build her sense of identity and self-worth (I have a husband, therefore I am; I have a superior husband, therefore I am superior too) is nowhere more brutally exposed than in the poet's response to her mother when Mrs. Plath sent her an endocrinologist's report on growth-stopping hormones shortly after Plath's daughter, Frieda, was born.

No more words about hormones and growth-stopping, please! . . . I'm surprised at you. Tampering with nature! What an American thing to feel measuring people to ideal heights will make them happier or not interfere with other things. Whatever height Frieda Rebecca is, I shall encourage her to be proud of it. My own height, 5'9", which so depressed me once is now my delight; and *I have a handsome, tall, living documentary of a husband to prove a tall girl need be nothing but fortunate in that line.*   (LH, 376–77; italics added)

It is hard to know what is more depressing in this passage: the lengths to which the grandmother was ready to go to insure that her granddaughter is socially acceptable as a woman or the fragility of the defense Plath offers of her own and Frieda's height.

By the standards society and her mother employed, the nature one should not tamper with had made Plath too tall, too bright, too superior, and certainly too highly motivated for a woman. If she was truly to be a woman with "a handsome, tall, living documentary of a husband to prove" her acceptability, then she would either have to search out, as her mother said, an *"extraordinary male counterpart"* to herself (LH, 181) or live a wasted and wasting life of lies and deceptions, pretending an inferiority she did not possess. Having tried this latter route from grade school through college — a period during which, her mother joyously reports, Plath would pride herself on fooling boys into believing she was not the all-A student she actually was (LH, 38) — Plath sensibly decided to look for the counterpart once she was on her own. But when Hughes, the superior one, the one to whom she rightfully submitted and with whom she ecstatically fused, deserted her in Devon six years after their wedding, the whole foundation upon which her identity as a woman was built fell in on her like a pack of cards and left her nothing positive on which she could rebuild.

Because she identified autonomy with feelings of rage and self-destruction, Plath could not take full hold of the freedom Hughes's desertion actually offered her. However positive the effect on her poetry, to be separate unleashed in her the demons of self-hatred and despair that had haunted her ever since Nauset. These were the disquieting muses, "Mouthless, eyeless, with stitched bald head," that nodded at her bedside and broke into her dreams. Ultimately she could not escape them.

While Sylvia Plath knew better than anyone that she was not the good girl her mother wanted her to be, there is no evidence anywhere in Plath's published writings that she ever seriously questioned the rightness of her mother's and society's position: Only good girls were deserving of love and approval and therefore only good girls won the right to life through fusion. Unlike Emily Dickinson, for Sylvia Plath the writing of great poetry could never be enough.

5. Bonds of Women

. . . .
. . . .
. . . .

The attainment of heterosexuality . . . is the major traditional oedipal goal for girls. For boys the major goal is the
achievement of personal masculine identification with
their father and a sense of secure masculine self.
— Nancy Chodorow

Being born a woman is my awful tragedy.
— Sylvia Plath, 1951

In her only completed novel, *The Bell Jar,* written
two years before her death, Sylvia Plath translates the social and psychological consequences of the split that dominated her interior life and her
relationship with her mother into a *bildungsroman* for American womanhood. As Plath's surrogate fictional self, Esther Greenwood's air of simplic-
ity or naivete is purest sham.[1] Guest editor of a magazine she secretly
despises, financée to a man she loathes, Esther knows perfectly well what
she has done to get where she is. The purity and goodness she longs for are
qualities she gave up long ago and can never, short of death or psychological
annihilation, recover.

I plummeted down past the zigzaggers, the students, the experts,
through year after year of doubleness and smiles and compromise, into
my own past.
People and trees receded on either hand like the dark sides of a tun-

nel as I hurtled on to the still, bright point at the end of it, the pebble at the bottom of the well, the white sweet baby cradled in its mother's belly. (BJ, 108)

Esther's self-annihilating plunge down the snowy Adirondack mountainside ends with a broken leg. It could just as well have ended with a broken neck, and the author's judgment—"This is what it is to be happy"—would not have changed. For Plath's fictional self, hurtling toward the inescapable confrontations of an emotional breakdown, death was a cheap price for purification. To strip away year after year of compromise, of doubleness and smiles, of zigzagging for grades and prizes, dates and friends, meant a return to the womb in any case, that is, to the "still, bright point" before the process of socialization began and with it the lying, pretending, and suppressing from which Esther's double self developed. Anything short of such a return could not, and as Plath found out in her own life, would not work.

The Bell Jar's accuracy in depicting the duplicity of Plath's relationship to the world at large during her high school and college years is supported by everything friends and acquaintances have said about her as well as by comments she makes about herself in her journals and elsewhere. To the world, as to her mother, Plath was relentlessly the good girl, the golden all-around American beauty whose "high, pure string of straight A's" in no way implied she was anything but "Okay" (JP, 54, 55). As she explained in a late essay, "America, America" (1963), this was the image she knew everyone—teachers, administrators, friends, and dates alike—wanted. And it was the image to which she felt compelled to conform if she wished to get ahead—get into college, get dates, be popular, win prizes, get married—in short, be the girl her mother hoped and expected she would be.

Told by a high school guidance counselor that she might be "just too dangerously brainy," that is, not sufficiently well rounded, for easy college admittance, Plath by her own account "became a rabid teenage pragmatist," joining the girls' basketball team and the school newspaper, "painting mammoth L'il [sic] Abners and Daisy Maes" for the school dances, and "leveling [her] bobbysocks to match those of [her] schoolmates" (JP, 54).

It was not just her bobbysocks she leveled. Her aim was to gain "admittance to the cherished Norm," to have "an Okay Image" (JP, 55). To this end she joined a high school sorority, an in club, whose activities, apart from a brutally humiliating initiation rite, consisted, she says, of eating cake and catting about dates. Though in "America, America," written from the perspective of her final crisis-laden year of life, Plath claims that the sorority's tailoring did not take, Nancy Hunter Steiner's memoir of Plath during the poet's last two years at Smith, *A Closer Look at Ariel,* suggests the contrary. With her first suicide attempt well behind her, Plath impressed Steiner, a junior-year transfer, as deliberately cultivating "her clothes and manner . . . to disguise any distinction" or divergence from "the prevalent stereotype."[2] "We pursued boys, clothes, and entertainment," Steiner writes, "as energetically as we pursued an education."[3] As scholarship students, both of them ardently desired "to appear well rounded" and part of "the mainstream of campus life."[4] Plath was so successful in creating this impression that Steiner comments, "Except for the penetrating intelligence and the extraordinary poetic talent she could have been an airline stewardess or the ingenuous heroine of a B movie."[5]

Although she was Plath's roommate and close friend, Steiner found it difficult to believe that Plath "had ever felt a self-destructive impulse." "She did not appear tortured or alienated," Steiner writes. Rather, she seemed to be "the typical American girl, the product of a hundred years of middle-class propriety" and to clinch her middle-class, well-rounded status, "she actively disliked the little band of rebels in the house [Lawrence House at Smith]. Their bare feet, rude manners, and coarse language offended her."[6]

Steiner's portrait of Plath is supported by virtually everyone who knew the poet at Smith. "The public portrait of her that emerges," Edward Butscher says of his interviews with Smith faculty and alumnae, "is . . . that of a normal, happy, brilliant young girl dedicated to duty, art, and scholarship, an outgoing student who could play tennis, bang out popular tunes on the piano, paint, date Ivy League men, and write sophisticated poems and stories in her spare time. . . . the all-American college girl at her best."[7] Plath "obviously wanted to paint" this portrait, Butscher notes. Just as obviously, however, the portrait depicts the daughter Aurelia Plath wanted to mother. Hardly a dark line appears in it. From what we know of Plath's interior life, her bald, disquieting muses, hardly a true one does either.

Plath's recently published journals make it clear that she herself was painfully aware, at least during her first two years at Smith, of just how much her "Okay" image was actually a front and how vulnerable it was. In the diaries that have survived from these years—those written after her breakdown are unfortunately missing—she habitually alternates between two states: brief but ecstatic highs, when she is feeling successful and her image is intact, and prolonged lows, when internally her image crumbles and she loses all confidence in everything she has done.

During the highs she would actively try to convince herself that she really was the optimistic, cheerful, giving, constructive person most people believed her to be. In such moods the sins of the past would be wiped away to be replaced, however temporarily, by her mother's bromides and solutions. "Look at that ugly dead mask here and do not forget it," she wrote of a small photograph of herself that she pasted in the margin of her journal in early January 1953, shortly after meeting a new man:

It is a chalk mask with dead dry poison behind it, like the death angel. It is what I was this fall, and what I never want to be again. The pouting disconsolate mouth, the flat, bored, numb, expressionless eyes: symptoms of the foul decay within. Eddie wrote me . . . I had better . . . get psychiatric treatment. . . . I smile, now, thinking: we all like to think we are important enough to need psychiatrists. But all I need is sleep, a constructive attitude, and a little good luck.

Thanksgiving I met a man I could want to see again and again.   (J, 67)

During the lows, on the other hand, usually following some failure like taking the wrong course or losing a boy friend, she would squarely confront the hollow self she knew lay behind her golden image.

How to justify myself, my bold, brave humanitarian faith? My world falls apart, crumbles, "the centre cannot hold." There is no integrating force, only the naked fear, the urge of self-preservation.

I am afraid. I am not solid, but hollow . . . I never wrote, I never suffered, I want to kill myself.   (J, 60)

Such passages, so poignant in their contradictions, suggest that by the time Plath reached Smith she had in fact lost touch with her emotions. Having geared her life to meet the expectations of others, first her mother, then by extension, the world at large—from guidance counselors to dates and friends—she no longer knew who she was or what she wanted. Of such young people, Alice Miller writes in *The Drama of the Gifted Child:*

He cannot rely on his own emotions, has not come to experience them through trial and error, has no sense of his own real needs, and is alienated from himself to the highest degree. Under these circumstances he cannot separate from his parents, and even as an adult he is still dependent on affirmation from his partner, from groups, or especially from his own children. . . . This is no obstacle to the development of intellectual abilities, but it is one to the unfolding of an authentic emotional life.[8]

Like Miller's patients, Plath had absorbed parental values as her own and was alienated from her true self as a result. Her social and academic accomplishments did nothing for her self-esteem because they were designed to meet the needs and expectations of others. To her, therefore, they could only be lies. Behind the facade of the all-American girl who had achieved everything a mother might desire or a teacher ask, there came to wallow a young woman obsessed with failure and the "blank hell" of her real self, a self that she desperately feared might, at any point, break through.

> I sit here, crying almost, afraid, seeing the finger writing my hollow futility on the wall, damning me—God, where is the integrating force going to come from? My life up till now seems messy, inconclusive, disorganized: I arranged my courses wrong, played my strategy without unifying rules. . . . I am drowning in negativism, self-hate, doubt, madness—and even I am not strong enough to deny the routine, the rote, to simplify. No, I go plodding on, afraid that the blank hell in back of my eyes will break through, spewing forth like a dark pestilence, afraid that the disease which eats away the pith of my body with merciless impersonality will break forth in obvious sores and warts, screaming "Traitor, sinner, imposter."[9]   (J, 61)

In committing herself both privately and publicly to an image that was utterly alien to her real needs, Plath had in effect set herself up. She was too brilliant, too ambitious, too intense, or, as she summed it up in "America, America," "too weird" (JP, 55) for the good girl image to stick just as she was too depressed and too filled with self-hatred for the false self to survive.[10] Under the stress of extreme negative emotional experience, precipitated first by the disillusionment that attended her guest editorship at *Mademoiselle* and later by the breakdown of her marriage, the false persona shattered completely. The "real" Sylvia Plath, the one neither her mother nor the world was allowed to see, the one who wrote nasty books and outraged poems and considered suicide a valid way out, hurtled into view.

With the sensitivity of seismographs, *The Bell Jar,* which was written seven years after the events that it depicts, and Plath's last poetry, *Ariel* and *Winter Trees,* record the eruptions of Plath's other self. In these works, where Plath's autonomous fantasy is finally freed, she gives voice to all the negative, offensive emotions that her good girl, all-around American image did not allow her to express. If the content of these works is ugly and painful, this ugliness and pain is, I believe, in direct proportion to the amount of negativity that Plath felt she had to suppress not only as her mother's daughter but also as a woman in this society. However one regards them as works of art, as documents recording one woman's rage at the intellectual and emotional sacrifices she felt she had to make in order to win love and social approval, *The Bell Jar* and Plath's last poetry are in my opinion without parallel in our culture to date.

. . .

Even given the powerful fusion relationship that existed between Sylvia and Aurelia Plath, it is possible that the poet could ultimately have found some way to break the bond with her mother—and thus integrate her personality—had she lived in a society that supported and encouraged autonomy as a goal for female psychological development. As *The Bell Jar* makes painfully evident, however, United States society in the 1950s did neither, and for Plath there was therefore no escape.

While Plath pays some attention to Esther's relationship with her parents in *The Bell Jar,* the novel's principal focus is on the heroine's interaction with the world at large and particularly on the pressure put on young women in our culture to conform to a stereotyped view of femininity if they wish to achieve social, as opposed to professional, success. Although Plath deals with her first suicide attempt in the novel, the orientation of the book is sociological rather than psychological. Indeed, psychologically speaking, *The Bell Jar* is distressingly thin, almost the "pot-boiler" Plath claimed it to be (LH, 472). The text's significance lies not in the light it sheds on Plath's inner dynamics, about which she has very little to say, but in the brilliance with which it delineates the oppressive atmosphere of the 1950s and the soul-destroying effect this atmosphere could have on ambitious, high-minded young women like Plath.

Plath's *Bell Jar* is a book about women.[11] More specifically, it is a book about growing up as a woman in a culture that is fundamentally unfair and hypocritical in its inequality. Through most of the novel, Esther, sick unto death of her good girl image but unwilling or unable to shed it, flounders in a hate-filled void: despising women because they comply with a system that divides and exploits them, despising men because they claim and exercise the benefits of a superiority not truly theirs, despising herself above all for having no way out of this dilemma. Esther's quest for a woman who can show her how to resolve this conflict successfully is one of the novel's major themes. Her goal is to find a means to be both feminine and equal, that is, to be socially acceptable as a woman while still retaining her power as an autonomous individual and a potential professional. Her dilemma is resolved, however factitiously, in the final section of the novel through her contact with Dr. Nolan, the "good mother," and through her acquisition of a diaphragm, the contraceptive device that will presumably allow her to exercise her feminity without fear of accidentally falling under the domination of a man by becoming pregnant and therefore dependent, as, in effect, Plath's mother did.

Esther's problems, according to Plath, come to a head in New York City after she has won a fashion magazine contest. Under the hot klieg lights of *Ladies Day* more than crabmeat sours. Esther discovers that the image on which she has depended for the first nineteen years of her life is a fraud. The golden girl is ash:

> I was supposed to be having the time of my life.
> I was supposed to be the envy of thousands of other college girls just like me all over America.   (BJ, 2)

But the "size-seven patent leather shoes . . . bought in Bloomingdale's . . . with a black patent leather belt and black patent leather pocketbook to match" leave Esther numb. So do the martinis, the dance dresses, the "anonymous young men with all-American bone structures" and all the other paraphernalia designed presumably to appeal to her femininity but appealing in fact to her developing consumer lust. (Denied the power to earn, middle-class American women in this century have been encouraged to spend in prodigious quantities, usually, as here, on items designed to make them attractive to the wage-earning male.)

Esther is supposedly fulfilling the dream for which any healthy, all-American girl would be willing to sell her soul. But having sold her soul, or at any rate, her artistic ability, Plath's heroine finds that she has received a mess of potage in return.

> We had all won a fashion magazine contest, by writing essays and stories and poems and fashion blurbs, and as prizes they gave us jobs in New York for a month, expenses paid, and piles and piles of free bonuses, like ballet tickets and passes to fashion shows and hair stylings at a famous expensive salon and chances to meet successful people in the field of our desire and advice about what to do with our particular complexions.   (BJ, 3)

Although Plath never specifies why Esther goes numb in New York

City, the bizarre juxtaposition in this passage of the trivial and the serio
telling. In the Madison Avenue world of *Ladies Day,* everything
reduced to the lowest common female denominator. Famous poets
great artists, a number of whom Plath met while at *Mademoiselle,* are
par with recipes for crabmeat and avocado salad and snappy effects
mink tails. A well-made story or hat are equally rewarded. And
rewards, no matter how demeaning, are what any girl will suppos
cherish for they are the kinds of things that make girls girls. "Instea
tests or books or grades," Sandra Gilbert writes of her own experience
guest editor at *Mademoiselle,* ". . . they gave us *clothes.* . . . Later they ga
new hairdos; makeup cases . . . sheets and bedspreads; dances on sta
rooftops; and much, much more. On those long, hot June afternoons we
around in our pastel, air-conditioned seminar room discussing these obj
and events as if they were newly discovered Platonic dialogues."[12] The
and brightest women in Plath's and Gilbert's generation, so the Mad
Avenue message read, were ultimately as seducible as any street-co
bobbysoxer with a crush on a movie star and a yen for glamour. Wom
were all the same underneath. They wanted to be loved.

For Esther this message comes, apparently, as a devastating sho
Under the best of circumstances, she had been insecure about her femin
ity. She was too tall, too brainy, and generally too awkward in many of
female graces to feel completely comfortable in her all-American, coll
co-ed role. Now here she was in New York City with everything a true
was supposed to want laid out before her, hers for the taking, and sh
miserable, not elated. More than that, having sacrificed a good part of
integrity for this success, she feels dirty and polluted. She no longer kn
who she is. Confronted by her boss, Jay Cee, on her plans for the future,
girl who spent "nineteen years . . . running after good marks and prizes
grants" (BJ, 31) answers only " ' I don't really know' " (BJ, 35). What
of career can possibly be meaningful to a woman if women are what *La
Day* perceives and encourages them to be? Yet if Esther rejects the *La
Day* version of womanhood, supported as that version is by her mother,
college friends, the boys she dates, the experts she consults, the books
reads, the movies she sees, and the songs she hears, then who or what is
anyway?

It is this conundrum that causes Esther to grind to a halt in *The Bell
Confronted by the gulf between her gender or being and her aspirations,
is left feeling numb, stuck, as she says over and over again, in a dark, air
sack like an aborted fetus under its glass bell. Looking at the choices m
by the women she knows, she can find no acceptable alternative for hers

Women either embrace the role society designates and betray themselves in the process (her mother, Mrs. Willard, Dodo, Betsy, Doreen, and the nameless girls in the college dormitory who shun Esther when she has no steady date or acts too much like a grind) or they pursue their careers, their independent lives, at the expense of their womanhood (Jay Cee with her "plug-ugly looks," the lesbian poet at Esther's college, and Joan with her horsey smell). Neither kind of woman presents Esther with a model for herself or an example she wishes to follow. At best she merely oscillates between them, listening to the advice they give but unable to follow the paths they take.

> When I had told the poet [the "famous woman poet" at Esther's college who is one of her principal mentors] I might well get married and have a pack of children someday, she stared at me in horror. "But what about your *career?*" she had cried.
>   My head ached. Why did I attract these weird old women? There was the famous poet, and Philomena Guinea, and Jay Cee, and the Christian Scientist lady and lord knows who, and they all wanted to adopt me in some way, and for the price of their care and influence, have me resemble them. (BJ, 247–48)

Like the prototypical neurotic whom her financée, Buddy Willard, describes to her, the man who cannot decide whether he wants to live in the city or the country (BJ, 103–4), Esther wants two mutually exclusive things at once: marriage and a career, "a pack of children" and poetry. In her fantasies she flies back and forth between these alternatives, unable to pick one because she cannot bring herself to give up the other.

> I tried to imagine what it would be like if Constantin were my husband.
>   It would mean getting up at seven and cooking him eggs and bacon and toast and coffee and dawdling about in my nightgown and curlers after he'd left for work to wash up the dirty plates and make the bed. . . . and I'd spend the evening washing up even more dirty plates till I fell into bed, utterly exhausted.
>   This seemed a dreary and wasted life for a girl with fifteen years of straight A's. (BJ, 93)

In the last sentence Esther slams up against the truth that stops her every time she tries to take one of her own domestic fantasies seriously. With probably the same ingenuous spirit in which Adlai Stevenson exhorted Plath's graduating class at Smith to go out and use their education to become better wives and mothers ("We loved it," Nancy Hunter Steiner recalls),[13] Buddy Willard had told Esther that "after [she] had a child . . . [she] wouldn't want to write poems any more." Both men were handing down the wisdom of the day, truths Esther saw moreover lived out in the daily lives of the married women around her.

> I knew that's what marriage was like, because cook and clean and wash was just what Buddy Willard's mother did from morning till night, and she was the wife of a university professor and had been a private school teacher herself.   (BJ, 93)

No matter how many A's she got or how enlightened the man that she married was, if she wished to get married and have children, this would be her fate as well. Yet if she did not marry, what kind of empty, unpleasant, "plug-ugly" existence did she have to look forward to?

After her return from New York City, Esther's growing recognition of the mutual exclusivity of her goals drives her into a deeper and deeper depression. Paralleling Plath's own experience at *Mademoiselle,* the guest editorship at *Ladies Day* was supposed to have been the high point in Esther's budding career, but what it revealed to her was the hollowness of her efforts, the fact that given the society in which she lived, her aspirations were ash. After Esther comes home from New York, she can neither care for her looks, her femininity, nor pursue her studies, that is, continue to ready herself for a career. Debarred from summer school, her one tenuous hope for a meaningful summer, she lets her hair and clothing go. She stops reading. She can't write. She wonders if she is competent even to wait on tables or to type.

Esther sees herself sitting in the crotch of a fig tree, "starving to death, just because [she] couldn't make up [her] mind" which fig to choose (BJ, 85). Esther is indeed starving. Surrounded by women at school, at the women's hotel in New York, at *Ladies Day,* and in her own home, where she breathes in "the motherly breath of the suburbs" (BJ, 126) and shares a room with her mother, there is not one woman, until Dr. Nolan successfully makes contact with her, who can feed or nurture Esther or to whom she can successfully relate. It is not simply Esther's mother who fails her, but womanhood itself.

And inevitably, therefore, Esther's anger and disillusionment with womanhood turns against herself in the ultimate act of self-destruction. If she cannot take shorthand or write novels, go on dates or read James Joyce—all activities she attempts after her return from *Ladies Day*—

without debilitating internal conflict, then there is, in effect, nothing she can do. As a woman she has no clear purpose in living.

> I could see day after day after day glaring ahead of me like a white, broad, infinitely desolate avenue.
> It seemed silly to wash one day when I would only have to wash again the next.
> It made me tired just to think of it.
> I wanted to do everything once and for all and be through with it.   (BJ, 143)

She might as well be dead.

In the final section of the novel, Plath has Dr. Nolan, the good mother, show Esther the way out of this dilemma by providing her with the long-sought model to follow. Dr. Nolan is perfectly suited to her role as surrogate parent. Unlike Esther's first psychiatrist, Dr. Gordon, the bad father, who keeps a picture of his happy family plus dog on his desk and mishandles Esther's shock treatments, Dr. Nolan is the essence of straight-forward professional concern. Yet her professionalism is softened by nurturing warmth: She provides "milk" along with shock therapy. To Esther she is the one woman able to fuse femininity with intellect, an attractive appearance and manner with successful dedication to a career. The picture Esther draws of her has an almost movie star ring. Dr. Nolan steps out of a film from the late forties, fancy spectacles and all.

> I was surprised to have a woman. I didn't think they had woman psychiatrists. This woman was a cross between Myrna Loy and my mother. She wore a white blouse and a full skirt gathered at the waist by a wide leather belt, and stylish, crescent-shaped spectacles.   (BJ, 210)

Like the fairy godmother of the childhood fantasies that Plath adored (J, 20–21), Dr. Nolan is able to free the princess from the spell that holds her bound, immobilized, in place. But the sad fact is that the wand she uses is a diaphragm. Into Esther's otherwise unchanged hands, she places the instrument meant to secure Esther's sexuality while releasing her from the paralyzing fear of its consequences. Without a baby "hanging over [her] head like a big stick, to keep [her] in line," Esther believes she no longer has to fear coming "under a man's thumb" (BJ, 249). She can pursue her all-American, good girl image and her career simultaneously, confident that having one will not necessarily jeopardize the other.

To Esther the diaphragm means freedom, "freedom from fear, freedom from marrying the wrong person, like Buddy Willard, just because of sex, freedom from the Florence Crittenden Homes [for unwed mothers]" (BJ, 251). But as Lynda Bundtzen has recently noted, nowhere in the text does Plath suggest that Esther's deeper problems have been solved by the acquisition of this device or by the various forms of therapy she received along with it.[14] On the contrary, to judge by the Irwin episode, Esther's attitude toward men is, if anything, even more rigid and vindictive after her suicide attempt than it was before. Nor, as far as one can tell, has her concept of marriage or her definition of womanhood been substantially altered. Although Plath saw many of the problems connected with her view of marriage and womanhood clearly when she wrote *The Bell Jar* in 1961, she was still not prepared to deal with these issues completely then—no more than she had been able to in 1954.

At the conclusion of *The Bell Jar,* Joan, the overt lesbian and Esther's "wry, black image" (BJ, 246), hangs herself. Since Joan, who was a patient at the same hospital as Esther, was also presumably making progress, the suicide is unexpected and Plath offers no explanation for it. The inclusion of this event appears, consequently, to be a cathartic act on Plath's part, necessitated not by the novel's plot, themes, or characters but by Plath's own emotional understanding of her text. Joan, the woman who loves other women and who, therefore, can pursue a career and an independent life without benefit of men or marriage, must be disposed of if the demons that haunt Plath's/Esther's mind are to be exorcised as well. While it might seem that Joan—horsey, awkward, overly intellectual, and thoroughly unfeminine—is well got rid of by an author/protagonist about to embark upon a new, integrated life, it is a sad note of historical irony that the woman upon whom Joan Gilling is loosely based actually, according to Butscher, "went on to become a highly respected psychologist." Her suicide, he writes, is "the only purely imagined event in the book."[15]

Plath ends *The Bell Jar* with Esther exiting triumphantly stage left, bearing her diaphragm aloft while Joan, the defeated, is laid to rest beneath the pearly snow. Particularly in light of later events, this conclusion is unbearably factitious. Yet given Esther's/Plath's determination after her first breakdown to reconcile the irreconcilable—to maintain her image while still pursuing her career—it was perhaps the only option available to the author. Certainly the diaphragm brought one aspect of Esther's second-class status into line, namely the double standard. And given the society in which Esther (and Plath) lived, for the author this may well have seemed victory enough.

But beyond sexual freedom, which, according to Butscher, Plath exploited to the hilt after her return to Smith, and which, according to her *Journals,* she continued to exploit until her marriage to Hughes, Plath herself seems to have gained little from her experience at the psychiatric hospital. She returned to Smith, Butscher writes, "as disoriented as ever, still committed to disguise as a fundamental mode of behavior and composition,"[16] still, I would add, hollow and unintegrated at her core.

•   •   •

Plath's *Journals* support Butscher's contention that the therapy the poet received at McLean Hospital did little to change her basic orientation. To be sure, she had gotten "permission," as she was later to say, "to hate [her] mother" (BJ, 229; J, 266). And hating her mother freed her to some extent to explore hitherto suppressed areas of herself, in particular, as *The Bell Jar* suggests, her sexuality. (Aurelia Plath's attitudes toward sexuality were, not surprisingly, quite conservative.) But the fundamental split in her personality structure remained the same and with it the set of social assumptions about woman's nature and fulfillment which made both her image and her false self so dangerous to her ultimate well-being and survival.

In May of 1955 Plath graduated from Smith with highest honors. Her mother had just had a subtotal gastrectomy, the end product of an ulcer she developed while nursing Otto Plath through his final illness, and she attended Plath's graduation on a mattress. In a letter Plath wrote to her mother just before graduation, she toted up the "list of prizes and writing awards for this year" just so her mother could "remember." She won eleven in all, ranging from a hundred dollars from the Academy of American Poets for ten poems to five dollars from the *Alumnae Quarterly* for an article on Alfred Kazin, one of Plath's more notable instructors at Smith. The sum came to $470 "plus much joy!" (LH, 176). The golden girl was golden again and the long-suffering mother plenteously rewarded for her pains.

In the fall Plath went to England on a Fulbright scholarship to Newham College, Cambridge, where, in the words of the editors of her *Journals,* the "great successes at Smith were not so easily duplicated" (J, 90). But the poet's avidity to succeed both socially and academically was in no way diminished. On the contrary, she appears, if anything, to have become more fiercely competitive than ever, pouring herself into her studies and simultaneously into her search, as her mother put it, for "an extraordinary male counterpart" to herself.

As if to prove "a [smart] girl need be nothing but fortunate in that line," she modeled fashions for the local college newspaper. In the photographs, which Mrs. Plath reproduces in *Letters Home,* she poses like a would-be Hollywood vamp, a country girl who didn't quite make it, and signs herself "Betty Grable." She worried constantly about other women whom she habitually saw as rivals—not friends—and as always, she remained pathologically dependent upon the approval of others for good feelings about herself. Whether it was a question of getting the right man or getting published in the right journal, rejections sent her plummeting into depression, while acceptances left her high as a kite.

What is most disturbing, however, is that to a far greater degree than at Smith, Plath now appears to have become committed to the concept of femininity which as a seventeen-year-old she had so doubted and even despised. In the Cambridge journals all her anxieties over marriage are gone, replaced by her obsession with the fact that she was still single though all of twenty-three and a half.

> Save me from that, that final wry sour lemon acid in the veins of single clever lonely women.
> Let me not be desperate and throw away my honor for want of solace; let me not hide in drinking and lacerating myself on strange men. . . . Even twenty-three and a half is not too late to live anew. . . . I honestly hope that in five years I can make a new life if he is not coming; I certainly cannot just go on blindly thinking of ways in which to fill enough years so that he will come.   (J, 124)

Blindly she went on. At one point she berates herself with the notion that if she could write "really good" poems, then she would catch a "really good boy" (J, 108). Another time, she embarks on an elaborate "self-improvement" project designed to help her "win friends and influence people" (J, 137–38), that is, make her more attractive to the longed-for but elusive "he." The stipulations of the project: *"Don't drink much,"* *"Be chaste,"* *"Be friendly and more subdued,"* *"Work on inner life to enrich,"* *"Don't blab too much,"* *"Keep troubles to self,"* *"Don't criticize anybody,"* "be nice but *not too enthusiastic,"* "Be stoic when necessary and *write,"* mingle all too predictably Plath's real needs with the needs she developed in her efforts to conform to what she later called "rules . . . rules . . . rules" (CP, 206).

Unhappily, these passages only add further confirmation to Butscher's thesis. Therapy may have helped Plath distance herself quite literally from her biological mother, but it had done little, if anything, to affect the "mother" within. Despite everything she knew about the hazards involved,

Plath still felt she must have it both ways, still believed both marriage and a career were absolutely essential for fulfillment, and as a result still sought frantically by manipulation and disguise to arrange for both. Indeed, it is arguable that through her contact with "Dr. Nolan"—a portrait that appears to blend her psychiatrist with a teacher at Cambridge whom she especially admired—Plath's problems had been exacerbated rather than helped. For now she was convinced that as a woman she could have both a marriage and a career—if only she played her cards right and was lucky enough to find the right man. There was nothing therefore to stop her from engaging totally in the grand pursuit as she called it. The agonizing doubts and questions that plagued her first two years at Smith and that she brilliantly records in *The Bell Jar* were over, replaced by her obsessive, frenetic need to find the right "he." More than that, she was now ready, as she had not been prior to her first suicide attempt, to put the entire responsibility for her reality as a woman and a human being upon her capacity to catch a "really good boy," her ability as a poet notwithstanding. "I long," she wrote pathetically in her journal after an unpleasant incident in Cambridge when schoolboys threw dirty snowballs at her,

> to permeate the matter of this world: to become anchored to life by laundry and lilacs, daily bread and fried eggs, and a man, the dark-eyed stranger, who eats my food and my body and my love and goes around the world all day and comes back to find solace with me at night. Who will give me a child, that will bring me again to be a member of that race which throws snowballs at me, sensing perhaps the rot at which they strike? (J, 102)

Where the self should have been in Plath, there was still only rot. But she was now firmly convinced that the love of a husband and child could give her the reality she could not possess on her own and thus fill the void that her bond to her mother had made.

In ways that are uncomfortably like the normal women whom Carol Gilligan describes in *In a Different Voice,* Plath had come, in short, to define herself entirely in terms of her ability to love and to be loved. Of this "fusion of identity and intimacy" in even "highly successful and achieving women," Gilligan writes:

> Measuring their strength in the activity of attachment ("giving to," "helping out," "being kind," "not hurting"), these . . . women do not mention their academic and professional distinction in the context of

describing themselves. If anything, they regard their professional activities as jeopardizing their own sense of themselves, and the conflict they encounter between achievement and care leaves them either divided in judgment or feeling betrayed.[17]

So for Plath, only in "the activity of attachment" could she feel or be real. To live, she had to be able to exercise her capacity to care, to "anchor" herself, as she said, in lilacs and fried eggs. Without a husband or child, neither her academic nor her professional distinction could affect the hollowness that lay at her core. She might be a poet, but she could not be a woman or truly feel she had an identity or self.

It is very possible that in trying to put an end to her self-hatred and sense of difference, Plath decided that this was the kind of normalcy that she should work for in therapy, independent of anything Beuscher actually felt or believed.[18] But whether it was Plath's or her therapist's responsibility, by the time she reached Cambridge the poet had clearly resolved her concerns over her femininity by deciding to make her "desires and emotions and thoughts center around what the normal woman's center around" (J, 312), no matter how poorly that particular shoe might fit or how limited she knew this vision of normalcy was. Unlike Emily Dickinson, she would base her mature sense of self on being *like,* rather than different from, other women. Thus the young woman who had dreaded marriage and hated babies now longed passionately, even hysterically, for both. And the brilliant young student who had dreamed of an independent life now despised those who led one. As "Two Sisters of Persephone" makes clear, by the time Plath met Hughes in Cambridge, there was in her mind only one life for a woman, that lived in the red blaze of the male sun as his bride and mother to his brood.[19]

> Two girls there are: within the house
> One sits; the other, without.
> Daylong a duet of shade and light
> Plays between these.
>
> In her dark wainscoted room
> The first works problems on
> A mathematical machine.
> Dry ticks mark time
>
> As she calculates each sum.
> At this barren enterprise

Rat-shrewd go her squint eyes,
Root-pale her meager frame.

Bronzed as earth, the second lies,
Hearing ticks blown gold
Like pollen on bright air. Lulled
Near a bed of poppies,

She sees how their red silk flare
Of petaled blood
Burns open to sun's blade.
On that green altar

Freely become sun's bride, the latter
Grows quick with seed.
Grass-couched in her labor's pride,
She bears a king. Turned bitter

And sallow as any lemon,
The other, wry virgin to the last,
Goes graveward with flesh laid waste,
Worm-husbanded, yet no woman.
                        (CP, 31–32)

Nothing Plath wrote captures more perfectly the degree to which she and Emily Dickinson diverged at the end of adolescence or the extent to which Plath, unlike Dickinson, had absorbed the ethos of her culture and was prepared to reflect it back. To be fruitful, to be productive—whether as mother or poet—a woman needed to be loved. This is what her society taught her. This is what Plath, ever her mother's daughter, conditioned herself to believe. Only the intensity of the poet's language and the franticness of her approach make her efforts to achieve normalcy in the Cambridge journals seem in any way extreme.

•   •   •

When A. Alvarez met Plath, now Mrs. Hughes, in London six years after her breakdown, the false self that carried her through so much of her life was still firmly in place. Indeed, the British author's description of Plath exhibits the same glowing fidelity to surface that characterizes Nancy Hunter Steiner's memoir of Plath at Smith. The image that Alvarez draws of a bright young housewife is little more than an elaboration of the bright young student with whom Steiner had roomed.

> In those days Sylvia seemed effaced, the poet taking a back seat to the young mother and housewife. She had a long, rather flat body, a longish face, not pretty but alert and full of feeling . . . She wore jeans and a neat shirt, briskly American: bright, clean, competent, like a young woman in a cookery advertisement, friendly and rather distant.[20]

Reading this passage one cannot help but be reminded of Lowell's description of Plath "dim against the bright sky of a high window,"[21] for there is hardly a woman here at all. Instead, Plath appears as a mannequin, a "bright, clean, competent" imitation of the real article, not unlike a picture torn from the pages of one of the slick women's magazines for which she was trying to write. In fact, Alvarez's description of her sounds remarkably like a photocopy of one of her own pop heroines, either Esther in "Mothers" or Ellen in "Day of Success." Only the breakup of her marriage with its many stereotypical details—the wandering husband, newly blessed with success, the bewildered young mother, tied to kids and kitchen, the other woman, an alien seductress—remained to complete the lineaments of what was in too many ways a B-movie fate.

Whatever Hughes may or may not have wanted from their marriage, *Letters Home* makes clear that Plath brought into it a set of romantic expectations that rivaled the worst pap found on the pages of *Seventeen* and *Mademoiselle* and were probably drawn from those sources. Despite her authentic genius as a poet and all the doubts she had once entertained, Plath had managed successfully to shape herself into a daughter of her time. Dorothea Krook, Plath's philosophy teacher at Cambridge and the only woman instructor Plath ever unequivocally admired, had introduced the poet to D. H. Lawrence. Plath's letters to her mother during the early years of her marriage reflect Lawrence's views on women and love, although, one is tempted to say in fairness to Lawrence, as seen through a B-movie lens. In their juvenility and superficiality, Plath's effusions on her new role and the joy it was giving her make painful but instructive reading.

> We have mystically become one. I can appreciate the legend of Eve coming from Adam's rib as I never did before; the damn story's true! That's where I belong. Away from Ted, I feel as if I were living with one eye lash of myself only. Everything I do with and for Ted has a celestial radiance, be it only ironing and cooking. (LH, 276)

With her marriage, presumably everything had fallen into place for Plath. She and her mother no longer need fear that she would end up a career girl. For all her brains, she would not dry out and become a spinster or "grotesque" like the women dons at Cambridge whom she satirized so mercilessly in her journals and letters home.[22] With Hughes, whose own capacity to fuse or solicit fusion appears to have been enormous, she would achieve full life. In his love, male love, she had at last become fully a woman and therefore, she believed, fully herself.

> Ted is up here this week and I have become a woman to make you proud. It came over me . . . the sudden shock and knowledge that although this is the one man in the world for me, although I am using every fiber of my being to love him, even so, I am true to the essence of myself, and I know who that self is. . . . and will live with her through sorrow and pain, singing all the way. (LH, 243)

To Plath, as to Lawrence, a woman's life was completed by a man and therefore effectively given over to him. There could be no "loyalty" among women, "even between mother and daughter," Plath wrote in a striking passage from her *Journals,* shortly before meeting Hughes, because all women fight for their men, "for the father, for the son, for the bed of mind and body" (J, 100). To the male she owed and should give all.

For Plath that all ended up including a great deal. For her marriage she gave up America for England, independent travel for housekeeping, and writing for children. Although she recognized throughout this period that her "deepest health" lay in her art (LH, 298), the facts of her daily life, particularly after the move to England and her first child's birth, spelled out a young mother's worst nightmare: trying to care for infant children, write, clean, wash, and cook all together, two babies in less than two years, little or no domestic help, few domestic conveniences, four major moves in five years, reams of her husband's manuscripts to type along with her own, his and her own mail to handle, cramped quarters, and to top it off, a constant stream of household guests largely, if not exclusively, his. Reading *Letters Home,* we are left with the impression that Plath did these things joyously; but it is a strange life indeed for a woman who at seventeen wished she were God and at twenty-nine declared in her only novel, "I hated the idea of serving men in any way." Like her mother before her, Plath had become "a slave in some private, totalitarian state" (BJ, 94), but it was a state largely of her own making. Unable to separate from her mother, Plath had become the woman her mother had wanted and expected her to be. After having "worked, bled, [and] knocked [her] head on walls to break through," Sylvia Plath was normal (J, 312).

Whatever else can be said about the breakdown of her marriage, it freed the poet to write and to express in her poetry all the pent-up rage she felt at what she perceived to be her victimization at society's—and her mother's—hands. It also freed her to draw from the ashes of her old life and old lies a new image of self, suited to a new woman, a woman capable of drawing her value solely from herself and from the fact of her womanhood. "In the image of the rising lioness/Virgin/red comet," Margaret Uroff writes, Plath "identified a female figure violent enough to triumph in a world that Plath imagined would reduce the woman to a jade statue—but a female also with creatively violent powers of her own."[23] Plath's new woman—the voice of her final poetry—is in many ways a terrifying figure, for she is wedded to separation and therefore, in Plath's mind, to death. But insofar as she draws her creative power entirely from herself, dependent on neither husband nor children, she embodies the freedom and autonomy that might well have saved Plath's life had she been able unambivalently to embrace them.

6. The Lioness

. . . .

. . . .

. . . .

It is one of the turning points in analysis when the narcis-
sistically disturbed patient comes to the emotional insight
that all the love he has captured with so much effort and
self-denial was not meant for him as he really was. . . . In
analysis, the small and lonely child that is hidden behind
his achievements wakes up and asks: "What would have
happened if I had appeared before you, bad, ugly, angry,
jealous, lazy, dirty, smelly? Where would your love have
been then?"
—Alice Miller

Fury jams the gullet and spreads poison, but, as soon as I
start to write, dissipates, flows out into the figures of the
letters: writing as therapy?
—Sylvia Plath, 1958

"I, sitting here as if brainless, wanting both a baby
and a career but god knows what if it isn't writing," Plath wrote in her
journal on February 19, 1959, during a period of bleak frustration. "What
inner decision, what inner murder or prison break must I commit if I want
to speak from my true deep voice . . . and not feel this jam-up of feeling
behind a glass-dam fancy-facade of numb dumb wordage" (J, 297).

Plath's difficulties in arriving at her own true deep voice were
monumental. After a precocious beginning, which she later realized had
not necessarily worked to her advantage, the poet found herself in maturity

alternating between brief spasms of intense creative furor and long stretches of poetic drought. A new love affair, an acceptance from a prestigious magazine, a return to therapy, interest in a new poetic model, would temporarily lift her writer's block, but then the "glass caul" (J, 297) would descend again, freezing her words. There was little poetry she wrote that she liked for long. "At each move we made," Ted Hughes writes, "she seemed to shed a style" (CP, 16).

Plath went through many styles in the long years between 1956, when she married Hughes, and 1960, when she first began to hear the throbbings of her own deep voice. Marianne Moore, D. H. Lawrence, Virginia Woolf, Theodore Roethke, Adrienne Rich, Robert Lowell, Anne Sexton, and, of course, Hughes himself, to name only the most important, all provided inspiration for her at one point or another during this time. Sometimes she seemed to try their idiosyncrasies on like overcoats: "Wrote a Grantchester poem of pure description. I must get philosophy in. Until I do I shall lag behind A[drienne] C[ecile] R[ich]" (J, 296). At other times, she seems to have gone to them sincerely searching for a pathway that would lead her to her self, "I felt mystically that if I read Woolf, read Lawrence (these two, why? their vision, so different, is so like mine) I can be itched and kindled to a great work: burgeoning, fat with the texture and substance of life" (J, 196). But just as each author superseded his or her predecessor in their influence upon her, always, it seemed, their writing remained just that much better than her own.

Plath leaned so heavily on the writings of others at this time because, quite simply, she did not care for the way she herself wrote: that is, the style of writing she developed at Smith and which is represented largely, but not exclusively, by the selection of juvenilia reprinted at the back of *The Collected Poems*. "My main difficulty has been overcoming a clever, too brittle and glossy feminine tone," she wrote to her mother in 1958. "I am gradually getting to speak 'straight out' and of real experience, not just in metaphorical conceits" (LH, 343). Similarly, in her journal she berates herself for having a "slick shiny artificial look" (J, 170) and a "bland ladylike archness or slightness" (J, 172). She is constantly fighting her own drive toward formalism—which she felt lessened her poetry's power (J, 296)—and toward saying small things perfectly in small, "crystal-brittle," "sugar-faceted" ways (J, 194).

Plath's harsh assessment of her early style is, in my opinion, difficult to quarrel with. Taking lines almost at random from the juvenilia, in "April Aubade" we read:

Worship this world of watercolor mood
in glass pagodas hung with veils of green
where diamonds jangle hymns within the blood
and sap ascends the steeple of the vein.

(CP, 312)

And in "Circus in Three Rings":

In the circus tent of a hurricane
designed by a drunken god
my extravagant heart blows up again
in a rampage of champagne-colored rain.

(CP, 321)

Sugared over with clever epithets like "watercolor mood" and curious images like "circus tent of a hurricane," such poems are every bit as "crystal-brittle" as she says.

In the almost uncannily revealing "Aerialist," based, perhaps, on an actual dream image, she compares herself to a tightrope acrobat. "Cat-clever" and adroit, the speaker performs, like a circus animal, to the "whipcrack" of "her maestro's will:"

Each night, this adroit young lady
Lies among sheets
Shredded fine as snowflakes
Until dream takes her body
From bed to strict tryouts
In tightrope acrobatics.

Nightly she balances
Cat-clever on perilous wire
In a gigantic hall,
Footing her delicate dances
To whipcrack and roar
Which speak her maestro's will.

(CP, 331)

But beyond adroitness, most of Plath's early poems have little stylistically-speaking to offer. While some like the "Aerialist" do express in covert terms Plath's ironic, anxiety-filled view of the world, even the best of these poems are too tense and too brittle for her real feelings to come through.

The language does not match the vision or rather it filters the vision through a formal lens that deprives it, as Plath herself acknowledged, of immediacy and power.

Despite her comment to her mother, however, Plath did not turn to real experience in her effort to break through this "glass-dam . . . of numb dumb wordage," which made it so difficult for her to speak "straight out." Rather, she turned compulsively, even frantically, to writers she considered more successful than herself.

> Have rejected the Electra poem from my book. Too forced and rhetorical. A leaf from Anne Sexton's book would do here. She has none of my clenches, and an ease of phrase, and an honesty.   (J, 301–2)

Honesty did not come naturally to Sylvia Plath, artifice did. To be "honest," she had to take a "leaf from Anne Sexton's book." Without someone to imitate or follow, she had no way to express, let alone reach, herself. Given Plath's genius for making other people's visions her own by absorbing them and reflecting them back, this imitation was not necessarily a bad thing for her art. On the contrary, some of the poems she wrote under the influence of other writers during the years from 1956 to 1960—"Point Shirley" (Lowell), "Medallion" (Lawrence), "Metaphors" (Sexton), and "Poem for a Birthday" (Roethke)—are generally grouped among her best work. If they do not represent her "true deep voice," as writing, they are certainly a major improvement over the poems contained in the Smith juvenilia. Imitating these poets, so much more candid and direct than herself, eased Plath's "literariness," allowing her to express some of the idiosyncrasies of her vision in a language that was almost, if not quite, her own. Thus, in "Poem for a Birthday," for example, we find Roethke ("Water mollifies the flint lip") mingling not at all uncomfortably with hints of late Plath ("My swaddled arms and legs smell sweet as rubber").

> Water mollifies the flint lip,
> And daylight lays its sameness on the wall.
> The grafters are cheerful,
>
> Heating the pincers, hoisting the delicate hammers.
> A current agitates the wires
> Volt upon volt. Catgut stitches my fissures.

A workman walks by carrying a pink torso.
The storerooms are full of hearts.
This is the city of spare parts.

My swaddled legs and arms smell sweet as rubber.
Here they can doctor heads, or any limb.

(CP, 137)

Such imitation did not—and given her other issues could not—solve the problem of acquiring her own deep voice. Nor, consequently, did the poems she wrote in this manner satisfy her for long. But as a liberating technique, imitation unquestionably helped pave the way for that acquisition to occur.

It took real experience, ironically, experience every bit as violent as the inner murder she feared, for Plath to achieve what she desired most: the final emergence in her poetry of the true self, the self, the voice, that lay behind "the jam-up of feeling," the "glass-dam . . . of numb dumb wordage," the "fancy facade" that had protected her and done such damage to her for so long.

• • •

While the change in Plath's writing is generally dated after February 1961, when the poet suffered a miscarriage,[1] a good deal of evidence both in *Letters Home* and in the few poems she managed to produce in 1960 suggests that the change had already begun before the turn of the year. Chief among the factors contributing to this change was the birth of the poet's daughter, Frieda Rebecca, on April 1, 1960. With Frieda's birth (rather than the hoped for and expected son—she was sure it would be "a Nicholas Farrar," Plath wrote her mother two months before the baby was born {LH, 364}), everything changed in Plath's life, as it generally does in the lives of young mothers.

For all the happiness the baby presumably brought—Frieda was, after all, the consummation of Plath's dreams of normalcy— 1960 was a year of intense, often bitter, frustration for the poet. In her letters to her mother, she complains regularly of loneliness, homesickness, exhaustion, lack of sleep, having too many distractions, too much to do, and not being able to find the time or space in which to write. Always the rigid perfectionist in everything she did, from poem writing to baby tending, Plath was not one to tolerate failures, mistakes, or slovenly work. Yet her letters after Frieda's birth read like a litany of vain, abandoned attempts to organize herself in order to write. On May 11, for example, she tells her mother that Ted is now using a friend's study to work, "which is a great relief for both of us. It is impossible for him to work in this little place with me cleaning and caring for the baby, and when he is out, I have the living room and desk to myself and can get my work done." His work is her "first concern," she adds: "I . . . don't mind that my own taking up of writing comes a few weeks later" (LH, 381). But a few weeks later, it is clear that the system has not worked. "The baby's feedings and keeping the house clean, cooking, and taking care of Ted's voluminous mail, plus my own, have driven me so I care only for carving out hours where I can start on my own writing" (LH, 384). A month later finds her "exhausted by noon" and using Ted's borrowed study in the mornings in search of "a solid hunk of time off, or, rather, time on, a day" (LH, 386). In mid-August she employs a "rigid housework schedule — laundry and market Monday, iron Tuesday, etc., to counteract the otherwise helterskelter days." But she still has "little energy for writing in anything but [her] diary and a few light poems" (LH, 391). By month's end she poignantly echoes Virginia Woolf and declares "I really hunger for a study of my own out of hearing of the nursery where I could be alone with my thoughts for a few hours a day. I really believe I could do some good stories if I had a stretch of time without distractions" (LH, 392).

She apparently never got that stretch of time. In 1960 she produced one publishable story, "Day of Success," and twelve poems, her lowest production rate in ten years. More than that, for every setback to her own work, Ted appears to have had a matching success: voluminous production, as well as mail, a growing reputation and acceptance among Britain's literary elite (T. S. Eliot, W. H. Auden, Louis MacNiece, Stephen Spender), a second book published with great fanfare while Plath's first, *The Colossus*, was still in press, and regular requests from the BBC for readings. No wonder during this period Plath saw her own poems as being born "dead" as in "stillborn":

O I cannot understand what happened to them!
They are proper in shape and number and every part.
They sit so nicely in the pickling fluid!
They smile and smile and smile and smile at me.
And still the lungs won't fill and the heart won't start.

(CP, 142)

Nor is it surprising that even the forthcoming publication of her first volume, *Colossus,* in October failed to rouse her from her depression. Like the tortured victim in "The Hanging Man," which she wrote, astonishingly enough given its appropriateness to the mood of *Ariel*, a scant two months after Frieda's birth, "A vulturous boredom pinned" her in place. As the mother of an infant daughter, she passed her time in "A world of bald white days in a shadeless socket" (CP, 141). And a sour note enters her poetry that will never leave thereafter. It is the disillusioned note of a woman who finds herself confined to the concrete world of babies, bottles, and laundry, and who as a result has come to despise the inflated abstract realities of the three wise men or Magi.

> The abstracts hover like dull angels:
> Nothing so vulgar as a nose or an eye
> Bossing the etheral blanks of their face-ovals.
>
> Their whiteness bears no relation to laundry,
> Snow, chalk or suchlike. They're
> The real thing, all right: The Good, the True—
>
> Salutary and pure as boiled water,
> Loveless as the multiplication table.
> While the child smiles into thin air.
>
> (CP, 148)

From the "Magi" it would appear that Frieda's birth had made Plath realize what her marriage in and of itself had not: that she had been had. The world for which she had prepared herself at college and university, where with Dorothea Krook she studied "the Good" and "the True," was not the world to which she, as a woman, was most fitted. Nor was it the world to which after marriage and motherhood she would be consigned. Like her daughter, she belonged to another realm, one that addressed a very different set of truths:

> Six months in the world, and she is able
> To rock on all fours like a padded hammock.
> For her, the heavy notion of Evil
>
> Attending her cot is less than a belly ache,
> And Love the mother of milk, no theory.
> They mistake their star, these papery godfolk.

They want the crib of some lamp-headed Plato.
Let them astound his heart with their merit.
What girl ever flourished in such company?
                                        (CP, 148)

Like so many of Plath's early poems, the "Magi" is a woman's poem, only with a difference. In the Smith juvenilia Plath had dealt with her anxieties as a woman at three artistic removes. In the poetry she wrote after arriving at Cambridge—poetry that appears to reflect her ardent desire to achieve normalcy—she deals with her womanhood largely in the romanticized terms of Gravesian or Laurentian myth: "I shall be . . . fully a rejoicing woman. . . . and my songs will be of fertility of the earth" (LH, 256). The "Magi," on the other hand, is bluntly rooted in the "bald white" realities of a woman's life: babies, laundry, boiled water, milk, cribs, and belly aches. In the poem, Plath opposes the "wisdom" that comes from such realities with the traditionally sanctioned wisdom she learned at school and from men or male-identified women like Krook. If the poem's wit seems to ameliorate the anger within it, the many denigrating similes: "salutary and pure as boiled water," "loveless as the multiplication table," convey more bitterness than, perhaps, Plath meant to suggest.

    There is, in fact, a good deal of Plath's later style in this poem: sarcastic, colloquial, direct—not literary and public, but confidential and real. Her diction and rhythm are flexible instruments to measure the precise gradations of her tone: "They're/The real thing, all right: The Good, the True—" How different from the tense artifice of the "Aerialist" or the exquisite but finally arch beauty of the concluding stanza of the Lowellian "Point Shirley."

I would get from these dry-papped stones
The milk your love instilled in them.
The black ducks dive.
And though your graciousness might stream,
And I contrive,
Grandmother, stones are nothing of home
To that spumiest dove.
Against both bar and tower the black sea runs.
                                        (CP, 111)

Compared to such lines, "Magi" is quintessentially Plath. In diction, rhythm, imagery, and idea, it bears her indisputable mark, the echo of her true deep voice.

    The "Magi" suggests that by the end of 1960, Plath's real voice and with it, her true self, were on the edge of breaking through. The slovenly chaotic nature of motherhood had won out against Plath's "carefully constructed facade." Confronted with real experience at last, gallant tales of happy homemakers from the sleek pages of the *Ladies' Home Journal* would no longer do. "Flowers and bluebirds that never were" could not compensate the frustrated and disillusioned poet for the inequities she was suffering in her own life. As "The Disquieting Muses" forewarned, her balance was precarious:

> I woke one day to see you, mother,
> Floating above me in bluest air
> On a green balloon bright with a million
> Flowers and bluebirds that never were
> Never, never, found anywhere.
> But the little planet bobbed away
> Like a soap-bubble as you called: Come here!
> And I faced my traveling companions.
>
> Day now, night now, at head, side, feet,
> They stand their vigil in gowns of stone,
> Faces blank as the day I was born,
> Their shadows long in the setting sun
> That never brightens or goes down.
> And this is the kingdom you bore me to,
> Mother, mother. But no frown of mine
> Will betray the company I keep.
> (CP, 75–76)

After her miscarriage in February, Plath could no longer conceal her frown. The disquieting muses possessed their own.

•　　•　　•

"In Plaster," written on March 18, 1961, indicates that Plath knew her facade was cracking. Like its stronger twin, "Tulips," written on the same day, "In Plaster" was, Ted Hughes observes, the "first sign of what was on its way." Both poems were, apparently, composed "without her usual studies over the Thesaurus, and at top speed, as one might write an urgent letter," a method of composition she was to employ from then on.[2] More than "Tulips," however, "In Plaster" presents a clear, unequivocal picture of the struggle going on inside the poet between her two selves. The "close, explicit, and murderous" relationship between these two selves forms, as

George Stade has said,[3] the substance and theme of this extraordinary and, for Plath, artistically novel poem.

> . . . There are two of me now:
> This new absolutely white person and the old yellow one,
> And the white person is certainly the superior one.
> She doesn't need food, she is one of the real saints.
> . . . .
> I didn't mind her waiting on me, and she adored it.
> In the morning she woke me early, reflecting the sun
> From her amazingly white torso, and I couldn't help but notice
> Her tidiness and her calmness and her patience:
> She humored my weakness like the best of nurses.
>
> (CP, 158–59)

To the increasingly angry and frustrated body living inside the plaster cast, there is nothing admirable about the saint's "slave mentality." Her tidiness, calmness, and patience are, the body now realizes, merely masks covering an intense resentment. "Secretly," the body declares, "she began to hope I'd die." For all the cast's "whiteness and beauty" and her proclivities to play the nurse, "living with her," the ugly and hairy body decides, "was like living with my own coffin" (CP, 159, 160). The body has had enough.

The pitched antagonism between the body and the cast is not resolved at the end of the poem. The body recognizes that it is dependent on the cast. The two are, in fact, mutually dependent: the body gives the cast life; the cast gives the body protection and, even more important, holds it together. Nevertheless the body is "collecting [her] strength." It is only a matter of time before, ugly and hairy, she will break through. "Now I see it must be one or the other of us" (CP, 160), the body ominously concludes. The time was fast approaching for Plath when it could not be both.

Although not as specifically, virtually all the poems Plath wrote in 1961 suggest the same sense of isolation, frustration, and internal division as "In Plaster." The titles alone seem to evoke Plath's sense of self-alienation and inner loneliness: "Zoo Keeper's Wife," "Face Lift," "Barren Woman," "I am Vertical," "Insomniac," "Widow," "Wuthering Heights," "The Surgeon at 2 a.m.," "Last Words," and "The Moon and the Yew Tree." In these poems, as in poems with more innocuous titles including "Parliament Hill Fields," "Morning Song," "Stars Over the Dordogne," and "Blackberrying," the poet presents herself as alone in a landscape. She is cut off not just from that "country far away as health" (CP, 162), but apparently from all human contact and consolation. In "Parliament Hill Fields," she stands on "this bald hill," her grief over her miscarriage dealt with in solitude, deliberately separate from the "lit house" where her live child waits (CP, 152, 153). In "Zoo Keeper's Wife," the speaker describes herself as "Cold as an eel," "a dead lake," "lungless/And ugly." Her marriage to the keeper of animals (Hughes and his animal poems) has soured. He lies "face-to-the-wall," unable to deal with his wife's "grievances," while nightly, she flogs "apes owls bears sheep/Over their iron stile" in a futile effort to get some sleep (CP, 154–55). In "Morning Song," she is a statue in a "drafty museum," blank as a wall and no longer part of the child she mothers (CP, 157). In "Wuthering Heights" she is "the one upright/Among all horizontals," a solitary figure walking through the night (CP, 168). And in "Blackberrying," based on an actual family outing, there is "Nobody in the lane, and nothing, nothing but blackberries." Whatever the real circumstances of the event, in the poem the speaker confronts the "intractable" sea by herself (CP, 168, 169).

Plath's sense of isolation and self-alienation culminates in "The Moon and the Yew Tree," written in October 1961, two months after she and Hughes moved to Devon. In an article devoted to Plath's poetry, Hughes confesses that reading this poem depressed him greatly, even though he originally suggested the idea for it.[4] His response is understandable enough for in "The Moon and the Yew Tree," "the powers in control of [Plath's] life" are made unmistakably clear. In accepting the "bald . . . wild" moon as her mother, Plath was in effect accepting the bald, wild side of herself, the side possessed by the disquieting muses and by all those impulses her false self (or "amazingly white torso") had been designed to hide.

> The moon is my mother. She is not sweet like Mary.
> Her blue garments unloose small bats and owls.

Poignantly, she declares,

> How I would like to believe in tenderness—
> The face of the effigy, gentled by candles,
> Bending, on me in particular, its mild eyes.
>   (CP, 173)

But she cannot. Such tenderness, love, and caring have no bearing on her particular life; she cannot believe in them because she cannot feel them, and despite Aurelia Plath's exorbitant devotion probably never had. She has "fallen a long way." Her fate is now irrevocably determined by the "message of the yew tree": "blackness and silence," death.

In her baldness, wildness, and complete indifference to human suffering ("The moon sees nothing of this" [CP, 173]), the moon-mother in "The Moon and the Yew Tree" is obviously a direct descendant of the bald-headed godmothers who control the poet's fate in "The Disquieting Muses." Even more significantly, however, she is the presiding moon-mother-muse of all the poetry Plath wrote from 1961 on.[5] In "Barren Woman" she is "Blank-faced and mum as a nurse," mother of a woman who in her emptiness has turned to stone (CP, 157). In "The Rival" she is "beautiful, but annihilating," a great light borrower with a gift for "making stone out of everything" (CP, 166). In "The Detective" she is "embalmed in phosphorus," the detached, indifferent observer of a strictly human tragedy, the "vaporization" of the wife (CP, 208–9). And in "Edge," Plath's last, bleakest, and perhaps most perfect poem, she stares "from her hood of bone" down upon the dead mother and children and "has nothing to be sad about":

> She is used to this sort of thing.
> Her blacks crackle and drag.
>
>   (CP, 273)

As a maternal surrogate, this moon-mother-muse stands in direct contrast to the real-life biological mother, the "Blubbery Mary," who in "Medusa," surely one of Plath's nastiest efforts, steams like a fat red placenta across the ocean uncalled for to paralyze "the kicking lovers" with the "eely" or strangulating "tentacle" of her love (CP, 225, 226). Insofar as Plath accepted this surrogate as her true mother, she also accepted, as "The Moon and the Yew Tree" makes clear, the ugliness of her own personality and the inevitability of her death. Succinctly, the daughter of such a mother would be a creature too wicked, too hate-filled, too tormented, too cut-off from humanity to live.

Although Plath tried to dismiss "The Moon and the Yew Tree" as an exercise, Hughes's initially anxious response to the poem was justified by what followed. The move from London to Devon had been intended to relieve some of the couple's marital difficulties. In particular Plath hoped to find in the large old house space as well as time to write. "I adore my own study," she wrote her mother in September, "and after I get my great plank table, paint the woodwork white, get a rug and maybe an upholstered armchair, it will be heavenly" (LH, 429). But by the following spring she had come to realize that in moving she had simply exchanged one form of imprisonment for another, overcrowded quarters for total isolation. "A curious desperate sense of being locked in among these people," she wrote in her journal, "longing toward London, the big world. Why," she asked, "are we here" (JP, 38)? Well she might ask. The housebound mother of two—one a newborn—and just past her thirtieth birthday, Plath was trapped. As the family breadwinner, Ted needed to maintain his freedom to work, travel, and meet people. But how was she "to unclutch the sticky loving fingers of babies," to have her "husband alone for a bit," and to purge herself "of sour milk, urinous nappies, bits of lints and the loving slovenliness of motherhood" (JP, 38)? Eternal woman's question: how, in short, was she to remain not only whole but attractive to her potentially erring mate? She was, after all, now over thirty.

Plath's response to this situation, recorded in the journal entries that Hughes published in *Johnny Panic and the Bible of Dreams*,[6] was not especially admirable, but certainly common and understandable. She became jealous: jealous of Ted's time, his freedom, and above all, his interest in other women. The response was, one suspects, counterproductive. In late February she could still delude herself into believing that managing a girdle, stockings, and heels could make her "a new person" as she confronted a sixteen-year-old rival over tea (JP, 41). But a month later in "Elm," love has become a "pale irretrievable" and Medusa's face—the mother-moon who turns everything to stone—glares out at her from the tree's "strangle of branches," a hideous mirror image of her own terror ridden soul (CP, 193).

On May 21, 1962, she wrote "Event," celebrating the end of the grand passion that had begun a scant six years before.

> I walk in a ring,
> A groove of old faults, deep and bitter.
>
> Love cannot come here.
> A black gap discloses itself.
> On the opposite lip
>
> A small white soul is waving, a small white maggot.
> My limbs, also, have left me.
> Who has dismembered us?
>
> The dark is melting. We touch like cripples.
>
> (CP, 195)

With "Event" and other poems written at this time, Plath was now working squarely in the confessional mode as she chose to carve it out for herself. All remaining touches of the good girl, the false self, had been purged and with them went the glass caul in which her poems had been wrapped. In a voice as sour as turned milk, as acid as urinous diapers, Sylvia Plath was ready to give birth from her own private anguish to a new poetic self.

. . .

The poems for which Plath is best known and which are generally considered her most distinctive work were almost all written between September 26, 1962, and February 5, 1963, a period of four months and nine days. After a rocky spring and summer, during which Ted had been "seeing someone else," as Aurelia Plath tactfully put it (LH, 458), Plath finally threw in the towel and on August 27 wrote her mother that she intended to ask for a legal separation. "I do not believe in divorce," she commented rather haughtily, possibly for her mother's sake,

> but I simply cannot go on living the degraded and agonized life I have been living, which has stopped my writing and just about ruined my sleep and my health.   (LH, 460)

Six months of agony were over. The final four months of her life and the richest, most complicated period of her creative output were about to begin.

The poems Plath wrote between September 1962 and the time of her death are by no means equally successful, nor do they always present a consistent point of view. Some are so cryptic in their personal reference or significance as to defy analysis. Others, although superficially clearer, seem painfully confused, even contradictory in the positions they assume. Where the poems succeed, and the majority do, it is because of the author's driving talent, the force and brilliance of her imagery, the depth of her voice, and the power of the myth she was in the process of forging. This myth, that of the red-bodied lioness with wings of glass, is not without severe internal contradictions, the product of Plath's highly ambivalent attitude toward antonomy. Nevertheless, the myth represents Plath's best effort to ground her sense of self and womanhood on something other than the love and approval of her mother, her society, or a man. If ultimately she was unable to free herself from the needs and attitudes which bound her to the past, this fact should not detract from the value of her struggle or from the more general significance that her struggle has for women more fortunate than herself. In many ways Plath's problems were peculiarly her own, and few women could or would want to match her intensity. But in confronting boldly and unstintingly the consequences of her commitment to "normal" womanhood—her need for attachment, her desire to please, her readiness to sacrifice herself for others—Plath spoke to, and perhaps for, us all.

Plath's lioness, her vision of herself as autonomous woman, springs directly from the loins of the "little toy wife" (CP, 233) she felt she had become. In poem after poem written in the four-month interval before her death, she excoriates the old image of herself, and with it the institution of marriage, which she believed made her what she was. In "A Birthday Present," she declares:

'Is this the one I am to appear for,
Is this the elect one, the one with black-eye pits and a scar?

Measuring the flour, cutting off the surplus,
Adhering to rules, to rules, to rules.

Is this the one for the annunciation?
My god, what a laugh!'

                                                    (CP, 206)

In "The Detective," she is "a case of vaporization," a woman tamped into a wall, wiped out, "The mouth first. . . . The breasts next" (CP, 209). In "Stings" she has "eaten dust" for years, allowing her "strangeness" to "evaporate," behaving like a "drudge" as she "dried plates with [her] dense hair" (CP, 214). In "Amnesiac" she is "The little toy wife—/ Erased" with barely a sigh (CP, 233). In "Purdah" she is a "Jade—/ Stone of the side" of an agonized "green Adam," a veiled woman and a "small jeweled/ Doll" (CP, 242, 244). In "Lady Lazarus" she is an "opus," a "valuable,/ The pure gold baby/ That melts to a shriek" (CP, 246)—all images that refer to woman's role as object or victim or both.

Marriage in these poems is described in complementary terms. It is a relationship of exploitation, a "wax house," a "mausoleum," an "engine" that kills ("Stings" [CP, 215]), where the woman is either kept for sexual purposes as in "Purdah" and "Lady Lazarus" or chained to domestic chores until her "strangeness," her self or spirit, evaporates as in "Detective,"

"Birthday Present," and "Amnesiac." Whichever way it goes, torture is involved. The toy wife is the perennial victim. She fulfills in herself the role that Plath now contends women have always played and wanted to play, that of Jew to their husband's/father's Nazi. In "Daddy," she even claims that it is precisely the father-husband's monstrous nature women love:

> Every woman adores a Fascist,
> The boot in the face, the brute
> Brute heart of a brute like you.

Insofar as they model themselves on their mothers and believe what their mothers tell them, this is the role that women were raised for.

> I made a model of you,
> A man in black with a Meinkampf look
>
> And a love of the rack and the screw.
> And I said I do, I do.
> (CP, 223, 224)

It is also the role Plath now wishes unequivocally to reject. To her mother she writes in "Medusa":

> Ghastly Vatican.
> I am sick to death of hot salt.
> Green as eunuchs, your wishes
> Hiss at my sins.
> Off, off, eely tentacle!
>
> There is nothing between us.
> (CP, 225–26)

The mother's "wishes," wishes that rendered them both impotent victims, no longer have power over the daughter. Like the demonic father in "Daddy," the mother in "Medusa," in whose victimization the daughter "communed," has finally been disowned. The pattern of replication is broken.

> A Communion wafer? Blubbery Mary?
> I shall take no bite of your body,
> Bottle in which I live.
> (CP, 225)

And the daughter, "poor and bare and unqueenly and even shameful," is ready at last to recover the self—the lion-queen—she now claims in "Stings" she actually is.

> . . . but I
> Have a self to recover, a queen.
> Is she dead, is she sleeping?
> Where has she been,
> With her lion-red body, her wings of glass?
>   (CP, 214, 215)

Finally awake to the fullness of her rage and the violations that have been perpetrated upon her, the little toy wife metamorphoses into Clytemnestra, a woman who is prepared to kill in order to satisfy her lust for revenge.

> I shall unloose—
> From the small jeweled
> Doll he guards like a heart—
>
> The lioness,
> The shriek in the bath,
> The cloak of holes.
>   (CP, 244)

Nowhere in Plath's work is the intimate cause-effect relationship between the poet's two selves, both the two sides of her personality and the two voices in which she wrote, more explicitly and succinctly stated than in these lines from "Purdah." Plath's lioness, her violent, autonomous woman poet, is the small jeweled doll unloosed, freed from the social and emotional restrictions that stifled her life and her art and made it impossible for her to bring her true feelings and her words together.

The lines gain added poignance and significance, however, when we remember that the primary cause for the murder of Agamemnon was not the king's adultery or Clytemnestra's lust for power but the sacrificial murder of their passive, doll-like daughter, Iphigenia. So for Plath, it was the recognition of the death or suppression of her self as woman and poet, that was the principal cause of her rage. This was the self she had sacrificed and denied for love and social approval virtually since birth. And for this woman-poet to write angry, violent, murderous poetry becomes, therefore, not just a means to revenge, but a way to re-create a new self, a self possessing all the power the old self had abjured. In autonomy, rage becomes redemption, a purification of all the old lies within her. In "Fever

103°'' her rage truly becomes, as Margaret Uroff has written, *creative* violence.

> Does not my heat astound you. And my light.
> All by myself I am a huge camellia
> Glowing and coming and going, flush on flush.
>
> I think I am going up,
> I think I may rise——
> The beads of hot metal fly, and I, love, I
>
> Am a pure acetylene
> Virgin
> Attended by roses
> . . . . . .
> (My selves dissolving, old whore petticoats)——
> To Paradise.
>
> (CP, 232)

Having finally and indisputably proved the uselessness of her "old whore petticoats"—the zigs and zags, the lies and doubleness, from which Esther, Plath's first surrogate fictional self, had been unable to escape—Plath's new self, her "pure acetylene/Virgin," is ready to rise entirely on her own. As Lynda Bundtzen notes, the masturbatory movement here is basic to the poet's intent.[7] In a wild burst of autoeroticism, of love of self, she makes her escape. Like a "White/Godiva" she will unpeel "Dead hands, dead stringencies" ("Ariel" [CP, 239]). As in "The Bee Meeting," she will make "The upflight of the murderess into a heaven that loves her" (CP, 212). As in "Lady Lazarus" she will rise like the phoenix from her own ash. Winged and terrible, she is a "red/Scar in the sky," a red comet flying "Over the engine that killed her" ("Stings" [CP, 215]), an arrow flying suicidally "Into the red/Eye, the cauldron of morning" ("Ariel" [CP, 240]). She "eat[s] men like air" ("Lady Lazarus" [CP, 247]).

This is the mythic backbone, the story, as it were, behind the poetry and the poetic of Plath's last four months. Stripped down, as presented here, it appears to be a consistent, even logical response to the dilemma of self confronting Plath at the time. As the extraordinary number of female referents and honorifics ("murderess," "virgin," "Godiva," "queen," "lady," "lioness") confirm, this myth involved Plath in a new definition of self as autonomous or self-empowered woman. Indeed, the myth rests on this redefinition. The winged lioness of "Ariel," like the queen bee of

"Stings" and "The Bee Meeting" and the acetylene virgin of "Fever 103°,"
is woman and woman-poet empowered—a being who carries within her
the capacity for flight and who, therefore, is capable of shattering all
preconceptions of what women are, or are supposed to be, as day shatters
night. In a moment of ecstatic union with herself, she becomes one with the
forces, "the active, creative impulses," that she owns.[8]

> Stasis in darkness.
> Then the substanceless blue
> Pour of tor and distances.
>
> God's lioness,
> How one we grow,
> Pivot of heels and knees!
> . . . .
> And now I
> Foam to wheat, a glitter of seas.
> The child's cry
>
> Melts in the wall.
> And I
> Am the arrow,
>
> The dew that flies
> Suicidal, at one with the drive
> Into the red
>
> Eye, the cauldron of morning.
>   (CP, 239–40)

Like the queen bee, she has the strength, the capacity, to rise above the
engine of the social system and marriage that would destroy her, to separate
herself irrevocably from it. Like the arrow, she becomes part of the "cauldron of morning," reborn even as, stripping off her old self ("The child's
cry/Melts in the wall"), she dies.

The difficulty in seeing Plath's myth as a simple, straightforward
celebration of the acquistion of womanly power and autonomy lies, however, precisely here: in the real nature of the presumably triumphant
upflight. As Sandra Gilbert notes, the flight of the queen bee is "terrible
because it is not only an escape, it is a death trip,"[9] the arrow's journey is
suicidal, a return to the dead past that destroys the future as well. While

Plath presents the flight as a victory, its true end is not the destruction of "the engine that killed her." It is the destruction of the polluted and abandoned self. Again and again, in "Ariel," in "The Bee Meeting," in "Stings," in "Fever 103°," the speaker's drive to fly up, her quest for victorious separation and purification merges imperceptibly with her need to kill off the offending self. Lady Lazarus's lifework, her true vocation, is the "art" of dying, the annihilation of her own "trash" (CP, 245). Even an injured thumb, as in "Cut," becomes a figure for suicide, a "Kamikase man" (CP, 235). In "Stings" and "Fever 103°," death is the necessary prerequisite for the speaker's ascent to paradise. Death is the obsessive theme of these poems, death to purify and redeem. Death becomes her way in "Getting There":

> And I, stepping from this skin
> Of old bandages, boredoms, old faces
>
> Step to you from the black car of Lethe,
> Pure as a baby.
> (CP, 249)

For a woman betrayed and abandoned, polluted both by her past compromises and by her present murderous rage, there was, as she saw it, no other way to achieve the renewal or re-creation of the self she so desperately wished.

Plath's extraordinarily confused attitude toward the autonomy she presumably celebrates in her final poetry is obviously the direct product of the conflicted attitude toward separation which she exhibits throughout her life and work. However destructive she now understood attachment to be, to be separated from those whom she loved and with whom she fused, whether mother or husband, meant to Plath separation from the good side of herself as well—the side that adhered to rules and did what others wanted. While part of her now desired autonomy, autonomy was, therefore, dangerous to her. She associated it only with what was bad in herself. It represented a violation of all the rules by which she believed women were supposed to live, and it opened her up to the charge of being strange or weird. In "Stings," she worries:

> I am no drudge
> Though for years I have eaten dust
> And dried plates with my dense hair.

And seen my strangeness evaporate,
Blue dew from dangerous skin.
Will they hate me,
Those women who only scurry,
Whose news is the open cherry, the open clover?

(CP, 214)

For Plath to achieve autonomy meant that she had to destroy the dependent, attachment-prone, side of herself. Once that self was destroyed, however, all that remained was a woman too wicked to live. If the "Plaster saint" was dead to begin with ("Perfection is terrible," Plath declares in "The Munich Mannequins," "it cannot have children" [CP, 262]), "old yellow," as George Stade calls the body, would die the minute she achieved an independent life. One could not survive without the other.

That Plath was nevertheless ready to reveal her bald or wild side to the world appears evident from an anecdote Butscher records in *Method and Madness*. According to Clarissa Roche, he writes,

after Ted's departure, Sylvia would collect her husband's letters and manuscripts from his desk, along with pieces of his fingernails, and burn them in the back yard. She then danced around the fire chanting the proper incantations for casting an evil spell on him.[10]

Whatever else may be said about this bizarre story, and since Plath was dabbling in spiritualism at the time, it may well be true, this is hardly the all-American apple pie image that the poet cultivated so assiduously throughout her college years: "the product of a hundred years of middle-class propriety." But the image does suit the witch-woman voice of the final poems, the voice of a woman who had taken the bald, wild moon for her mother and no longer expected or sought tenderness for herself.

Plath's inability either to separate her wicked feelings from her sense of autonomous self or to integrate them properly as Dickinson had done accounts for some of the least palatable poetry in *Ariel* and *Winter Trees*. The image of the lioness in flight, the core myth, has a triumphant aura about it that tends to overshadow the nasty, "bitchy" tone of many of the poems. It is tempting to ignore or downplay the significance of poems such as "An Appearance," "Amnesiac," "Eavesdropper," "The Other," "Words heard, by accident, over the phone," and "The Tour" because they are so ugly and petty in their personal attack that they hardly qualify as art. Poems such as "Lesbos" and "Medusa," while possessing much greater substance, are at bottom not much better. But to ignore such poems is to ignore an essential part of Plath and what was happening to her at this time. Whatever else may be said about them, these poems contain all the ugliness, all the viciousness, all the unwomanly, competitive, aggressive attitudes her good girl, plaster saint, toy wife image was meant to conceal. Like many of her journal entries, these poems are exercises in cruelty. And they make it clear just how much Sylvia Plath did have to hide from the world. Like her moon-mother-muse, her blue poet's garments could and did let forth small bats and owls, vermin and predators. For her, therefore, the good girl image, like the plaster cast in "In Plaster," was not just a disguise. It was a matter of survival. Without true integration of her opposing selves, it was the only means her ego had to control the destructive impulses within herself—impulses that had never been given an appropriate channel. To abandon this image—as she was forced to abandon it in maturity without compensating support—was an admission of defeat and a relinquishment to death. As she wrote in "The Moon and the Yew Tree":

> I have fallen a long way. Clouds are flowering
> Blue and mystical over the face of the stars.
> Inside the church, the saints will be all blue,
> Floating on their delicate feet over the cold pews,
> Their hands and faces stiff with holiness.
> The moon sees nothing of this. She is bald and wild.
> And the message of the yew tree is blackness—blackness and silence.
>
> (CP, 173)

In her last poem, "Edge," written on February 5, six days before her suicide in London, Plath could only repeat what is essentially the same idea, only now in the terse meters of a classical resignation.

> The woman is perfected.
> Her dead
>
> Body wears the smile of accomplishment,
> The illusion of a Greek necessity
>
> Flows in the scrolls of her toga,
> Her bare
>
> Feet seem to be saying:
> We have come so far, it is over.
>
> Each dead child coiled, a white serpent,
> One at each little

Pitcher of milk, now empty.
She has folded

Them back into her body as petals
Of a rose close when the garden

Stiffens and odors bleed
From the sweet, deep throats of the night flower.

The moon has nothing to be sad about,
Staring from her hood of bone.

She is used to this sort of thing.
Her blacks crackle and drag.

(CP, 272–73)

The stiff, holy beauty of the flowering world cannot touch the daughter of the moon. For someone as alien, as empty of the milk of nurturance, warmth, female compassion, and love as herself, there was only blackness and silence and death.

.   .   .

Hughes's desertion freed Sylvia Plath to write, and write voluminously, as she had never been able to do before. It also freed her as never before to express all the evil, the wickedness, inside her self. Her rage, greed, vindictiveness, pettiness, cruelty, envy, and despair all came pouring forth, the sum and substance of her true deep voice, released by the "prison break," the "inner murder." Separated from Hughes, she was also separated from her mother and all that her mother and husband stood for: the standard of "normalcy" that she had never really fit but that she had so desperately struggled to achieve. And the glass caul splintered into a thousand pieces.

In the poem "Wintering," Plath tried to find a way out of her predicament that did not involve her in destruction and death, but instead was based on woman's capacity to draw sustenance or nurturance from herself.

Winter is for women—
The woman, still at her knitting,
At the cradle of Spanish walnut,
Her body a bulb in the cold and too dumb to think.

Will the hive survive, will the gladiolas
Succeed in banking their fires
To enter another year?
What will they taste of, the Christmas roses?
The bees are flying. They taste the spring.

(CP, 219)

But, as she said in "Contusion," the bruise was too great. The heart shut. The sea slid back. The poet went numb, her destiny fixed, not by the stars to which she refers in "Words," but by the inner forces that made her what she was: a woman who could not live without the love of a man and the approval of her mother; a poet whose identity and creativity rested ultimately on neither.

The tragedy of Sylvia Plath is the tragedy of a woman who was split apart by her need to be what she thought others wanted her to be. Perhaps because like her mother she was an overachiever, Plath tried to fulfill in herself every aspect of what her society meant by the term "normal woman." From high school into marriage, she pursued this phantasm, this image. In order to appear "Okay" she bleached her hair, modeled fashions, chased boys relentlessly, prostituted her talent, and hid, not just from the world, but from herself, the burgeoning "weirdness," the "strangeness" that made her the poet she was. Disguise for her became a mode of being, just as unmasking brought about her shame-filled death: "Her wings torn shawls, her long body/Rubbed of its plush—" (CP, 214).

Plath pursued her "Okay" image so assiduously because she believed that both her mother and her society demanded such conformity as the price of love. Not to be a woman as the image defined womanhood was not to be loved, just as not to be loved meant in effect that she was not really a woman. As a woman, her "need [was] to be loved." All her other accomplishments, whether intellectual, academic, occupational, or creative, paled before this one great stipulation. Her role was not to be the best, but to cater to the male, to encourage and sustain in him the greatness she had no right to desire or achieve for herself. My "life work," she wrote to her mother, is "to make [Ted] into the best man the world has seen" (LH, 252). Only thus could she ever hope to prove herself the best woman.

Plath's commitment to the values of "normal" womanhood, values that resulted in her conviction that as a woman she must prove her worth vicariously through her attachments to others, made it impossible for her to live with herself. These values alienated her from her own most distinctive qualities: her anger, her questioning spirit, her need for autonomy, and her drive for greatness. They made her dependent on men and marriage and encouraged her not only to despise women as inferior to men, but also to fear them as potential rivals for the one man in her life. They filled her with distrust of her own responses as a woman living in a world unfairly biased toward the male. They led her to sacrifice her own needs—for space, freedom, even simple human contact—again and again. They left her, in short, with no way to understand herself or how she, with her anger, her brilliance, and her ambition, fit into the scheme of things. Finally, they made it impossible for her to love herself, women, or ironically, even men. She learned these values—as most women learn them—from her mother. [11]

In encouraging in her daughter the values of attachment—giving to, helping out, being kind, not hurting—Mrs. Plath did no more than most mothers do. And like most mothers, she asked no more of her daughter than what life had, in effect, asked of her. Aurelia Plath also had enjoyed what she called a state of "psychic osmosis" with her mother (LH, 32). From her introduction to *Letters Home*, it is clear that she too had been expected to play the good girl and to sacrifice her own career for the well-being of others. And thus, she also learned to define her identity not in terms of what she accomplished but in terms of whether and how she loved.

If, as Alice Miller asserts, Aurelia Plath could not empathetically listen to her daughter Sylvia's real needs, surely we may conclude that it was because her own needs had never been listened to —not by her parents who insisted that she take business courses, not by her husband who found in her a convenient and docile tool. It would be futile to expect that such a woman with such a history could facilitate in her daughter the autonomy and sense of personal freedom she herself had never been encouraged or permitted to enjoy. Beyond the sympathy that comes from a recognition of likeness, true empathy requires a respect for difference as well, and who had respected difference in Aurelia Plath? Who had helped her understand that learning sometimes not to give, not to help out, and not to be kind, is also necessary not just for growth but for survival? "Mother," Sylvia Plath wrote to her brother, Warren, in 1953, "would actually Kill herself for us if we calmly accepted all she wanted to do for us. She is an abnormally altruistic person . . . we have to fight against her selflessness as we would fight against a deadly disease" (LH, 112). Plath was referring only to the toll self-sacrifice was taking on Aurelia when she wrote these lines, but the poet spoke more truly than she knew. Parental giving unchecked by a recognition of boundaries is in its own way a form of abuse. Without a father present to model otherness or to balance Aurelia Plath's excess of devotion, Sylvia Plath was lost.

That Aurelia Plath loved her daughter is, I think, without question. That her love appears ultimately to have been destructive to her can, I believe, only be seen as tragic. It is a tragedy Mrs. Plath is by no means alone in experiencing.

Caught in a culture that devalued and disempowered her as a woman and bound to a mother who was never able to achieve the sense of separation and autonomy needed to help herself, let alone her daughter, Sylvia Plath burnt herself out in rage. Insofar as we recognize the enormous talent present in her final poetry—a talent never fully realized—there is no way for us to calculate what was lost in the death of this divided and tormented woman who bought the brief flourishing of her genius with her life.

ADRIENNE RICH

*Feminism and
the Integration of Self*

. . . .
. . . .
. . . .

7. Dutiful Daughter

· · · · · · · · · · · ·
· · · · · · · · · · · · · ·
· · · · · · · · · · · ·

Who in his daydreams does not prefer to see himself as a
leader rather than a follower, an explorer rather than a
cultivator and a settler? Unfortunately, the possibility of
realizing such a dream is limited, not only by talent but
also by time. . . . He who today climbs the Matterhorn,
though he be the greatest climber who ever lived, must
tread in Whymper's footsteps.
                                        —W. H. Auden, 1951

A thinking woman sleeps with monsters.
                              —Adrienne Rich, 1960

In a 1977 interview with the lesbian-feminist jour-
nal *Conditions,* Adrienne Rich told Elly Bulkin that she began her literary
career as "a dutiful daughter, doing my craft right."[1] Being exceptionally
skilled at her craft, Rich was handsomely rewarded: nomination for the
Yale Younger Poets series by W. H. Auden while she was still an undergraduate at Radcliffe, a *New Yorker* contract, a second book published
within four years. Rich managed to garner early the kind of success that
Sylvia Plath, despite all her efforts, was never able after college to achieve
and Emily Dickinson at no time permitted herself to consider. "Certified by
Auden when [she] was twenty-one years old,"[2] she was stamped and
approved by the literary establishment and earned its most sought-after
awards.

Rich's extraordinary success in a close to all-male medium was neither accidental nor fleeting. Even as late as 1974, when her commitment to feminism had become essential to her writing, an establishment critic such as Robert Boyers could still name her as one of three women poets whom "everyone who reads poetry in our time will approve the efforts of."[3] (Boyers also includes Plath and Bishop, along with seventeen male poets, in his select group of irreproachable writers.) Her reputation for craft and what Plath called "philosophy," that is, intelligence, was solidly based, and even her recent forays into radical lesbian-feminist politics have not entirely dislodged it. For many people besides the particular audience to whom she now writes, Adrienne Rich remains America's foremost living woman poet, a poet whose overall accomplishment cannot be challenged, however much aspects of her current political theory may, for some, narrow her appeal.

The great irony of Rich's success lies in the fact that in thus achieving and maintaining her status as a major woman poet, Rich has, albeit without wanting to, fulfilled not just her own but her father's dream. Unlike Dickinson and Plath, Adrienne Rich learned her craft at her father's knee. Precocious and docile, in the root sense of that word, she responded to his tutelage by flourishing early and agonizing in the complexities of her debt to him ever after. As a young poet Rich was the epitome of the dutiful daughter, and her struggle with this knowledge is fundamental to understanding the poetry she has written both prior to embracing feminism and—perhaps even more important—since. It is also fundamental to understanding generally the often painful ambiguities that afflict the successful woman practitioner in a male-dominated field, whatever that field might happen to be.

Adrienne Rich was born on May 16, 1929, in Baltimore, Maryland, the eldest daughter in what she now describes as a white, middle-class, racist, and patriarchal home (OL, 280). Her father, Dr. Arnold Rich, was a renowned expert on tuberculosis and chair of the department of pathology at Johns Hopkins University, a singular achievement for a Jew of his period. To a far greater extent than Sylvia Plath, whose father appears, on the whole, to have interacted very little with his family, Rich was raised in a home in which the father was blatantly, even morbidly, dominant. Brilliant, ambitious, and determined to "pass" in anti-Semitic postwar Baltimore, Arnold Rich treated his family with anything but benign neglect. The women who depended on him, a Christian wife and two Christian daughters, were his appendages and he expected them, at least so his eldest daughter claims, to conform in all things to his expectations and needs.

We — my sister, mother and I — were constantly urged to speak quietly in public, to dress without ostentation, to repress all vividness or spontaneity, to assimilate with a world which might see us as too flamboyant. . . . [W]hen Arnold took us out to a restaurant, or on a trip, the Rich women were always tuned down to some WASP level my father believed . . . would protect us all.   (NJG, 75)

In a way unlike that found in most American families, in the Rich household, Arnold Rich was, it seems, a true man of the house, molding and shaping every aspect of these women's lives. Neither mother nor daughters had at the time the strength to hold out against him or perhaps, despite Rich's later disclaimers, the will or desire.

In *Of Woman Born* Rich is extremely protective of her mother's situation. "Born in a southern town," she writes proudly of Helen Rich's early accomplishments, "mothered by a strong, frustrated woman, she had won a scholarship to study with the director at the Peabody Conservatory in Baltimore, and by teaching at girls' schools had earned her way to further study in New York, Paris, and Vienna." But the "unusual talent, determination, and independence" (OWB, 221) that Rich justifiably sees in this part of her mother's story (this was, after all, the American South in the twenties) seems to have had little appreciable effect on Helen Rich's behavior once married. Whether totally in connection to her husband's demands, as her daughter believes, or whether partly as a result of her own needs as well, she subordinated herself entirely to him, giving up her career as pianist and composer and living the life he wanted. For Rich the experience of her mother's capitulation and slow effacement at her father's hand remains demonstrably one of her most painful and bitter memories. In *Of Woman Born* she writes:

My father . . . assumed that she would give her life over to the enhancement of his. She would manage his household with the formality and grace becoming to a medical professor's wife, though on a limited budget; she would "keep up" her music, though there was no question of letting her composing and practice conflict with her duties as a wife and mother. She was supposed to bear him two children, a boy and a girl. She had to keep her household books to the last penny. . . . [S]he marketed by streetcar, and later, when they could afford a car, she drove my father to and from his laboratory or lectures, often awaiting him for hours. She raised two children, and taught us all our lessons, including music. (Neither of us was sent to school until the fourth grade.) I am sure that she was made to feel responsible for all our imperfections. (OWB, 221–22)

Of all the capitulations Helen Rich made, however, none appears to have had more serious or complicated consequences for her eldest daughter's psychological and intellectual development than her willingness to educate her husband's children at home. Like Bronson Alcott, Rich writes, her father wanted his children, even though both were, disappointingly enough, girls, raised "according to his unique moral and intellectual plan" to prove "to the world the values of enlightened, unorthodox, child-rearing" (OL, 222). But, again like Alcott, he left to his wife the actual day-to-day implementation of his child-rearing theories. For Rich, caught in a situation few children would suffer gladly, the consequences were devastating. "For years," she writes, "I felt my mother had chosen my father over me, had sacrificed me to his needs and theories" (OL, 222). And this feeling, which under the circumstances appears to have been justified, led, Rich claims, to "deep reservoirs of anger" toward her mother that even the compassion taught by feminism has not entirely dissolved:

> the anger of a four-year-old locked in the closet (my father's orders, but my mother carried them out) for childish misbehavior; the anger of a six-year-old kept too long at piano practice (again at his insistence, but it was she who gave the lessons) till I developed a series of facial tics . . . the anger of a daughter, pregnant, wanting my mother desperately and feeling she has gone over to the enemy. (OWB, 224)

The significance of Rich's early anger at her mother cannot be overestimated. In carrying out her husband's wishes so completely, Helen Rich, like Aurelia Plath, was presumably fulfilling what she believed to be the role of a good wife and possibly even a loving mother. But unlike Sylvia Plath, Adrienne Rich chose not to be a good daughter in return. Acutely aware of how much she felt her mother had failed her, she seems to have identified with her father instead, "'acting-out,'" as she writes in *Of Woman Born*, "the masculine roles" in the "childish . . . games" she and her sister played (OWB, 193) and generally endeavoring to become the favored son he wished her to be. "He and I," Rich writes in a prose section from *Sources* of her relationship with this loved and hated man, "always had a kind of rhetoric going with each other, a battle between us, it didn't matter if one of us was alive or dead" (S, 32). There is no evidence anywhere in Rich's work that she carried on a similar rhetoric or on-going attempt at persuasion with her mother. Nor given the manner in which she was reared, would such a rhetoric with her mother have made sense. Without Arnold Rich, Helen Rich, at least during her husband's lifetime, appears to have made no decisions on her own. She had, as a result, no influence on Rich's upbringing except in a negative sense. Between mother and child a gulf developed that, as Rich's own writing testifies, was filled only by the poet's rage.

For Rich, this situation, so fraught with irony, has been crucial. Although her mother taught her daily lessons, her father was responsible for both the worst and the best that her childhood had to offer. From him she learned both the pain of enforced will: her own helplessness as a child and a woman, and the high-minded idealism and love of learning that would one day set her free. While Rich has over the past fifteen years become an ardent and eloquent spokeswoman for motherhood and for the importance of the mother-daughter relationship, her understanding of women's profound need for this relationship is rooted in its very absence from her life (OL, 280).[4] From the time he taught her how to read around her fourth year, Adrienne Rich became her father's, not her mother's child. And in her struggle with the patriarchy and her rejection of the masculinist literary tradition, her lifelong quarrel with this strange, driven, and unhappy man is writ large.

• • •

Only recently in two pieces specifically dealing with her Jewish heritage, the essay "Split at the Root," in *Nice Jewish Girls: A Lesbian Anthology,* published in 1982, and the multisectioned poem *Sources,* written about the same time, has Rich finally started to deal openly and frankly with the double debt of love and hate she owes her father. This confrontation and admission have not come easily to her. And in the frequent awkwardness and flatness of their language, to a degree unusual for Adrienne Rich, both works show the signs of her discomfort as she explores what she now calls the sources of her strength:

> *a chosen people*
> of shopkeepers
> clinging by strategy to a way of life
> that had its own uses for them
>
> proud of their length of sojourn in America
> deploring the late-comers   the peasants from Russia

I saw my father building
his rootless ideology

his private castle in air

in that most dangerous place, the family home
we were the chosen people

In the beginning we grasp whatever we can
                              (S, 14)

In *Sources* Rich does not expand on what she means by her father's "rootless ideology" but in the essay that preceded the poem and appears to have inspired it, she spells out the details of this ideology and with them, the effect they had upon her as a growing child and nascent poet.

What Arnold did, I think, was call his Jewish pride something else: achievement, aspiration, genius, idealism. Whatever was unacceptable got left back under the rubric of Jewishness, or the "wrong kind" of Jews: uneducated, aggressive, loud. The message I got was that we were really superior: nobody else's father had collected so many books, had travelled so far, knew so many languages. . . . My father was an amateur musician, read poetry, adored encyclopaedic knowledge. He prowled and pounced over my school papers, insisting I use "grown-up" sources; he criticized my poems for faulty technique and gave me books on rhyme and metre and form. His investment in my intellect and talent was egotistical, tyrannical, opinionated and terribly wearing. He taught me nevertheless to believe in hard work, to mistrust easy inspiration, to write and rewrite; to feel that I *was* a person of the book, even though a woman; to take ideas seriously. *He made me feel, at a very young age, the power of language, and that I could share in it* [Italics added].   (NJG, 76–77)

No matter how one chooses to view Arnold Rich, from this passage one thing is clear. As a father he not only educated his eldest daughter, he filled her with his own sense of pride, power, and ambition. As a result of the interest he took in her, Adrienne Rich, despite her sex, became "a person of the book," a woman for whom language and learning were as much a part of life as the air she breathed. Egotistical, tyrannical, and opinionated he may have been, but for her development as a poet, he was also crucial.

A physically small man of extraordinary intellect, Arnold Rich was also, particularly for a medical doctor, a man of unusual cultural breadth.

According to his obituary in the *New York Times*, Rich was a musician and composer as well as a poet and pathologist.[5] His father, Samuel Rich, an immigrant from Austria-Hungary, owned a shoe store in Birmingham, Alabama. His mother, Hattie Rice, was of Sephardic background and came from Vicksburg, Mississippi. Like many ambitious parents of their generation, they passed on to their son their own desire to partake of America's blessings, sending him to military school in Tennessee, "a place," Rich writes, "for training white Southern Christian gentlemen" (NJG, 68), and later to the University of Virginia. If any financial sacrifices were involved in these decisions, their son repaid them tenfold by becoming the esteemed "exception" and entering the professional class. "Never, in describing these experiences," Rich adds, "did he ever speak of having suffered—from loneliness, cultural alienation, or outsiderhood. I never heard him use the word, 'anti-Semitism'" (NJG, 68).

Unable truly to feel accepted by those among whom he had achieved professional success, Arnold Rich, according to his daughter's account, turned to "that most dangerous place, the family home" for psychological satisfaction and the exercise of personal power. Having married a gentile wife and sired two daughters, whom he eventually sent to Christian schools and had confirmed in the Episcopal church, it was with these women that he sought "emotional connectedness" and among whom he built his "private defense system" (NJG, 77), his "castle in the air." But perhaps because he was a man, trained to live for the mind, Arnold Rich had only one way to relate to the women who surrounded him, namely intellectually. Jewish and Southern, his attitudes toward the body, particularly the female body, were conflicted at best. "My father talked a great deal of beauty and the need for perfection," Rich writes in *Of Woman Born*. "He felt the female body to be impure; he did not like its natural smells. His incorporeality was a way of disengaging himself from that lower realm where women sweated, excreted, grew bloody every month, became pregnant" (OWB, 220).

As with many men of similar attitude, Arnold Rich's discomfort with femaleness manifested itself toward his eldest daughter in a tendency to treat her as a genderless son, a child not of the body but of the mind.

> . . . I saw myself,
> the eldest daughter raised as a son, taught to study but not to pray,
> taught to hold reading and writing sacred: the eldest daughter in a house
> with no son. (S, 15)

He enveloped her in an education the net effect of which seems to have been to obliterate from her mind, at least for a while, the fact of her gender. To all intents and purposes, Adrienne Rich throughout her childhood was her father's favorite son, with all that this might imply in a Jewish family. She became the woman he wanted her to be: intellectually oriented, filled with the sense of her own prowess, imbued with a thorough knowledge and love of the language she would, as she declares in *Sources,* someday "use . . . against him" (S, 15). As Rich confesses in a little-known interview in *Island,* a small poetry magazine of the sixties, it was her doctor father, not her teacher mother, who, for whatever selfish and narcissistic reasons, tended and nurtured the budding poet in her and who, therefore, in a profound sense is responsible for the writer she is today.

> I started writing verses the way I suppose a lot of literary children do. My father was tremendously interested in literature. He taught me to write by copying out Blake and Keats every day. And then, when I was still writing children's verses, he used to criticize me and try to get me into more regular meters and rhymes. . . . So I was very much encouraged as a child . . . and when people told me later, when I was writing in college, that I had all this technical competence, I took it for granted because this was something I learned the way people learn arithmetic or to play scales.[6]

My point is not to defend Arnold Rich and his child-rearing practices. However important they were for Rich's development, the methods he employed were in other respects every bit as cruel as she claims them to be. For all his love of Keats and Tennyson, Rossetti and Swinburne, he imposed this love in a selfish manner, ignoring not only the fact of his daughter's gender but any needs she might have had as a young woman growing up in the middle of the twentieth century. And it is no wonder that the oppressive weight of his encouragement—as she suggests in one of her rare, early confessional lyrics, "Juvenilia"—led her prepubescent mind to "unspeakable fairy tales" of blood.

> Your Ibsen volumes, violet-spined,
> each flaking its gold arabesque!
> Again I sit, under duress, hands washed,
> at your inkstained oaken desk,
> by the goose-neck lamp in the tropic of your books,
> stabbing the blotting-pad, doodling loop upon loop,
> peering one-eyed in the dusty reflecting mirror

of your student microscope,
craning my neck to spell above me

A DOLL'S HOUSE   LITTLE EYOLF
    WHEN WE DEAD AWAKEN

Unspeakable fairy tales ebb like blood through my head
as I dip the pen and for aunts, for admiring friends,
for you above all to read,
copy my praised and sedulous lines.

Behind the two of us, thirsty spines
quiver in semi-shadow, huge leaves uncurl and thicken.

(SDL, 32)

But we should not allow the murderous fantasies that crowd the child's mind as she stabs the blotting pad, draws (hangman's?) loops, and squints one-eyed into her father's microscope (as into the sight of a gun?), to obscure what is also going on in this remarkable little exercise in Plathian gothic. For the father who has forced the child to sit at his ink-stained desk and copy her "sedulous lines" is also the father who placed the pen in her hand. And the leaves of the volumes that line his shelves, that seem to uncurl and threaten her, threaten him far more. For, as we now know, it was precisely from authors such as Ibsen that Rich would one day gather the strength to rebel. Not only did they inspire her to fight for a "right to an emotional life and selfhood beyond [her father's] needs and theories" (OWB, 222), but they provided her with the weapons she needed to destroy the view of life and literature on which his world of books, so magisterial, so male, was based. In short, her father gave her the tools not just to free herself, but to murder him, in the form of the patriarchy, as well.

A full appreciation of Arnold Rich's "Victorian paternalism, his seductive charm and controlling cruelty" (OWB, 223) is, therefore, necessary to any understanding of the particular direction Adrienne Rich's life and art have taken. Just as Dickinson's development revolved around her quarrel with her society, and Sylvia Plath's revolved around her quarrel with her mother, so Adrienne Rich's development can be understood only when the importance of the "rhetoric" she carried on with her father has been fully grasped. And the true nature of this rhetoric can only be grasped when the very great debt she owed him has first been taken into account. If this debt is not acknowledged, then much of the significance and all of the poignancy of her struggle to find a self and a language outside her father's needs and theories will be lost. In her love of literature, her respect for the power of language, her dedication to work and devotion to the life of the mind, her high-minded, often opinionated, idealism,[7] Adrienne Rich remains, however changed, her father's daughter to this day.

In the poem "Power" in *The Dream of a Common Language,* Rich deals in a curiously inverted way with the irony of her own situation while presumably meditating on the fate of Madame Curie, the discoverer of radium.

> Today I was reading about Madame Curie:
> she must have known she suffered   from radiation sickness
> her body bombarded for years   by the element
> she had purified
> It seems she denied to the end
> the source of the cataracts on her eyes
> the cracked and suppurating skin   of her finger-ends
> till she could no longer hold   a test-tube or a pencil
>
> She died   a famous woman   denying
> her wounds
> denying
> her wounds   came   from the same source as her power
> (DCL, 3)

Read within the context of the volume in which it appears, "Power" is an unambiguous poem. It deals with the fate of the token woman, that is, the woman who through luck or diligence has gained access to male power in our society and who is corrupted and destroyed by it. As a depiction of the deficit side of tokenism, the poem is disturbing but hard to quarrel with. That women in positions of power suffer from wielding that power is too well established to require supporting evidence here. From Ken Kesey's Big Nurse to Britain's Margaret Thatcher, such women are all around us. This is in any case the price traditionally exacted in Western society by power itself, as Rich is at some pains to show in *The Dream of a Common Language* as a whole.[8]

But when "Power" is read within the context of the poet's own life, the poem presents a very different, far less scrutable, face. For if, as Rich claims, the token woman's wounds come from the same source as her power, then, as Rich has finally admitted in the poem ironically entitled *Sources,* the reverse in her case also holds true. Her power comes from the same source as her wounds: her father's all too passionate, all too tyrannical commitment to the life of the mind. And most ironically, perhaps, like the power that Marie Curie sought to purify, the power that Rich wields, the so-called patriarchal power of language, the male logos, also has the capacity to heal as well as to destroy its possessors. It cannot simply be abjured.

For Rich as, presumably, for Curie, the acceptance of these ambiguities has not been an easy matter. But the consequences that flow from them, particularly as they affect Adrienne Rich's attitude toward language and her definition of her role as artist, have had a primary influence in shaping her career. Indeed, the entire course of her career may be viewed as an outgrowth of the poet's struggle to come to grips with her father's power and make it finally, indisputably, her own.

> After your death I met you again as the face of
> patriarchy, could name at last precisely the principle
> you embodied, there was an ideology at last which let
> me dispose of you, identify the suffering you caused,
> hate you righteously as part of a system, the kingdom
> of the fathers. I saw the power and arrogance of the
> male as your true watermark; I did not see beneath it
> the suffering of the Jew, the alien stamp you bore,
> because you had deliberately arranged that it should
> be invisible to me. It is only now, under a powerful,
> womanly lens, that I can decipher your suffering and
> deny no part of my own.   (S, 15)

Feminism, the "powerful womanly lens," has provided Rich with a new way to understand her power as a woman and a poet. In doing so, it has allowed her to reconcile with her father at last, to see his suffering, while denying no part of her own, and thus to begin true separation, not just rebellion, from him. It has, however, taken Adrienne Rich over fifty years to reach the point where this reconciliation may become possible. How she arrived here is in many ways the most important story her poetry has to tell. For in Rich's attempt to bring together the conflicting elements of her past—her father's power and her woman self—is mirrored the struggle for individuation and integration that is the primary task confronting thinking women in America today. Unlike both Dickinson and Plath, Adrienne Rich has not allowed the conflict between her gender and her creative power to split her life irrevocably apart. Nor has she yielded one or the other in order to have peace within herself. As a result, her struggle with these issues offers a model of possible healing not just to women poets, but to any woman who seeks to resolve the conflict between womanhood and power, attachment and creativity, and to make of her complicated being one whole.

*   *   *

In the poem "After Dark" in *Necessities of Life* (as by implication in "Juvenilia"), Rich states that her feelings toward her father were murderous during childhood; she "wanted" his death (NL, 29). But despite this rage, Rich entered adolescence to all intents and purposes her father's son. Split, she writes in *Of Woman Born,* from any real recognition of her gender, her physical being as a woman, her "mind lived on one plane, [her] body on another." She could know "exhilaration in language, in music, in ideas, in landscape, in talk, in painting" but "physical pleasure, even in sex, was problematic" to her, and her sense of her own womanhood appears to have been inchoate at best (OWB, 175).

Given her devotion to the life of the mind, Rich was able to pursue her intellectual development with apparently less internal conflict than most girls experience at that age. Like other adolescent girls, she had "spent hours trying to apply lipstick more adroitly, straightening the wandering seams of stockings, talking about 'boys,'" but "writing poetry, and [her] fantasies of travel and self-sufficiency, seemed more real" to her (OWB, 25). Whatever doubts she had about her authenticity as a woman, they were not sufficiently painful during this period to prevent her—as they had prevented Plath and even, to some extent, Dickinson—from single-mindedly devoting herself to the advancement of her career. In 1951 after six years of writing poetry, by her own account, "seriously" (OWB, 25), Rich's first book was published as part of the Yale Younger Poets series. The same year she graduated Radcliffe College Phi Beta Kappa. However poorly she got along with him, many of her father's hopes and expectations for her had clearly been fulfilled.

By the standards she has since set for herself, Adrienne Rich's early poetry makes curious reading. According to statements that she makes in the *Island* interview and elsewhere, she had already begun to break away from her father's largely Victorian taste in literature once exposed to modernists in college. But when read against the poetry she has since written, Rich's early efforts seem safe and old-fashioned in the extreme. Indeed, it appears to have been these very qualities of conservatism and clinging to tradition which made her verse so attractive to Auden in the first place. In the introduction to *A Change of World,* Rich's prize-winning volume, the master states his belief that this was the kind of poetry that young poets, living, he claimed, in the "middle," not at the beginning, of a historical epoch ought to write. Only "a radical change in human sensibility," Auden claims, could justify "significant novelty in artistic style" (CW, 8):

> So long as the way in which we regard the world and feel about our existence remains in all essentials the same as that of our predecessors [for Auden, the poets who lived through the great revolutionary crises that marked the end of the last century] we must follow in their tradition; it would be just as dishonest for us to pretend that their style is inadequate to our needs as it would have been for them to be content with the style of the Victorians. (CW, 9)

To Auden, Adrienne Rich, careful, conservative, was the epitome of the well-bred young poet: content to "tread in Whymper's footsteps," disclaiming "any extraordinary vision," ensuring by her emphasis on craft "that whatever she writes shall, at least, not be shoddily made" (CW, 9–10). The poems in her book, he concludes, as if defending by means of analogy his selection of this very young woman poet,

> are neatly and modestly dressed, speak quietly but do not mumble, respect their elders but are not cowed by them, and do not tell fibs: that, for a first volume, is a good deal. (CW, 11)

While Auden's comments may strike us today as sexist, condescending, and even, in light of Rich's development over the past decade and a half, downright wrong, they all too aptly describe the kind of poetry she wrote early in her career—not just *A Change of World* but her second volume, *The Diamond Cutters,* as well. The poems in these two volumes are, consequently, worth pausing over, for they not only help us understand the course of Rich's development in its continuities and discontinuities, but equally important they epitomize the kind of poetry and poetic values she has since specifically chosen to repudiate. In the very perfection of their craftsmanship and control, the poems in these two volumes exemplify the standards that distinguish the poetry of the great tradition (the line that extends from Homer to Frost and is with very few exceptions both white and male) from the kind of poetry that others (women, ethnic minorities, amateurs) write. And in their narrowness and lack of personal authenticity, these poems make clear why Rich, as a woman poet now committed to using her whole self in her poetry, can no longer write such verse, however universal its supporters claim it to be.[9]

Along with craft, the qualities that most obviously characterize Adrienne Rich's early poetry are its derivativeness (the plethora of well-known male voices who echo through the poet's song) and its objectivity, or, put another way, its "fibs." In a beginning poet the derivativeness is to be expected. One learns from one's elders and though it is to be regretted that Rich chose to model herself in her early poetry on the likes of MacNeice, Ransom, Spender, and Frost, rather than on Dickinson, Lowell, and H. D., it is hardly surprising. These were the poets considered by her largely male instructors to be preeminent in their field.[10] As an ambitious young poet, she would naturally have gravitated to them, adopting their attitudes as well as aspects of their style. Where, after all, could imitating Emily Dickinson get you, except into trouble?

But Rich's commitment to objectivity in her early poetry is a more complex and difficult matter to assess. Given the aesthetic criteria of the period, to maintain distance was not simply an exercise in judgment and control. It also involved her, as she has since admitted, in active efforts at suppression and disguise. The credentials for this kind of suppression could not, of course, have been more impressive. "In a young poet, as T.S. Eliot has observed," Auden writes approvingly in his introduction to *A Change of World*, "the most promising sign is craftsmanship for it is evidence of a capacity for *detachment from the self and its emotions* without which no art is possible" (CW, 10; italics added). To young poets working in the early fifties, the height of the so-called new criticism, Eliot's dictum had become gospel: poetry was a made object. It bore at best an indirect relation to the author's emotions and self, his or her life. To truly qualify as a poet, one had to subordinate the particular in one's self to the universal in human experience. For a young woman such as Adrienne Rich, however, adherence to this principle could not help but result in some rather peculiar and stilted verse. In the poem "Afterward" from *A Change of World*, she writes, for example:

> Now that your hopes are shamed, you stand
> At last believing and resigned,
> And none of us who touch your hand
> Know how to give you back in kind
> The words you flung when hopes were proud:
> *Being born to happiness*

Above the asking of the crowd,
You would not take a finger less.
We who know limits now give room
To one who grows to fit his doom.
                    (CW, 43)

By any standard I am prepared to use, "Afterward" is not a good poem. It rhymes. It scans. It is literate. It is completely in control. It is in no sense amateur or unprofessional verse. But it might as well have been spoken by a Greek chorus. Attempting to get away from the false impression of universality in this poem, Rich reprints it in *Poems Selected and New,* substituting "her" for "his" in the final line; but the substitution does no good. The problem with "Afterward" lies not simply with Rich's use of the generic *he* in one line. Throughout the poem the voice of the poet, so aware of limits, is correspondingly without specific gender, wholeness, or identity. If, as one disgruntled male critic angrily notes, some of Rich's post-sixties poetry "could have been written by a small committee composed of Germaine Greer, Susan Brownmiller and Ti-Grace Atkinson,"[1] poems like "Afterward" could just as easily have been written by a committee of earnest professors. An abstract, chiseled variation on an ancient and overworked theme, the death of hope, neither the speaker nor her protagonist has any specificity or existential reality in the poem. "Afterward" is pure craft and little more.

While "Afterward" is an extreme example, it is typical of Rich's early work. Worldly wise and a little weary, careful, alienated, and occasionally ever so slightly ironic, but above all, distant and impersonal, the poet wanders through her first two volumes, mouthing the so-called wisdom of a safer if not saner past. Thus we are told in *A Change of World* that change can be foretold but not averted ("Storm Warnings"), that we live in a period of religious doubt ("Air without Incense"), and that nature is resistant to human meanings ("The Return of the Evening Grosbeaks"). Similarly, in *The Diamond Cutters* we learn that people are isolated from each other ("The Roadway"), that we all must die ("I Heard a Hermit Speak"), and that love is threatened daily by "those who shall be false by night" ("The Platform"). None of these observations, or the many like them, informs us about how the author herself actually feels about life, love, death, religion, or any of her other major themes. In this poetry such information would in fact be out of place, for this is not poetry written out of life. It is poetry written out of literature, the poetry of universal human experience, or, put more accurately perhaps, the poetry of the generic *he.*

In the essay "When We Dead Awaken: Writing as Re-Vision," Rich tries to rationalize the formalism of her early poetry by saying that it was "part of the strategy—like asbestos gloves, it allowed me to handle materials I couldn't pick up bare-handed" (OL, 40–41). And this explanation does seem to fit without difficulty certain of her early poems, in particular, poems such as "Living in Sin," "Autumn Equinox" (which presents an interesting slant on Rich's relationship with her father), and the brilliant "Aunt Jennifer's Tigers." Unlike "Afterward" and the other poems cited above, these poems do deal specifically with women's experience and, for all their control, they do have palpable substance that the formalism distances but does not destroy. "Aunt Jennifer's Tigers," especially, is a poem that can hold its own even today with Rich's finest work, an incisive, exquisitely accomplished commentary on the complicated and ambiguous relationship that obtains between the traditional woman artist and her power.

Aunt Jennifer's tigers prance across a screen,
Bright topaz denizens of a world of green.
They do not fear the men beneath the tree;
They pace in sleek chivalric certainty.

Aunt Jennifer's fingers fluttering through her wool
Find even the ivory needle hard to pull.
The massive weight of Uncle's wedding band
Sits heavily upon Aunt Jennifer's hand.

When Aunt is dead, her terrified hands will lie
Still ringed with ordeals she was mastered by.
The tigers in the panel that she made
Will go on prancing, proud and unafraid.

(CW, 19)

But the majority of Rich's early poems are not distinguished as this poem is by the control and distancing of real feeling. They are distinguished by feeling's absence. The universality for which Rich strove is not a state of being, but a state of nonbeing. The experiences described in these poems, even when they are fairly intimate in nature, such as a child's disillusionment with its parents in "The Middle-Aged" and a tourist's sense of perennial isolation in "The Tourist and the Town," are finally as genderless, as lacking in particular identity and character as the voice the poet employs.

Created by an author who presents her speaker as neither distinctively male nor distinctively female, who is without background or character, who exhibits neither lusts nor appetites, needs nor fears, and who writes above all in total unawareness of the physical self, the poems in Rich's first two volumes are the undiluted products of the tradition from which they derive. They were written by a woman who had "grown to fit" her father's mind, a woman without a body and without the psychological foibles that presumably beset her sex. No wonder Rich's early critics approved. By writing objectively, Rich had shown herself in this virtually all-male medium (whether Tillie Olsen's one out of twelve or Robert Boyers's somewhat more generous three out of twenty),[12] the most dutiful of dutiful daughters, the daughter who used her power to suppress all traces of strength within her womanself, the daughter who wrote as if she were a son.

• • •

In 1953, at the pinnacle of her early success, Rich went against her parents', or, rather, her father's wishes (NJG, 72–76) and married Alfred Haskell Conrad (né Cohen), a divorced professor of economics at Harvard University. Like his reluctant father-in-law, Conrad was a high-minded Jewish intellectual who exhibited substantial ambivalence concerning his ethnic and religious identity. From Arnold Rich's point of view, Conrad's Ashkenazi family also came from the wrong part of Europe and the "wrong part of history" (S, 25). The ill-sorted couple (Conrad was twenty-nine, came from Brooklyn, and had been reared in an observant family, Rich was twenty-three, came from the South, and was a Christian), settled in Cambridge and within a year the poet was pregnant with her first child, a son, David Conrad, born in 1955. That same year saw the publication of her second book, *The Diamond Cutters*. But Rich was not to publish again for eight years. Instead she gave birth in quick succession to two more children, Paul Conrad, born in 1957, and Jacob Conrad, born in 1959. Immediately following the birth of Jacob, a child that, Rich claims in *Of Woman Born* (OWB, 28), she did not originally intend to have, Rich had her tubes tied; but by then the dice were already cast. Poet though she might be, she also had become the mother of three, two of them in diapers.

From Rich's account of these years in *Of Woman Born*, it is clear that she was totally unprepared emotionally and intellectually for the role of mother which she had so impulsively taken upon herself: "A life I didn't choose," she wrote in "The Roofwalker" in 1961, "chose me" (SDL, 63). Not only had she been inadequately mothered by her own mother (Rich believes that "the most unconditional, tender, and . . . intelligent love" she received as a child came from a Black woman who nursed her until she was four years old [OL, 280]); but her own identity as a woman, let alone a mother, was hardly fixed in 1953. Indeed, there is very little evidence to suggest that Rich actually thought of herself as a woman prior to her marriage and the birth of her first child. Certainly, as she told David Kalstone in 1972, she had no desire at that time to be considered a woman poet. [13] Nor did she wish to be identified primarily in terms of her ability to fulfill a conventional woman's role. Why then did Rich marry?

If we are to believe the few statements she makes on the subject in *Of Woman Born,* she married, simply enough, out of guilt (OWB, 25). [14] Like Dickinson and Plath, although it seems far less intensely, Rich had suffered through adolescence the typical anxieties that beset a nascent "thinking woman" (SDL, 22). "From the age of thirteen or fourteen," she writes, "I had felt I was only acting the part of a feminine creature." And "this sense of acting a part created a curious sense of guilt" even though the poet knew "it was a part demanded for survival" (OWB, 25). With marriage and even more with her first pregnancy, this sense of guilt disappeared, albeit temporarily. "As soon as I was visibly and clearly pregnant," Rich declares,

> I felt, for the first time in my adolescent and adult life, not-guilty. The atmosphere of approval in which I was bathed — even by strangers on the street, it seemed — was like an aura I carried with me, in which doubts, fears, misgivings, met with absolute denial. *This is what women have always done.*   (OWB, 26)

Older than Plath by only a few years, Rich also had been subjected to the influence of "the family-centered, consumer-oriented, Freudian-American world of the 1950's" (OWB, 25). And like the younger poet she too had come to believe that marriage and motherhood were necessary not just for the fulfillment but the confirmation of her womanhood. To be "like other women," she explains in *Of Woman Born,* she felt she had to do *"what women have always done,"* and conversely — however illogical it may seem to us now — if she did not do what women have always done, she was not really a woman. She was only acting a part.

But as a ploy to deflect guilt, Rich quickly discovered that motherhood had a deadly capacity to boomerang. The reality of the experience of motherhood, a reality few middle-class women in our culture have any grasp of prior to the birth of their first child, sank in, displacing the myths that Rich, like so many before her, had believed about it. Becoming a mother, she found, might be a natural experience, but mothering was not, and Adrienne Rich, ambitious, aggressive, demanding, was not by nature especially well suited for it or, she believed, good at it.

Like Plath's post-*Mademoiselle* discovery of the gulf between her womanhood and her aspirations, Rich's realization that she was not by nature the all-patient, all-submissive, all-nurturant woman she believed she had to be in order to rear her children properly came as a terrible shock and a frightening revelation. In *Of Woman Born* she reproduces journal entries that testify again and again to the torment she suffered not only at her inability to meet her children's demands but, even worse in her eyes, her intense resentment of them. In November 1960 she wrote:

> Their voices wear away at my nerves, their constant needs, above all their need for simplicity and patience, fill me with despair at my own failures, despair too at my fate, which is to serve a function for which I was not fitted. (OWB, 21)

And six years later she berated herself in even more extravagant terms.

> Perhaps one is a monster—an anti-woman—something driven and without recourse to the normal and appealing consolations of love, motherhood, joy in others. (OWB, 22)

Totally ignorant of how common, even mundane, her "selfish" reactions essentially were, she began with the heightened imagination of a poet to see herself as a monster, a Medea, a Kali (OWB, 32), unnaturally turning on those who were by nature and by right totally dependent on her and whom, in other ways, she very much loved. In the first section of "Night-Pieces: For a Child," she explored these feelings in a poem that could easily serve as a companion piece to Plath's "Morning Song," so similar are the situations and, in some ways, the reactions of the mothers involved.

> You sleeping I bend to cover.
> Your eyelids work. I see
> your dream, cloudy as a negative,
> swimming underneath.
> You blurt a cry. Your eyes
> spring open, still filmed in dream.
> Wider, they fix me—
> —death's head, sphinx, medusa?

You scream.
Tears lick my cheeks, my knees
droop at your fear.
Mother I no more am,
but woman, and nightmare.

          (NL, 25)

"Haunted," Rich writes, "by the stereotype of the mother whose love is 'unconditional' . . . and by the visual and literary images of motherhood as a single-minded identity" (OWB, 23), she was for an extended period of time torn apart and stymied by her own ambivalence—loving her children yet unable to love herself as their mother, hating them because they made her feel so miserable about herself. Her determination "to prove that as a woman poet [she] could also have what was then defined as a 'full' woman's life" (OL, 42) had backfired. Guilt overwhelmed her once again.

The fact is that in opting for womanhood as conventionally defined, Rich, like Plath, had discovered too late that motherhood and poetry writing were not necessarily compatible occupations. Being "a female human trying to fulfill traditional female functions in a traditional way," she found, was "in direct conflict with the subversive function of the imagination," which required time to play, to experiment, in order to create (OL, 43). With three children at her heels, time was one item she did not have. And without it, she began to think she would go mad. Indeed, if we take literally one of her more recent, apparently confessional lyrics, "Mother-in-Law" (1980), she began to envy the freedom of those who were insane.

I've been trying to tell you, mother-in-law
that I think I'm breaking in two
and half of me doesn't even want to love
I can polish this table to satin because I don't care
I am trying to tell you, I envy
the people in mental hospitals their freedom
and I can't live on placebos
or Valium, like you
A cut lemon scours the smell of fish away
You'll feel better when the children are in school
I would try to tell you, mother-in-law
but my anger takes from yours and in the oven
the meal bursts into flames

          (WP, 31–32)

While outwardly she continued to lead the life of the good wife and loving mother, inwardly Adrienne Rich believed that she was dying. In the poem "Orion," written in 1965 and addressed to the constellation that to her symbolized the masculine or creative energy within her self (OL, 45), she mourned her loss. Unable to be sufficiently cold and egotistical like her distant half-brother Orion, she became convinced that her love for her children would ultimately consume what was left of her life.[15]

Indoors I bruise and blunder,
break faith, leave ill enough
alone, a dead child born in the dark.
Night cracks up over the chimney,
pieces of time, frozen geodes
come showering down in the grate.

A man reaches behind my eyes
and finds them empty
a woman's head turns away
from my head in the mirror
children are dying my death
and eating crumbs of my life.

Pity is not your forte.
Calmly you ache up there
pinned aloft in your crow's nest,
my speechless pirate!
You take it all for granted
and when I look you back

it's with a starlike eye
shooting its cold and egotistical spear
where it can do least damage.
                    (Lf, 11–12)

And it is true, particularly for the five years between the time her first child was born and the time when, according to the dating of her poems, she returned to serious work, Adrienne Rich, like Sylvia Plath, did give every appearance—however unwillingly and unintentionally—of recapitulating her mother's fate: giving up or sacrificing a promising career for the traditional role of wife and mother.

For the fact that she did not actually do so, she could thank her father. He had educated her too well to be his son, for her ever to rest content with her role as daughter (-in-law), no matter how much guilt she suffered because of her selfish need to have a life and career of her own. The "boredom and indifference" (OWB, 26) that she felt in the very early years of her life as mother toward her career as poet soon dissipated and, according to her journal entries in *Of Woman Born,* she became increasingly anxious to get back to work. In 1960 she applied for a Guggenheim fellowship, the first in that series of fellowships and grants which is so distinguishing a feature of her own, as of her father's, career. By 1962 she had enough poems for her third volume, *Snapshots of a Daughter-in-Law,* only a third of which was written prior to 1960.

But it is also clear from the poetry included in this volume that Rich's relationship to her craft had been irrevocably altered by her experience as a mother. The dutiful daughter might not be adequate to or happy in her role as daughter-in-law, but she now also had indisputable evidence that she could never truly be her father's son. With three children constantly there to remind her, Adrienne Rich as forced at last to confront her womanhood: its nature, its powers, and its limitations.

8. The Will to Change

You know, I've loved it as much as you have, I'm sure. I
really have, and I know how you feel about it. But I just
can't . . . I can't wake up at three in the morning and read a
poem by Yeats and feel somebody is talking to me whose
voice I need to hear. I just can't do that anymore.
                                        —Adrienne Rich, 1971

In a statement made at a poetry reading in 1964,
Adrienne Rich tried to capture the difference between the closed poetry she
wrote at the beginning of her career and the experientially open poetry she
began to write from about 1960 on.

> In the period in which my first two books were written I had a much
> more absolutist approach to the universe than I now have. I also felt — as
> many people still feel — that a poem was an arrangement of ideas and
> feelings, pre-determined, and it said what I had already decided it
> should say. There were occasional surprises . . . but control, technical
> mastery and intellectual clarity were the real goals.[1]

As she looked back over her early poetry, it now seemed, even at its best,
"queerly limited" to her. In many instances, she admits, she "had suppressed, omitted, falsified even, certain disturbing elements, to gain that
perfection of order,"[2] sacrificing truth to experience in the effort to impose
technical mastery, intellectual clarity, and control.

Rich no longer found her old poetry satisfying in 1964 because, as she explains in an interview given two years later, marriage and motherhood had taught her that experience was not as absolute and orderly as the poems she was writing in their very stylistic perfection made it seem. And this discovery had led her to read more sympathetically those poets like Charles Olsen who employed a more open, direct, and colloquial manner of approach. Her move to a "less formal style" after *The Diamond Cutters* was, she declares,

> the result of a lot of convergent things. I was changing a great deal emotionally through all sorts of experiences: marriage, having children, somehow getting into a much more complicated emotional world than I'd ever let myself in for. At the same time I was reading a lot of poets whose style and language were much more open and free, and who . . . made evident possibilities that the poets I first began to learn from hadn't.[3]

For Rich in the early sixties—an increasingly frustrated wife and miserably burdened mother—the perfection of order could not, in fact, exist. And the attempt to achieve it artificially in one's verse could, therefore, only be a lie, a fib. To be honest, poetry had to duplicate the raggedness, the complexity, the uncontrollability of experience. Indeed, the writing of poetry had itself become an experience for her, as open to surprise, new awareness, and change, as any other aspect of life. Writing poetry in this way, she told her audience at the 1964 reading, "engenders new sensations, new awareness in me" as the poems progress.

> Without for one moment turning my back on conscious choice and selection, I have been increasingly willing to let the unconscious offer its materials, to listen to more than the one voice of a single idea.[4]

Although it is unlikely that she was fully aware of all the implications involved in her move to this less formal technique, by 1964 Adrienne Rich had become committed to what Albert Gelpi has since, most appropriately, called "the poetics of change."[5]

•   •   •

Not surprisingly, both the content and the form of Rich's poetry were deeply affected by the poet's shift in aesthetic and philosophic position. In

A Change of World Rich had, despite the volume's title, taken a strong stand against the desirability — if not the possibility — of change. In the opening poem, "Storm Warnings," she had declared that if one could not prevent change, one could at least "close the shutters," "draw the curtains," and in other ways defend oneself "against the season" (CW, 18). In "The Uncle Speaks in the Drawing Room," a poem that Rich omits from *Poems Selected and New,* her own record of her growth, her conservatism is even more, perhaps embarrassingly, apparent. The "treasures handed down / From a calmer age passed on" are, the uncle declares, "in the keeping of *our kind"* (italics added). It is therefore the responsibility of the uncle and, presumably, his dutiful niece to

> stand between the dead glass-blowers
> And murmurings of missile throwers.
> (CW, 45)

Far from advocating any "radical change in human sensibility," both *A Change of World* and *The Diamond Cutters* were reactionary works. In their approach as in their form, they looked to the past for value and toward the future with apprehension.

In her third volume, *Snapshots of a Daughter-in-Law* (1963), on the other hand, Rich's attitude toward change has clearly undergone a profound rethinking. In this volume, change is no longer something that the poet seeks to defend against. On the contrary, it is accepted, even looked forward to. Indeed, in one of the most forceful and effective poems in the collection, "Prospective Immigrants Please Note," Rich treats the need for change as an ethical imperative, a call she can no longer afford to ignore.

> Either you will
> go through this door
> or you will not go through.
>
> If you go through
> there is always the risk
> of remembering your name.
>
> Things look at you doubly
> and you must look back
> and let them happen.

If you do not go through
it is possible
to live worthily

to maintain your attitudes
to hold your position
to die bravely

but much will blind you,
much will evade you,
at what cost who knows?

The door itself
makes no promises.
It is only a door.

                    (SDL, 59)

Having entered, without ever quite intending to, the "much more complicated emotional world" of a traditional marriage, Rich now knew that the old attitudes, the old position, no matter how worthy, could not suffice. And this discovery had placed her in the either-or situation reflected by the poem's syntax. She could choose, nevertheless, to stay where she had always been: safe, sheltered, poetically and emotionally a dutiful daughter, a compliant wife. Or she could take the gamble and explore the world that lay outside her father's door. Unlike Dickinson and Plath, she not only knew, she accepted the fact that she could not have it both ways and that ultimately the choice was one she would have to make.

In *Snapshots of a Daughter-in-Law*, Rich begins, albeit very tentatively, to explore the world of personal emotions and political concerns for which her dedication to the traditional values of craft and intellectual clarity, her father's values, had made so little room. In "The Roofwalker" she states bluntly that she can no longer live under the roof that she had once gone to such "infinite exertion" to lay. Her "tools are the wrong ones / for what [she has] to do."

I feel like them up there:
exposed, larger than life,
and due to break my neck.
· · · · · · · · · · ·
a naked man fleeing
across the roofs.

However vulnerable her need for change renders her, she still prefers this
danger to the living-death of security—her old detachment—which she
symbolizes at the conclusion of the poem by the man who "with a shade of
difference" could also be herself,

> . . . sitting in the lamplight
> against the cream wallpaper
> reading—not with indifference—
> about a naked man
> fleeing across the roofs.
>
> (SDL, 63)

Other poems in *Snapshots of a Daughter-in-Law*, while far less articulate
than "Prospective Immigrants" and "The Roofwalker," are similarly
permeated by the poet's growing sense of frustration and by her need to take
more of her own life, emotionally and politically, into her hands. In
"Antinoüs: The Diaries," she expresses through the mouth of Hadrian's
kept boy[6] the violence of her self-disgust at all that she has allowed to go to
waste.

> If what I spew on the tiles at last,
> helpless disgraced, alone,
> is in part what I've swallowed from glasses, eyes,
> motions of hands, opening and closing mouths,
> isn't it also dead gobbets of myself,
> abortive, murdered, or never willed?
>
> (SDL, 30–31)

Similarly, though on a less dramatic note, in "Passing On" she takes the
occasion of a move from one residence to another to bring up all the
opportunities she and her husband have missed.

> Soon we'll be off. I'll pack us into parcels,
> stuff us in barrels, shroud us in newspapers,
> pausing to marvel at old bargain sales:
> Oh, all the chances we never seized!
> Emptiness round the stoop of the house
> minces, catwise, waiting for an in.
>
> (SDL, 26)

But it is in the volume's extraordinary title poem that Rich's frustration
and her need for change, both generally and in her personal life, receive

their most vivid and unequivocal expression. Written under the inspiration of Simone de Beauvoir's *The Second Sex,* "Snapshots" represents Rich's first serious and undisguised attempt to get at the roots of the conflict that, according to *Of Woman Born,* was tearing her life apart at the time. Although she still could not use "I" in this poem when speaking of herself, Rich obviously identifies with the daughter-in-law in whose mind the poem occurs.[7] And the angels that chide the unhappy woman are the poet's own inner voices, warning her of what she must do if she is to save herself from ruin. The advice they give *("Have no patience," "Be insatiable," "Save yourself")* is advice of which Dickinson would have approved.

> Banging the coffee-pot into the sink
> she hears the angels chiding, and looks out
> past the raked gardens to the sloppy sky.
> Only a week since They said: *Have no patience.*
>
> The next time it was: *Be insatiable.*
> Then: *Save yourself; others you cannot save.*
> Sometimes she's let the tapstream scald her arm,
> a match burn to her thumbnail,
>
> or held her hand above the kettle's snout
> right in the woolly steam. They are probably angels,
> since nothing hurts her any more, except
> each morning's grit blowing into her eyes.
>
> (SDL, 21)

Reading de Beauvoir had, apparently, made Rich cognizant not only of how self-destructive her own behavior was (the repressed rage of "Aunt Jennifer's Tigers" now surfacing in the images of the scalded arm, the hand above the kettle's snout), but, equally important, how common this kind of repression and self-destructiveness was among women generally. Whether the poet contemplated what appears to be her own mother's response to marriage—

> Your mind now, mouldering like wedding-cake,
> heavy with useless experience, rich
> with suspicion, rumor, fantasy,
> crumbling to pieces under the knife-edge
> of mere fact
>
> (SDL, 21)

—or the mythical Corinna, forever poised with her lute, preparing to sing words and music that were not her own, what she saw were figures of waste and exploitation. "Pinned down / by love, for you the only natural action" (SDL, 23), women were not only unable to express their rage, they were unable to express their legitimate gifts, their creative potential, as well:

> Knowing themselves too well in one another:
> their gifts no pure fruition, but a thorn,
> the prick filed sharp against a hint of scorn . . .
> Reading while waiting
> for the iron to heat,
> writing, *My Life had stood—a Loaded Gun—*
> in that Amherst pantry while the jellies boil and scum,
> or, more often,
> iron-eyed and beaked and purposed as a bird,
> dusting everything on the whatnot every day of life.

Victims of the society in which they lived, women were encouraged to view each other as rivals and enemies.[8]

> The argument *ad feminam,* all the old knives
> that have rusted in my back, I drive in yours,
> *ma semblable, ma soeur.*
> (SDL, 22)

And their very strengths were undermined by the way in which their "mediocrities" were "over-praised."

> indolence read as abnegation,
> slattern thought styled intuition,
> every lapse forgiven, our crime
> only to cast too bold a shadow
> or smash the mould straight off.
> (SDL, 24)

Composed in snatches over a two-year period, "during children's naps, brief hours in a library, or at 3:00 A.M. after rising with a wakeful child," "Snapshots," as the title suggests, is a compendium of Rich's new insights, a brief anthology of her gripes. It was, she claims, "an extraordinary relief to write" (OL, 44–45). In its long loose line, its direct manner of address, its fragmented style, it is also, formally speaking, the most advanced poem in the volume and a clear signal of the direction Rich's development would soon take.

But in many ways "Snapshots" also represents a moment whose time had not yet come. At the conclusion of the poem, Rich presents her vision, based on a passage in de Beauvoir,[9] of the new woman, "at least as beautiful as any boy / or helicopter," upon whom her hope for the future is placed. It is an exquisite vision:

> Well,
>
> she's long about her coming, who must be
> more merciless to herself than history.
> Her mind full to the wind, I see her plunge
> breasted and glancing through the currents,
> taking the light upon her
> at least as beautiful as any boy
> or helicopter,
>   poised, still coming,
> her fine blades making the air wince
> but her cargo
> no promise then:
> delivered
> palpable
> ours.
>
>   (SDL, 24–25)

But even as the images of the boy and helicopter which she employs in this passage suggest, Rich herself was still not free of the old attitudes, the old beliefs. Lacking the support of a formalized feminist theory to guide her in a totally new direction and supplant the "rootless ideology" that had been her father's bequest, Rich was still dependent on most of her earlier, male-identified values, still anxious as she has since admitted to maintain the approval of the literary establishment to which she felt she owed so much, still unable to put words such as *woman* and *power* together. While Rich knew the door was there, she had not yet fully stepped through it.

The embryonic feminism that Rich expresses in *Snapshots of a Daughter-in-Law* had, therefore, little specific effect on the poetry she wrote over the next seven or eight years, before her involvement in the women's movement. In the *Island* interview in 1966 she could still name Randall Jarrell, who had just died, as her ideal reader. In its very paradoxicality, the string of epithets which she uses to eulogize Jarrell—"so incredibly intelligent and so full of feeling, so full of sympathy, so ruthless, so unsparing, and yet so aware of all the potentialities in what you've done"[10] —makes the deceased poet-critic sound remarkably like an idealized version of Arnold Rich. And rankling under bad reviews the woman-centered material in *Snapshots* received, it was for such male readers that she continued to censor her work, controlling, though by no means eliminating, the amount of personal and woman-oriented material in it. Of her feelings during this period, Rich told Elly Bulkin in the 1977 *Conditions* interview:

> I realized I'd gotten slapped over the wrists and I didn't attempt that kind of thing for a long time again.
> I wrote a lot of poems about death and that was my next book [*Necessities of Life*], but I think I sensed even then that if there's material you're not supposed to explore, it can be the most central material in the world to you but it's going to be trivialized as personal, it's going to be reduced critically, you're going to be told that you're ranting or hysterical or emotional. The reception of *Snapshots* did make a deep impression and in some way deepened my sense that these were important themes, that I had to deal with them. But it certainly didn't encourage me to go on with them at that point. I had no sense that there was going to be an audience for them.[11]

In the criticism directed toward *Snapshots*, Rich had, in fact, come smack up against the limits drawn by the literary establishment around the woman poet. It was acceptable for a woman to lay claim to serious attention as a poet but only if she kept certain central aspects of her womanhood out of her art—if she detached her poetry from her (woman)self and all its personal emotions. Without an alternative poetic theory or an audience for whom such material might actually be relevant and meaningful, Rich was left with the choice of either writing in ways and on themes that met with establishment approval or writing without hope of being heard. Understandably, she took the former course. "I put a lot [in my journals]—about my life as a mother—that I couldn't put into poetry at the time," Rich says in the *Conditions* interview, "largely because by the male standards which were all I knew, motherhood was not a 'major theme' for poetry."[12]

Caught between her need for growth on the one hand and her continued desire for establishment approval on the other, and unable to deal frontally with many of the issues that were of greatest concern to her as an individual, Rich, for all her extraordinary ability and drive, in many ways did a poetic tailspin after *Necessities of Life*, her last fully acceptable volume by establishment standards, [13] as her work became increasingly fragmented, solipsistic, and difficult to follow. While she became more and more convinced of the necessity for change, no systematic view of the kind of change needed controls her poetry. Rather, each poem seems to stand on its own, a separate stab made by the poet to get at what was bothering her—her own sense of internal fragmentation and the fragmentation or "splittings," as she has since called them, in the world around her.

In *Leaflets,* published in 1969, three years after *Necessities of Life,* thoughts of her own vulnerability and lack of a stable base obsess her. Rich's father had died in early 1968, after a lingering illness that destroyed his mind as well as his body. Rich and her father had never completely reconciled. She claims that his continued demand for "absolute loyalty, absolute submission to his will" after her marriage always stood between them, making full reconciliation impossible (NJG, 79). Perhaps because of this, and because of the bitter and divisive political throes American society was undergoing in the mid to late sixties, she was no longer able to make a meaningful connection to the past, and her poetry hangs in a curiously suspended temporal void.

In "Abnegation," written in 1968, she compares herself to a red vixen, who has

> . . . no archives,
> no heirlooms, no future
> except death.

Like the animal, she lives only for the present and to keep "every hair on her pelt alive." "What does she want," Rich asks, speaking both for herself and the fox,

> with the dreams of dead vixens,
> the apotheosis of Reynard,
> the literature of fox-hunting?

And what does the poet want with the historical "birthright" that she has been given, "a redstained, ravelled / afghan of sky." "I could," she concludes,

> . . . be more
> her sister than theirs

who chopped their way across these hills
—a chosen people.

(Lf, 38)

In "In the Evening" Rich is no less adamant in her rejection of the once unassailable past. Only here it is her cultural, not her historical legacy that she abjures.

> . . . We stand in the porch,
> two archaic figures: a woman and a man.
>
> The old masters, the old sources,
> haven't a clue what we're about,
> shivering here in the half-dark 'sixties.

(Lf, 15)

The authors in whom her childhood had been steeped cannot be used as guides to the way we live now. Guides do not exist, not when so many changes have occurred and are still occurring.

Cut off from the consolations and support of her culture and history, Rich presents herself in these poems as alien and alienated. Dreams of war haunt her; "The radio had just screamed / that Illinois was the target." And even tenderness seems "futile . . . / . , in a world like this" (Lf, 20, 21). She lives, in fact, in the dark, and night pervades these poems, a night symbolic not only of the fragmentation of society but of the numb isolation that has overtaken individual lives, including the poet's own. In this world, even the break of day, a "white / scar," brings no relief.

> The enemy has   withdrawn
> between raids   become invisible
> there are
>   no agencies
>   of relief
> the darkness becomes utter
> Sleep   cracked and flaking
> sifts over the shaken   target
>
> What breaks   is night
> not day   The white
> scar   splitting

over the east
The crack weeping
Time for the pieces
          to move
dumbly back
        toward each other.
              (Lf, 49)

"How," she asks her husband, in the last poem in the volume,

    did we get caught up fighting this forest fire,
we, who were only looking for a still place in the woods?
                      (Lf, 77)

Like the title of the book in which they appear, the poems in *Leaflets* suggest a world of fugitive moments, a world concerned only with "tidings of the immaculate present" (Lf, 38), a world in which the author's primary concern is simply to survive. There is, Rich declares at the conclusion of "Charleston in the 1860's," "No imagination to forestall woe" (Lf, 25). Like the past, the future is a blank. Even the words she writes are "vapor-trails, / by the time I write them out, they are whispering something else" (Lf, 62).

In *The Will to Change,* the hopelessness with which Rich viewed her own situation and the fate of her society affects her treatment of poetry as well. Indeed, in "Images for Godard" (1971), Rich takes up the theme announced so briefly in *Leaflets* ("These words are vapor-trails") and pushes it, poetically speaking, as far as she can. The poem becomes no more than a set of notes mirroring the process that is occurring in the poet's mind at the moment of writing.

Interior monologue of the poet:
the notes for the poem are the only poem

the mind collecting, devouring
all these destructibles

the unmade studio couch the air
shifting the abalone shells

the mind of the poet is the only poem
the poet is at the movies

dreaming the film-maker's dream but differently
free in the dark as if asleep

free in the dusty beam of the projector
the mind of the poet is changing

the moment of change is the only poem
                                        (WC, 49)

However beautifully crafted these lines are, with their balanced repetitions of "dreaming" and "dream," "changing" and "change," they also assert Rich's loss of faith in the poetic process. In them, the poet has retired almost entirely into her own dream world, a world that does not extend beyond the flickering beams of the "movie projector" that is her own mind playing over the isolated fragments of her experience: "the unmade studio couch . . . the abalone shells" (a coded reference, I believe, to her husband's infidelity), as it collects and devours "all these destructibles."

While "Images of Godard" is extreme, it is not atypical of the attitude Rich assumes toward her medium in *The Will to Change*. In the poem which precedes it and helps decode it, "Photograph of the Unmade Bed," she is, for example, only slightly less remote, indirect, and fragmented in her handling of the marital difficulties that were having such immediate and terrible consequences for her personal life and to which "Images" refers only in the most oblique way, if at all.

Cruelty is rarely conscious
One slip of the tongue

one exposure
among so many

a thrust in the dark
to see if there's pain there

I never asked you to explain
that act of violence

what dazed me was our ignorance
of our will to hurt each other
                          . . . .
                          In a flash I understand
                          how poems are unlike photographs

(the one saying   This could be
the other   This was

The image
isn't responsible

for our uses of it
It is intentionless

A long strand of dark hair
in the washbasin

is innocent and yet
such things have done harm
. . . .
These snaphots taken by ghetto children
given for Christmas

Objects blurring into perceptions
No "art," only the faults

of the film, the faults of the time
Did mere indifference blister

these panes, eat these walls,
shrivel and scrub these trees—

mere indifference? I tell you
cruelty is rarely conscious

the done and the undone blur
into one photograph of failure.
. . . .
This crust of bread we try to share
this name traced on a window

this word I paste together
like a child fumbling

with paste and scissors
this writing in the sky with smoke

this silence

> this lettering chalked on the ruins
> this alphabet of the dumb
>
> this feather held to lips
> that still breathe and are warm
> (WC, 45–46)

In this poem Rich uses the image of the photograph to help give substance to what is otherwise presented as a totally private and internal moment of failure between herself and, one assumes, her husband. But even with this concrete symbol, "Photograph of an Unmade Bed" is an unusually distant and abstract work. The act of adultery that presumably lies at its core is reduced to a single image, the "long strand of dark hair / in the washbasin." The husband himself is faceless and without presence in the poem. And though Rich mentions the violence and harm they have done each other, these events seem more mental than real. They are part of the poet's interior world of thought as she contemplates the uses of imagery, the ineffectuality of language, and the nature of the cruelty that has occurred between them. Even the "snapshots taken by ghetto children" are objects that blur into perceptions, just as "the done and the undone blur / into one photograph [or perception] of failure." Everything that happens in the poem seems, in short, to happen inside the poet's head or is reduced to a mental event. No matter how specific and real the biographical circumstances behind what she writes, we are once again in her interior world, "dreaming the film-maker's dream," overhearing a monologue in which neither we nor the actors in the poem seem to have a concrete part.

That Rich was saved from moving into completely solipsistic writing during this period was due only to her commitment to politics and to the larger world in which her private tragedy, her own "moment of change," was being acted out. As her marriage had disintegrated during the sixties, so, on a considerably larger scale, did America's faith in itself. For Rich, who, like her husband, was a passionate supporter both of the Black movement and the antiwar movement, the two events became inextricably linked together, one standing symbol for the other and both symbolic of the failure of our culture, our language and literature, to provide the means by which human beings could in Rich's terms live decent, honorable, and courageous lives. In the brilliant conclusion to "The Burning of Paper Instead of Children," a poem inspired by an actual book-burning incident in which one of her sons was involved, she brings these various strands together in a prose poem of exceptional force.

I am composing on the typewriter late at night, thinking of today. How well we all spoke. A language is a map of our failures. Frederick Douglass wrote an English purer than Milton's. People suffer highly in poverty. There are methods but we do not use them. Joan, who could not read, spoke some peasant form of French. Some of the suffering are: it is hard to tell the truth; this is America; I cannot touch you now. In America we have only the present tense. I am in danger. You are in danger. The burning of a book arouses no sensation in me. I know it hurts to burn. There are flames of napalm in Catonsville, Maryland. I know it hurts to burn. The typewriter is overheated, my mouth is burning, I cannot touch you and this is the oppressor's language. (WC, 18)

In this passage Rich's frustrations with her society, her education, her paternally inculcated childhood values, and her own situation as a confused and aggrieved wife all come together for the first time in the multiple meanings of the single phrase: "the oppressor's language." The power she had acquired as an ersatz son and wielded as a dutiful daughter now reveals itself as an open, festering wound. It healed nothing. Books healed nothing. Language was a map of our failures, personal and historical, nothing more. The broken syntax of the ghetto mother who declares, "Some of the suffering are," was finally more eloquent and possibly, like Frederick Douglass's English, purer than the language Milton wrote.

In the period between 1968 and 1970, when Rich wrote the poems included in *The Will to Change,* she had reached, in effect, the nadir of her relationship with language, with her father's power. Lacking any alternative way to use language or even to think about it, she saw it either as a tool for oppression or as an almost useless weapon in the struggle for change ("The typewriter is overheated, my mouth is burning"). Filled with rage at the disintegration of her society and at the disintegration of her marriage, but unable to prevent either, she used her poems almost exclusively to explore her wounds. Much of her work teeters on the brink of incoherence. It is as if there was no way, with language and all that language had once represented to her—the "great tradition," the "old sources"—that she could now articulate her ideas in a logical, accessible manner. In "The Blue Ghazals" (loosely modeled on a poetic form invented by the nineteenth-century Urdu poet Mirza Ghalib—who also wrote, she declares, "in an age of political and cultural break-up" [Lf, 59]), thoughts of Christ's sacrifice at Christmas time become:

Frost, burning. The city's ill.
We gather like viruses.

The doctors are all on their yachts
watching the beautiful skin-divers.

The peasant mind of the Christian
transfixed on food at the year's turning

Thinking of marzipan
forget that revolutionary child.

Thought grown senile with sweetness.
You too may visit the Virgins.

In the clear air, hijacked planes
touch down at the forbidden island.
                                    (WC, 23)

And in "Shooting Script," Rich's most extreme experiment in the "poetics of change," she flashes single, seemingly unrelated, lines or sentences before the reader, using them as if they were images on a movie screen to express through linguistic discontinuation not only her alienation from her own experience but her inability to make sense of the whole.

I was looking for a way out of a lifetime's consolations.

We walked in the wholesale district: closed warehouses, windows, steeped in sun.

I said: those cloths are very old. You said: they have lain in that window a long time.

When the skeletons of the projects shut off the sunset, when the sense of the Hudson leaves us, when only by loss of light in the east do I know that I am living in the west.

When I give up being paraphrased, when I let go, when the beautiful solutions in their crystal flasks have dried up in the sun, when the lightbulb bursts on lighting, when the dead bulb rattles like a seed-pod.

Those cloths are very old, they are mummies' cloths, they have lain
in graves, they were not intended to be sold, the tragedy of this
mistake will soon be clear.

Vacillant needles of Manhattan, describing hour & weather; buying
these descriptions at the cost of missing every other point.

(WC, 65)

If this chain of associations had a coherent meaning for Rich, she did not
choose to make it available to the reader. On the surface, at least, "Shooting
Script" is as arbitrary and random as the world it describes.

The language of the fathers, her father's language, was all Rich had. And
that language, like the world it mirrored, the world the fathers made, was
rapidly failing her: "the tragedy of this / mistake will soon be clear." Her
commitment to politics had prevented her from turning inward completely, but it could not prevent her from seeing in the larger outer world a
reflection of her own dissolution or mirroring that dissolution in the poetry
she wrote. Given the high degree of fragmentation in the poems composing
The Will to Change, her last volume before *Diving into the Wreck*, it is an open
question, which Rich herself asks, whether she could have gone on writing,
let alone growing as a writer, had she not been able to find a new center from
which to write in 1971.[15] Like the mummy cloths in the window, emotionally and intellectually Rich had reached a dead end in *The Will to
Change,* the title of the volume notwithstanding—the dead end of the
world the fathers had made and the language of the fathers reflected.

Enraged by war, by waste, by the hyprocrisy of those with power who
could use their power to heal and didn't, and frustrated almost beyond
endurance by her own inability to communicate, to break out of the
"cellblock" in which she was confined, Rich in 1968 could only dream of
the freedom possessed by the woman who had volcanoes to protect her. She
could not emulate it. In an exquisite and now, sadly, ironic poem on the
late Dian Fossey, Rich wrote:

Completely protected on all sides
by volcanoes
a woman, darkhaired, in stained jeans
sleeps in central Africa.
In her dreams, her notebooks, still
private as maiden diaries,
the mountain gorillas move through their life term;
their gentleness survives

observation. Six bands of them
inhabit, with her, the wooded highland.
When I lay me down to sleep
unsheltered by any natural guardians
from the panicky life-cycle of my tribe
I wake in the old cellblock
observing the daily executions,
rehearsing the laws
I cannot subscribe to,
envying the pale gorilla-scented dawn
she wakes into, the stream where she washes her hair,
the camera-flash of her quiet
eye.

(Lf, 47)

"Rehearsing . . . laws" she could not subscribe to, Adrienne Rich was
still at this time in some profound sense her father's daughter, no matter
how disillusioned she had become with his world or with the values in
which he had taught her to believe. She still sought to wield power by his
standards, although it was a power she now both loved and hated, and she
still spoke, in effect, to an audience composed of men like him. It took the
women's movement to help Rich understand that as a woman this power
could also be hers in a womanly way. "When I speak," she writes at the
conclusion of *Sources,*

of an end to suffering I don't mean anesthesia.
I mean knowing the world, and my place in it, not in
order to stare with bitterness or detachment, but as a
powerful and womanly series of choices: and here I
write the words, in their fullness:

powerful;   womanly

(S, 35)

For Rich to write these words "in their fullness" required first that she
confirm in herself and in other women that women could indeed have
power—and that that power need in no way reflect the male-identified or
patriarchal social and personal values of the world in which she lived.

. . .

Sometime in 1970, as she was working on the last poems of *The Will to Change,* Rich, by then under the influence of the women's movement, left her marriage of seventeen years. In "Tear Gas," written in 1969 but not published until 1975, in *Poems Selected and New,* she anticipated the separation and explored the feelings of anger and frustration that led to it.

> Trying every key in the bunch to get the door even ajar
> not knowing whether it's locked or simply jammed from long disuse
> trying the keys over and over then throwing the bunch away
> staring around for an axe
> wondering if the world can be changed like this
> if a life can be changed like this
> · · · · · · · · · ·
> The will to change begins in the body not in the mind
> My politics is in my body, accruing and expanding with every
>   act of resistance and each of my failures
> Locked in the closet at 4 years old I beat the wall with my body
> that act is in me still.

> (PSN, 140)

There was no way for change wrought only in the mind to maintain its meaning for Adrienne Rich, especially as she came to understand the extent to which her body had determined her destiny. And it was, therefore, to the politics of the body—a politics built into her, as it were, by her early childhood education—that she now turned. Feminism led her to "a place where," as she told Conrad, "we can no longer be together," however much in some ways she continued to love him.

> I mean that I want you to answer me
> when I speak badly
> that I love you, that we are in danger
> that she wants to have your child, that I want us to have
>   mercy on each other
> that I want to take her hand
> that I see you changing
> that it was change I loved in you
> when I thought I loved completeness
> that things I have said which in a few years will be forgotten
> matter more to me than this or any poem
> and I want you to listen
> when I speak badly
> not in poems but in tears

not my best but my worst
that these repetitions are beating their way
toward a place where we can no longer be together
where my body no longer will demonstrate outside your stockade
and wheeling through its blind tears will make for the open air
of another kind of action.

(PSN, 141)

For Rich, both she and Conrad had changed too much in ways they could not control for any other kind of action to work. The body, the womanhood, that she had neglected, suppressed, and misunderstood for so many years had finally taken charge of her life.

Not many months after the separation, Conrad, apparently depressed over the dissolution of his marriage and over career difficulties that he was having at the time, drove up to Peacham, Vermont, in a rented car and shot himself in a meadow near the cabin in Barnet which they owned together.[16] Rich has said very little publicly about her feelings over Conrad's suicide. In *Sources,* one of the few poems in which she speaks directly to him, she claims that her silence has been due to her desire to protect him, not to use him "merely as a theme for poetry or tragic musings" (S, 32). And this silence should be respected

But it is also clear that her husband's death marked the close of a chapter in Adrienne Rich's life as well. Between July 1970, when she wrote the final sections of "Shooting Script," and 1971, when she began composing the poems that went into *Diving into the Wreck,* Rich appears to have written no poetry. When she picked up writing again, her voice and style had once more changed profoundly but this time in ways that would allow her, finally, to make her power her own.

9. A Woman of Our Time

. . . .
. . . .
. . . .

To me [Adrienne Rich] was the poet, after the suicides of Sylvia Plath and Anne Sexton, my generation of women writers could depend on—the wise woman we could safely choose to follow.
—Joyce Greenberg, 1978

There must be ways, and we will be finding out more and more about them, in which the energy of creation and the energy of relation can be united.
—Adrienne Rich, 1971

Of the poems Adrienne Rich wrote prior to her active involvement in the women's movement, she chose only one, "Planetarium," to publish in a feminist journal.[1] In light of her later development, however, the choice could not have been a more apposite one.

Ostensibly, "Planetarium" is dedicated to Caroline Herschel, the sister of the astronomer William Herschel, and a highly capable astronomer in her own right. But the poem is of a piece with many poems Rich has written since 1971 which, as Helen Vendler complains, while putatively about others, are actually about the poet herself.[2] The woman astronomer and her fate, hidden from history by the greater glory of her brother, are merely the springboards for Rich's far more immediate concern: her own situation in life and her place in the history of the times. In "Planetarium," she is anything but self-effacing in her treatment of these themes.

Heartbeat of the pulsar
heart sweating through my body

The radio impulse
pouring in from Taurus

    I am bombarded yet   I stand

I have been standing all my life in the
direct path of a battery of signals
the most accurately transmitted most
untranslateable language in the universe
I am a galactic cloud so deep   so involuted that a light wave could take 15
years to travel through me   And has
taken   I am an instrument in the shape
of a woman trying to translate pulsations
into images   for the relief of the body
and the reconstruction of the mind
                  (WC, 14)

Like Whitman, who claimed to contain multitudes, Adrienne Rich presents herself in this passage as considerably larger than life. And like Milton, who took upon himself the awesome task of justifying the ways of God to man, Rich also has assumed a difficult if not impossible burden of translation: the task of converting the pulsations of our period, our time in history, into images that will relieve the body and reconstruct the mind.

What makes this poem particularly suitable for a feminist journal is, of course, the fact that it is a woman who is saying these things. In "Planetarium," Rich, a woman poet, is claiming special powers for herself, powers that, except under the most unusual circumstances, women have historically been denied. They are, moreover, powers which she can no more extricate from her womanhood ("I am an instrument in the shape / of a woman"), than Milton and Whitman could have separated their power from the knowledge that they were men. No longer the "monster" ("death's head, sphinx, medusa") of her early self-alienating fears, Rich collapses the traditional division of the sexes where poetry is concerned, and becomes, in effect, her own muse.

A woman in the shape of a monster
a monster in the shape of a woman

the skies are full of them
. . . .
Galaxies of women, there
doing penance for impetuousness
ribs chilled
in those spaces   of the mind
. . . .
every impulse of light exploding
from the core
as life flies out of us
. . . . . .
What we see, we see
and seeing is changing
                              (WC, 13, 14)

In writing "Planetarium," Rich was establishing a new relationship to
her lyric voice, her poetic persona, and to her readers — to whom she is now
speaking directly for the first time as woman prophet or seer. As she
observes in "When We Dead Awaken," "the woman in the poem and the
woman writing the poem" have finally "become the same person" (OL, 47).
But like the title poem in *Snapshots of a Daughter-in-Law*, "Planetarium,"
written in 1968, stands alone in the volume in which it appears. Apart from
this one poem, *The Will to Change* is dedicated either to private, solipsisti-
cally experienced pain or to fragmented visions of the outer world. Another
three years were to elapse before Rich began to write feminist poetry in
earnest and put herself as woman at the center of her verse.

.   .   .

The effect feminism had on Adrienne Rich's poetry can be grasped quickly
by an examination of one of the more explicitly political poems in *Diving
into the Wreck*, "Translations," written in 1972.

You show me the poems of some woman
my age, or younger
translated from your language

Certain words occur: *enemy, oven, sorrow*
enough to let me know
she's a woman of my time

obsessed

with Love, our subject:
we've trained it like ivy to our walls
baked it like bread in our ovens
worn it like lead on our ankles
watched it through binoculars as if
it were a helicopter
bringing food to our famine
or the satellite
of a hostile power

I begin to see that woman
doing things: stirring rice
ironing a skirt
typing a manuscript till dawn

trying to make a call
from a phonebooth

the phone rings unanswered
in a man's bedroom
she hears him telling someone else
Never mind. She'll get tired.
hears him telling her story to her sister
who becomes her enemy
and will in her own time
light her own way to sorrow

ignorant of the fact this way of grief
is shared, unnecessary
and political.
                    (DW, 40–41)

It hardly needs saying that "Translations" is a quintessentially feminist poem. It is spoken by a woman. It is about a woman. It describes a situation with which virtually all women, at least in our culture, are familiar and from which many, if not most, have suffered one way or another at one time or another in their lives. The poet's concern in the poem is not, as it was in her earlier poems on her husband's infidelity, to show the male the error of his ways—he has, it seems, been given up as hopeless—but to make women realize the error of theirs. Through their exclusive dedication to love—or to what Rich calls the "energy of relation" (OL, 43)—women have not only sacrificed themselves and their creative potentials; they have, ironically, sacrificed one another as well. It is to this theme that the poem is devoted. It is a theme to which Rich, as both a poet and a woman, obviously has a deep personal commitment, a commitment she intentionally stresses by the use of self-referential pronouns within the poem itself.

> You show *me* the poems of some woman
> *my* age, or younger
> translated from your language
>
> Certain words occur: *enemy, oven, sorrow*
> enough to let *me* know
> she's a woman of *my* time.
>   (italics added to pronouns)

It is also a theme that, for better or worse, has been very narrowly defined in its appeal.

For many people, reading a poem like "Translations" can prove a disturbing experience. Unless, like Rich, you are committed to feminist values, you may very well feel left out. In his review of *Diving into the Wreck* for the *New York Times,* Harvey Shapiro speaks for many readers when he questions the poem's final lines: "But how is it 'political' and in what scheme of things will it become 'unnecessary'? The refusal to explain, if it is that, is the patronizing attitude of those saved for those who are not."[3]

But in raising this protest Shapiro has ignored the purpose of the poem as the poet conceived it. For women who have experienced the situation Rich describes in "Translations" and who are determined at last to step back from their lives and understand their actions, the last lines of the poem carry a shock of recognition that cannot be denied. It is to these women that Rich as a woman is writing. Her *semblables* have become her intended readers. In its very exclusivity, therefore, "Translations" fulfills the purpose for which it was written. Its aim is not to appeal to the general, undifferentiated reader but to move women who like the poet herself have been taught throughout their lives to accept victimization in their relationships with men as their lot, to move these women specifically to think — to move them to ask Is this necessary? And if it is not, then to ask What have I done to myself? What have I done to other women?

From the point of view of craft, there is no way to say that "Translations" is more successful as poetry than most of Rich's earlier work. While it does not represent her writing at its strongest, its most affective, it is certainly well written, exhibiting a good control of structure, imagery, and, for those in sympathy with what it has to say, tone. Like the earlier work it achieves its end. But it is a very different kind of poetry. Until *Diving into the Wreck,* Rich's work, even at its most political, had been directed toward a general audience and had emphasized themes like the disintegration of society, the ineffectuality of language, and the pain of infidelity, to which most readers, male and female, could relate. "Translations," on the other hand, is clearly and exclusively a woman's poem. It is directed toward a limited audience and it emphasizes the poet's commitment to a specific set of values which as a woman she wishes to share with others like herself. What matters here is that from Rich's point of view, writing political poems such as "Translations," that is, writing poems from a specifically woman-centered point of view, has not only provided her with a much-needed framework by which to understand her experience, but it has allowed her to reach an audience she did not know was there before. As a result it has had a distinctly liberating effect on her art as well as on her life.

In a 1977 interview with Blanche Boyd in the gay publication *Christopher Street,* Rich explains how the discovery of this limited audience, this women's community, has affected the way she relates to her readers and the way she feels about herself as a woman artist.

> I think women go to women's readings for a reason that goes back to the oldest source of art: in search of community, of a place where words will be spoken that all can hear and share in, words they aren't hearing in other places, in classrooms or workplaces or in the world at large
> *Boyd:* To be a woman artist before the women's movement was almost a contradiction in terms.
> *Rich:* It was possible only for a few, and you were always asking yourself whether you were in some way a monster. . . . I live most of my life now in a female cognitive community, which means both an aesthetic and a political community. . . . There is so much happening, it's so rich, and I need it — for my life and for my work. I was starved for it for forty years.[4]

By turning her focus to this community, Rich has freed herself not just to own her power but to use it in new ways: to write the words that women do not hear in other places — the topics, like motherhood and lesbianism, that she had long considered taboo — and to write about herself openly and directly as a woman for the first time. The taking of these freedoms has radically changed her art, just as it has in many respects ended her prolonged isolation as an artist.

It is, I believe, because this community exists that Rich has at last been able to come to grips with her self, her wounds and her power, in her verse. Contrary to much critical opinion, Rich's feminist poetry is not all of a piece, nor is it entirely self-consistent. Rather, like so much of her earlier work, it presents a record of the poet's continued growth, her changes and discoveries. What has altered, however, is the scope and direction of the poet's inquiry. For in writing to the women's community, Rich has profoundly altered the focus of her verse and with it the very substance of the kind of poetry she writes. If not all of this poetry succeeds, it is nevertheless this work, not her earlier writing, that has made Rich truly a "woman of [our] time" and "wise woman"⁵ for so many in the next generation of women writers.

•   •   •

As Rich noted in *Sources,* the most immediate impact feminism had on her was to give her an ideology by which to understand the principle her father embodied, "the face of the patriarchy" he wore. Through the seventeen years of her marriage, Rich had struggled with her misery as wife and, more particularly, as mother, without, it appears, truly grasping the way her father's values continued to control her life as woman and poet. Now armed with theory, she could, she believed, "hate [him] righteously as part of a system, the kingdom of the fathers" (S, 15). And hate she did.

The feminism of *Diving into the Wreck* consists principally of the poet's righteous indignation, her barely mitigated rage. In "Merced," Rich — a baleful presence — walks the streets of her city alone, furiously aware of her moral and intellectual isolation in a world "masculinity made / unfit for women or men."

> For weeks now a rage
> has possessed my body, driving
> now out upon men and women
> now inward upon myself
> Walking Amsterdam Avenue
> I find myself in tears
> without knowing which thought
> forced water to my eyes
> To speak to another human
> becomes a risk
> I think of Norman Morrison
> the Buddhists of Saigon
> the black teacher last week

who put himself to death
to waken guilt in hearts
too numb to get the message
in a world masculinity made
unfit for women or men
Taking off in a plane
I look down at the city
which meant life to me, not death
and think that somewhere there
a cold center, composed
of pieces of human beings
metabolized, restructured
by a process they do not feel
is spreading in our midst
and taking over our minds
a thing that feels neither guilt
nor rage: that is unable
to hate, therefore to love.

(DW, 36–37)

In "Incipience," she imagines herself as a neurosurgeon with "a stern, delicate face like Marie Curie" (DW, 12), dissecting a man's brain.

We are his dreams
We have the heads and breasts of women
the bodies of birds of prey
Sometimes we turn into silver serpents

(DW, 11, 12)

In "The Phenomenology of Anger," in one of the most controversial passages in the entire volume, she becomes a blow torch, white acetylene "effortlessly released" from her body.

perfectly trained
on the true enemy

raking his body down to the thread
of existence
burning away his lie
leaving him in a new
world; a changed
man

(DW, 29)

And in "Burning Oneself Out," she depicts herself as burning up, her mind a fire her whole life has fed.

> or, as tonight, the mirror of the fire
> of my mind, burning as if it could go on
> burning itself, burning down
>
> feeding on everything
> till there is nothing in life
> that has not fed that fire
>
> (DW, 47)

Reading such passages, one can understand why even sympathetic critics, including some feminist critics, have found *Diving* too militant for their taste. "The voice of *Diving*," Karen Whitehill writes, quoting perhaps unfairly from "The Phenomenology of Anger," does "not go beyond 'self-hatred, a monotone in the mind. / The shallowness of a life lived in exile.'"[6] Yet for Rich, as for feminist writers generally, this outpouring of rage has been the necessary first step in the creation of a verifiably woman-centered vision, a feminist poetic.

In the 1971 essay "When We Dead Awaken: Writing as Re-vision," her most important prose statement on her art, Rich tries to explain the significance of anger for the woman poet. Her starting point is an off-hand comment made by the British anthropologist Jane Harrison in a 1914 letter to Gilbert Murray, a prominent classical scholar:

> By the by, about "Women," it has bothered me often—why do women never want to write poetry about Man as a sex—why is Woman a dream and a terror to man and not the other way around? . . . Is it mere convention and propriety, or something deeper? (OL, 36, as quoted by Rich)

To Rich, Harrison's casually put query is all-embracing, touching not only "the myth-making tradition, the romantic tradition" but the relationship between men and women and "the psyche of the woman writer." In particular, she argues, it explains the special qualities and appeal of writers like Plath and Wakoski and, by extension, herself.

In these poets, Rich writes, "Man appears as, if not a dream, a fascination and a terror; and . . . the source of the fascination and the terror is, simply, Man's power—to dominate, tyrannize, choose, or reject the woman." It is, she concludes,

finally the woman's sense of *herself*—embattled, possessed—that gives
the poetry its dynamic charge, its rhythms of struggle, need, will, and
female energy. Until recently this female anger and this furious awareness of the Man's power over her were not available materials to the
female poet, who tended to write of Love as the source of her suffering,
and to view that victimization by Love as an almost inevitable fate. Or,
like Marianne Moore and Elizabeth Bishop, she kept sexuality at a
measured and chiseled distance in her poems.   (OL, 36)

While Rich's statement does not, in my opinion, give enough credit to
Dickinson, who also depicted the masculine as "a fascination and a terror,"
it certainly helps explain her own writing and that of Plath. In their
"furious awareness" and their sexual energy, these two poets have been able
to break through not only the layers of convention and propriety to which
Harrison alludes, but, even more important, through that "something
deeper" which the British anthropologist does not name but which, I would
suggest, is woman's own sense of self as "Other."

In its very extremism, the anger in *Diving into the Wreck* is consequently
fundamental to the value of the work. A way of seeing and a way of being, it
defines both who and what the poet is.

Looking as I've looked before, straight down the heart
of the street to the river
walking the rivers of the avenues
feeling the shudder of the caves beneath the asphalt
watching the lights turn on in the towers
walking as I've walked before
like a man, like a woman, in the city
my visionary anger cleansing my sight
and the detailed perceptions of mercy
flowering from that anger

if I come into a room out of the sharp misty light
and hear them talking a dead language
if they ask my identity
what can I say but
I am the androgyne
I am the living mind you fail to describe
in your dead language
the lost noun, the verb surviving
only in the infinitive

the letters of my name are written under the lids
of the newborn child

(DW, 19)

Rich does not include this poem in *Poems Selected and New*—presumably
because of the reference to androgyny in it—but "The Stranger" nevertheless represents a critically important way station in her evolution from
dutiful daughter to spokeswoman for a totally woman-centered lesbian
vision.[7] In claiming to be both male and female in her understanding, Rich
has, in effect, established a new identity for herself: one that is based not on
how she is perceived but on *how she perceives*. No longer the other—neither the
monster of male nightmares nor the passive subject of his dreams—she
becomes the actor instead, the one who names. Specifically through her
capacity as androgyne to see, feel, and record what others because of their
allegiance to traditional sex roles refuse to acknowledge, she has been able
to cleanse her sight and take the power of language, the traditionally
male-defined logos, to herself.

For Rich, the act of seizing language, which she describes in "The
Stranger," is both crucial and deliberate. In an unpublished interview with
Wendy Martin in 1978, she declared, "When the woman writer takes pen
in hand, she has been in some way, even if in only a small way, seizing
power—seizing some of that male power, that logos, and saying 'I.' Both
Bradstreet and Dickinson were extremely conscious of seizing power
through poetry and used language to create self-hood."[8] What is true of the
earlier writers is more than true of Rich herself. In *Diving into the Wreck,* the
seizing of language—or, more precisely, the written word—becomes the
means by which the cleansed self in its "furious awareness" is re-created,
becoming perceiver and namer at once. By using her poetry to insist on her
"I," Rich has acknowledged individuation, what she is as a totality, and has
empowered the woman and the woman vision inside her self, thus making
full integration of her womanhood and her poetic gift, her gender and her
genre, possible.

Although Rich no longer supports the poem in which these terms
appear, it is not too much to say, therefore, that all the poems in *Diving into
the Wreck* are poems of visionary anger, cleansed sight. Like the harsh
opening lines of "The Stranger," they are poems that almost without
exception are deliberately void of the softening effects of poeticalness.
Rooted in the city Rich both loves and hates, and vibrating with the tensed
nerves of Vietnam America, they look with a gaze that is almost too steady

straight into the heart of our lies as if they would burn them out. In their blunt earnestness they hover on the brink of prose.

> In a bookstore on the East Side
> I read a veteran's testimony
>
> the running down, for no reason
> of an old woman in South Vietnam
> by a U.S. Army truck
>
> The heat-wave is over
> Lifeless, sunny, the East Side
> rests under its awnings
>
> Another summer
> The flames go on feeding
>
> and a dull heat permeates the ground
> of the mind. . . .
>   (DW, 46)

Exploding with a lifetime of suppressed or, better perhaps, dissociated rage, *Diving into the Wreck* reads in many ways like a long female *Howl*. Like the wild boy from Aveyron, whose story concludes the volume, Rich rejects the civilized values thrust upon her—"glossed oak planken," the "glass / whirled . . . / to impossible thinness," the "names for things / [he] did not need," including, most significantly, books (DW, 55). She is unable to tell whether her scars, like the slash on the boy's throat, "bear witness / . . . to repair / or to destruction" (DW, 58). Her poems have become a "hierogylph for scream" (DW, 59). The only hope she holds out in this extraordinary volume is the promise of her own internal change and the vague suggestion that something may come of this destruction after all.

> I walk the unconscious forest,
> a woman dressed in old army fatigues
> that have shrunk to fit her, I am lost
> at moments, I feel dazed
> by the sun pawing between the trees,
> cold in the bog and lichen of the thicket.
> Nothing will save this. I am alone,
> kicking the last rotting logs

with their strange smell of life, not death,
wondering what on earth it all might have become.

(DW, 8)

• • •

The rage and sense of futility that permeate *Diving into the Wreck* are due
primarily to the poet's decision to focus her writing on the world that, as she
says in "Merced," "masculinity made / unfit for women or men" (DW,
36). In the work she has written since *Diving, The Dream of a Common
Language* (1974–77), *A Wild Patience Has Taken Me This Far* (1978–81),
Sources (1981–82), and the loose poems collected in *Poems Selected and New*
(1975) and *The Fact of a Doorframe* (1984), she balances this vision by
exploring the possibilities for re-creation and re-vision that lie within her
sexual and political commitment to women. For Rich the move to lesbianism has meant considerably more than simply a switch in sexual preference.
It has also meant, as she declared in a highly controversial speech before the
Modern Language Association in 1976, "desiring [her]self . . . choosing
[her]self" as a woman and choosing her bond or connection to other
women. "Even before I wholly knew I was a lesbian," the poet told this
predominantly heterosexual audience of English professors,

> it was the lesbian in me who pursued that elusive configuration. And I
> believe it is the lesbian in every woman who is compelled by female
> energy, who gravitates toward strong women, who seeks a literature that
> will express that energy and strength. It is the lesbian in us who drives us
> to feel imaginatively, render in language, grasp, the full connection
> between woman and woman. It is the lesbian in us who is creative, for
> the dutiful daughter of the fathers in us is only a hack.   (OL, 200–201)

From Rich's point of view lesbianism has brought the possibility of new
energy and strength into her verse. In "the full connection between woman
and woman," as she told Elly Bulkin in the *Conditions* interview, she has
found "a new center from which to voice compassion, human caring, [and]
the protection of life"[9] and thus a means, so long sought, to bring the
"energy of relation" and the "energy of creation" (her autonomous creative
potential and her need for love, whether for adults or children) finally into
harmony with each other.

For Rich this has meant the possibility of "a whole new poetry beginning
here," a poetry dedicated not to the world masculinity made but to "the

many-lived, unending / forms in which [as a woman] she finds herself," a poetry not of the cold, isolated ego but of her own enduring connection to the *materia* of this world. In the magnificent conclusion of "Transcendental Etude," she writes:

Vision begins to happen in such a life
as if a woman quietly walked away
from the argument and jargon in a room
and sitting down in the kitchen, began turning in her lap
bits of yarn, calico and velvet scraps,
laying them out absently on the scrubbed boards
in the lamplight, with small rainbow-colored shells
sent in cotton-wool from somewhere far away,
and skeins of milkweed from the nearest meadow—
original domestic silk, the finest findings—
and the darkblue petal of the petunia,
and the dry darkbrown lace of seaweed;
not forgotten either, the shed silver
whisker of the cat,
the spiral of paper-wasp-nest curling
beside the finch's yellow feather.
Such a composition has nothing to do with eternity,
the striving for greatness, brilliance —
only with the musing of a mind
one with her body, experienced fingers, quietly pushing
dark against bright, silk against roughness,
pulling the tenets of a life together
with no mere will to mastery,
only care for the many-lived, unending
forms in which she finds herself,
becoming now the sherd of broken glass
slicing light in a corner, dangerous
to flesh, now the plentiful, soft leaf
that wrapped round the throbbing finger, soothes the wound;
and now the stone foundation, rockshelf further
forming underneath everything that grows.

(DCL, 76–77)

No longer blinded by her exclusive commitment to her father's values, Rich is now seeking in the specifically nontranscendental world[10] of the body, the womanly or maternal body she ignored for so long, a new way to use and heal her mind and thus to reconcile the father and the mother within herself—what she once called her male and female sides. In lesbianism, as "Sibling Mysteries" reveals, Rich has found a way to recover the pre-oedipal mother, the mother she never really had, and to draw from her woman's body a different kind of poetry and strength. To her sister and sisters she writes:

> Remind me how we loved our mother's body
> our mouths drawing the first
> thin sweetness from her nipples
>
> our faces dreaming hour on hour
> in the salt smell of her lap   Remind me
> how her touch melted childgrief
>
> how she floated great and tender in our dark
> or stood guard over us
> against our willing
>
> and how we thought she loved
> the strange male body first
> that took, that took, whose taking seemed a law
>
> and how she sent us weeping
> into that law
>
> (DCL, 48)

By her own account Rich decided to act on her sexual feelings for women only after reading a book or, rather, a poem. Home sick with the flu in January 1974, she came upon Judy Grahn's "A Woman Is Talking to Death" in *Amazon Quarterly,* a now-defunct lesbian literary journal of unusually high quality. Grahn's poem is a tour de force, one of the most remarkable pieces yet to come out of the feminist poetry movement. According to Rich (OL, 250), writing the poem frightened Grahn herself, so powerful is its vision of female self-betrayal and the need for commitment among women. But for Rich, it was precisely this message that she had been waiting to hear. "It was," she tells Elly Bulkin,

> the power of the poem, it was the meshing of the poem with where I was at that point, it was as though I had been waiting for that, as though I'd been waiting for something, certain words in a certain order. . . . in some way it had to be confirmed through language. There were plenty of

women with whom it could have happened and nearly did, but it had to happen first in that way. . . . in that sense, I could say that a poem changed my life. My life would have changed anyway, but language was the catalyst.[11]

Reduced to its simplest terms, Grahn's point in "A Woman Is Talking to Death," a very long and complicated poem, is that as long as women continue to give their love, their loyalty, their obedience, or even their attention to men rather than to each other, they are giving it to death. Forced into an awareness of her own choices, her lifetime of betrayals, by witnessing a freak accident, which she describes in the poem, Grahn vows never again to participate in the patriarchal system that has exploited and oppressed women and separated them from each other. "To my lovers," she writes in the poem's grotesquely gothic conclusion,

>   I bequeath
> the rest of my life.
> I want nothing left of me for you, ho death
> except some fertilizer
> for the next batch of us
> who do not hold hands with you
> who do not embrace you
> who try not to work for you
> or sacrifice themselves or trust
> or believe you, ho ignorant
> death, how do you know
> we happened to you?
>
> wherever our meat hangs on our own bones
> for our own use
> your pot is so empty
> death, ho death
> you shall be poor[12]

In her 1977 introduction to Grahn's poetry, Rich observes that the point here "is not the 'exclusion' of men; it is [the] *primary presence of women to ourselves and each other*" (OL, 250). Like Mary Daly, whom she cites, Rich believes that it is only in this *"primary presence"* that "the crucible of a new language," a truly woman-centered poetry, will be found. And, indeed, it is precisely from this "primary presence of women to ourselves and each other" that much of Rich's own new poetry has been drawn.

The poems that Rich has written since *Diving into the Wreck* are filled with the lives of other women. To name them almost at random: Marie Curie, Elvira Shatayev, Paula Becker, Clara Westhoff, the woman who died in her forties, the frontier women, the weavers and spinners, Ethel Rosenberg, Rich's mother, her grandmothers, her mother-in-law, her sister, her past and present lovers, Julia Penelope in Nebraska, Willa Cather, Simone Weil, the Hohokam, Mary Jane Colter, Emily Dickinson, the Black girl falsely arrested by the Boston police, Falconetti's Saint Joan, Audre Lorde, refugee women, an alleged murderess, Makeba, the goose girl, Citizen Kane's mother, the landscape architect in her fourth month, Ellen Glasgow, the nineteenth-century suffragists whom she lists by name in "Culture and Anarchy," the *"exceptional / even deviant"* nineteenth-century women of "Heroines," and the "ordinary" women of "Natural Resources." These women, both fictive and real, are the dark and the bright, the silk and the rough, out of which the poet attempts to pull "the tenets of a life together." To them, in the person of Elvira Shatayev, leader of the all-woman climbing team that died on Lenin peak in August 1974, Rich attributes her own most deeply held belief in the necessity for bonding or community among women. To the poet this bonding now appears more important than physical survival itself.

> *We know now we have always been in danger*
> *down in our separateness*
> *and now up here together   but till now*
> *we had not touched our strength*

> In the diary torn from my fingers I had written
> *What does love mean*
> *what does it mean   "to survive"*
> *A cable of blue fire ropes our bodies*
> *burning together in the snow   We will not live*
> *to settle for less   We have dreamed of this*
> *all of our lives*
>
> (DCL, 6)

And it is this belief, this dream, that her poems, like a "cable of blue fire," now celebrate. As she declares in "Origins and History of Consciousness," "the true nature of poetry" lies in "The drive / to connect. The dream of a common language" (DCL, 7). And this drive, this dream, has become the motivating power behind her verse. It is a drive that, as "Sibling Mysteries" makes clear, Rich cannot separate from the recovery of the missing and silenced mother within herself.

In the long poem "From an Old House in America," written in 1974 but collected only in her volumes of selected poetry, Rich's determination to connect herself through language to other women receives its most elaborate and powerful expression. Set in the Vermont farmhouse she and her husband once shared, and which still haunts her with memories of their failure and his suicide, the poem gradually moves from the poet's contemplation of her immediate situation, surrounded by the detritus of the past and frustrated by her incomplete connections with the dead, to a meditation on her power to raise the "undead," to bring the women of America "back on the road of birth" (PSN, 238). In the course of the poem she becomes all these women—the original immigrant populations who crossed the Bering Strait from Siberia to Alaska at the end of the last ice age, the Black women shipped here under intolerable conditions to be slaves, the refugee women who accompanied their husbands to the United States in the nineteenth century, looking for a better life —all women who, willingly or unwillingly, have helped to people this continent.

> shipped here to be fruitful
>
> my body a hollow ship
> bearing sons to the wilderness
>
> sons who ride away
> on horseback, daughters
>
> whose juices drain like mine
> into the *arroyo* of stillbirths, massacres
>
> Hanged as witches, sold as breeding-wenches
> my sisters leave me
>
> I am not the wheatfield
> nor the virgin forest
>
> I never chose this place
> yet I am of it now
>
> (PSN, 238–39)

Whatever their circumstances, however alone, however cut off from other women or indeed from their own womanhood, they accepted the conditions under which they lived and did what they had to do in order to survive.

> In my decent collar, in the daguerrotype [sic]
> I pierce its legend with my look
>
> my hands wring the necks of prairie chickens
> I am used to blood
>
> When the men hit the hobo track
> I stay on with the children
>
> my power is brief and local
> but I know my power
>
> I have lived in isolation
> from other women, so much
>
> in the mining camps, the first cities
> the Great Plains winters
>
> Most of the time, in my sex, I was alone
>   (PSN, 239)

Yet, though she is compassionate toward the suffering these women endured, Rich does not allow herself to romanticize them. If their willingness to accept their labor and their isolation was their strength, enabling them individually to survive, it was their weakness as well. Unwilling or unable to bond together, they remained the perennial victims of male needs, only making do, in effect, with what men offered. However real their power was, therefore, it was also "brief and local." Separated from each other, they remained at the mercy of men, obedient to male law and to the control men exercised over their sexuality.

> Her children dead of diphtheria, she
> set herself on fire with kerosene
>
> (O Lord I was unworthy
> Thou didst find me out)
>
> she left the kitchen scrubbed
> down to the marrow of its boards

"The penalty for barrenness
is emptiness

my punishment is my crime
what I have failed to do, is me . . ."
                    (PSN, 241)

In "From an Old House in America," Rich wants more, therefore, than simply to connect herself to the past. The study and assimilation of the past—one's identification with it—is, she argues, the foundation upon which the future must be built. If "the order of things" is to be changed (PSN, 244), if men are no longer to be able to treat women merely as objects of "lust and fear" (PSN, 242), using them as they see fit, then, Rich contends, women today must recognize that they too are "in danger" (PSN, 242). Difficult or frightening as it may be, they must give up their isolation and assert their connections with each other, as mothers and daughters, as sisters, lovers, and friends.

and yes, we will be dangerous
to ourselves

groping through spines of nightmare
(*datura* tangling with a simpler herb)

because the line dividing
lucidity from darkness

is yet to be marked out

Isolation, the dream
of the frontier woman

leveling her rifle along
the homestead fence

still snares our pride
—a suicidal leaf

laid under the burning-glass
in the sun's eye

Any woman's death diminishes me
                    (PSN, 244–45)

In appropriating Donne's great line to conclude her own poem, Rich has undoubtedly offended a number of literary critics. But within the context established by the poem, Rich's use and "re-vision" of this line is justified not only because she is referring specifically to women but because whatever its defenders say, the generic *he* that Donne employs ("Any man's death diminishes me") does not and never has included women. Women were outside the rights and laws that provided the foundation for human liberty in this country and declared all "men" created equal. Women's needs and desires were not part of the thinking that went into the conquest of this land where "man fought," as the historical marker outside Red Cloud, Nebraska, says, "to establish a home" (WP, 16). Women's inclusion in Donne's line is, therefore, no more axiomatic than it was axiomatic for the framers of the Declaration of Independence and the Constitution to include women in their thinking about "equal rights" or for the frontiersman to be concerned with the loneliness and labor he imposed on his wife in his drive to fulfill his own personal destiny to "conquer the land" and the aboriginal peoples living on it.

By taking over and rewriting Donne's famous admonition, Rich is in effect warning women that only when they have broken through the isolation imposed on them socially, psychologically, and linguistically by patriarchal assumptions that a priori do not include them will they be able to achieve the fullness of humanity that Donne, through his very use of the generic *he, takes for granted for men*. Only when women accept, that is, their bonds with other women, will they cease to be objects in their own eyes and in the eyes of others and become fully themselves.

> In the diary I wrote: *Now we are ready*
> *and each of us knows it   I have never loved*
> *like this   I have never seen*
> *my own forces so taken up and shared*
> *and given back*
>
> *After the long training   the early sieges*
> *we are moving almost effortlessly in our love*
>
> In the diary as the wind   began to tear
> at the tents over us   I wrote:
> *We know now we have always been in danger*
> *down in our separateness*
> *and now up here together   but till now*
> *we had not touched our strength*
>
> (DCL, 5–6)

• • •

For Rich the vision of community implicit in her love for women, like her recognition of patriarchal oppression, has been a liberating one. It has made it possible for her to draw on history, myth, and dream to give herself and other women a sense of womanly power. Equally important, it has allowed her to use language in new ways: as a source of connection and transcendence rather than simply, as in so much of her sixties poetry, as an instrument for the release, usually in disguised forms, of anger and pain. It has encouraged Rich to exploit the capacity for beauty and tenderness within her voice, and it has given her a concept of womanhood from which she has obviously drawn great personal strength. It has, in effect, restored her "mother" to her and allowed her to love the woman inside herself.

But as she suggests by the very title of the volume in which this vision of community first appears, *The Dream of a Common Language,* Rich is also keenly aware of just how difficult it will be to sustain these connections in the real world and among real people.

Although little has been made of it, there are two distinct strands in Rich's lesbian-feminist poetry. The first, which I have already discussed, is visionary. It presents the poet as "pioneer, witness, prophet."[13] But there is a second, equally important strand, which places the poet in quite a different, decidedly more complex and ambiguous light. In this poetry, a poetry of self-exploration and self-revelation, Rich appears less as a prophet or wise woman than as "a woman of [our] time," a woman not just "obsessed with Love our subject," but determined, often at great cost, to come to grips with her many, conflicting selves, with her past and present, her weakness as well as her strength. While this poetry usually lacks the beauty and fervor of Rich's finest visionary work, it compensates for this loss by complicating and enriching what otherwise might have become an entirely unquestioning, unworldly, and monolithic art.

In the poem "Splittings," written in 1974, at the time she came out, Rich promises herself a new start in lesbianism and an end to the old dichotomies between mind and body, love and action, the personal and the political, which, like her Christian-Jewish heritage, have left her "split at the root."

> The world tells me I am its creature
> I am raked by eyes   brushed by hands
> I want to crawl into her for refuge   lay my head
> in the space   between her breast and shoulder
> abnegating power for love

```
as women have done      or hiding
from power in her love      like a man
I refuse these givens      the splitting
between love and action      I am choosing
not to suffer uselessly      and not to use her
I choose to love      this time      for once
with all my intelligence
```
                                    (DCL, 11)

But it is a promise she has only fitfully been able to keep.

"Twenty-One Love Poems" in *Dream of a Common Language* is Rich's longest and most successful attempt to deal with the interface between love and action, between the lovers and the larger world with which they must contend on a daily basis. Yet as a love sequence, it ends with a failed relationship. The two women, who seek to root their "animal passion" in the city (DCL, 25), are defeated not only by the outside forces arrayed against them, but by their own inner unreadiness to cope with the dangers they must confront. They are not, as Rich reminds herself and her beloved, "heroines" "fated or doomed" like Tristan and Isolde "to love" (DCL, 33). They fail before the very ordinariness of love: the petty squabbles, the minor distances they cannot bridge, the choices they do not take responsibility for. As Rich herself says baldly at one point,

```
two women together is a work
nothing in civilization has made simple,
two people together is a work
herioc in its ordinariness,
the slow-picked, halting traverse of a pitch
where the fiercest attention becomes routine
—look at the faces of those who have chosen it.
```
                                    (DCL, 35)

Without the support of the society at large, which degrades them as women and condemns them as lesbians, the lovers cannot complete this work. Nor can they maintain this pitch. The hopefulness with which the sequence opens ("in these hands / I could trust the world" [DCL, 27–28]) gradually dissipates. At the end of the series, the poet finds herself once more, as so often in her life, alone. Unable to keep the one she loves from "drowning in secrets" (DCL, 35) or to close with words the huge gap that has developed between them, she is forced to choose again the circle of solitude and power in which so much of her own life has been spent, the circle of the mind.

> . . . this is not Stonehenge
> simply nor any place but the mind
> casting back to where her solitude
> shared, could be chosen without loneliness
> not easily nor without pains to stake out
> the circle, the heavy shadows, the great light.
> I choose to be a figure in that light,
> half-blotted by darkness, something moving
> across that space, the color of stone
> greeting the moon, yet more than stone,
> a woman. I choose to walk here. And to draw this circle
>
> (DCL, 35–36)

These are brave words, surely, strikingly reminiscent of Rich's brilliant description of Emily Dickinson in "'I am in Danger—Sir.'"

> you . . .
> chose to have it out at last
> on your own premises
>
> (NL, 33)

But they are also, finally, a measure of the poet's defeat. The healing of the mind-body split, which she captures so exquisitely in the sequence's unnumbered or "floating" poem ("Whatever happens with us your body / will haunt mine" [DCL, 32]—the only explicitly erotic poem Rich has ever published), is entirely undone. The poet once more confronts the world not only alone but internally divided. After a brief period of harmony, she has again become a "Philoctetes / in woman's form . . . / fighting the temptation to make a career of pain" (DCL, 28, 29).[14]

In her most recent works, *A Wild Patience Has Taken Me This Far, Sources,* and the few new poems collected in *The Fact of a Doorframe,* Rich has made coming to terms with her own internal division, her wounds and her power, a chief priority. While still works of impassioned political awareness, much of this poetry exhibits, as Helen Vendler claims, an overwhelming concern with "what it is to be Adrienne Rich in middle age—her investigations, her commitments, her memories, her outrage."[15] Indeed, these last three volumes contain the most directly biographical and confessional material Rich has written to date. And at points, as in the following lines from "Mother-in-law" and "Rift," the poet's honesty, her determination to expose and confront herself, may well strike the reader as too raw, too unmediated, as Vendler argues, by art.

> Your son is dead
> ten years, I am a lesbian,
> my children are themselves.
> Mother-in-law, before we part
> shall we try again? Strange as I am,
> strange as you are? what do mothers
> ask their own daughters, everywhere in the world?
> Is there a question?
> Ask me something.
>
> (WP, 32)

> When language fails us, when we fail each other
> there is no exorcism. The hurt continues. Yes, your scorn
> turns up the jet of my anger. Yes, I find you
> overweening, obsessed, and even in your genius
> narrow-minded—I could list much more—
> and absolute loyalty was never in my line
> once having left it in my father's house—
>
> (WP, 49)

It is almost as if (and it may well be) Rich has decided to follow the advice that, according to Joyce Greenberg, she gave to her students: "to include all the complexities, the imperfections, the confusions"[16] in their verse no matter what the formal cost. "Poetry," she told Greenberg, "is a way of expressing unclear feeling."[17] For Rich her recent poetry has become a way of expressing unclear feeling about the self, where she has been, where she is now, and what she has to look forward to.

As Greenberg—who found Rich's advice not a little disconcerting— seems to have recognized, in writing this way Rich is taking huge risks with her verse. Not only is she, as in the above quotations, jeopardizing linguistic control, but she is confiding more to her reader than most poets would consider it prudent to confess.[18] For better or worse, we learn of her weaknesses, her inner conflicts and her evasions. In the remarkable and poignant poem "Transit," Rich treats at gut level the way she has used her disabling arthritic condition to make a "career of pain," allowing her anger or self-pity to disable her further. In "Integrity" she deals with her longing for wholeness; in "Images" she describes her need for refuge: "I wished to cry loose my soul / into her, to become / free of speech   at last" (WP, 5). In "For Memory" she deals with accusations of disloyalty and betrayal that have been leveled against her. In "Rift" and *Sources* she levels these same accusations against herself.

And if my look becomes the bomb that rips
the family home apart

is this betrayal, that the walls
slice off, the staircase shows

torn-away above the street
that the closets where the clothes hung

hang naked . . ?

(S, 22)

If she still is, as she claims, a "woman with a mission, not to win prizes / but to change the laws of history," she is also the woman who has been "gripped" by "a desert absolute" and forced into choices not entirely her own. The child who copied her "sedulous lines" has become the poet who knows what it means to explode "the boundaries of perfection" and to betray those from whom her mission originally came.

The faithful drudging child
the child at the oak desk whose penmanship,
hard work, style will win her prizes
becomes the woman with a mission, not to win prizes
but to change the laws of history
How she gets this mission
is not clear, how the boundaries of perfection
explode, leaving her cheekbone grey with smoke
a piece of her hair singed off, her shirt
spattered with earth . . . Say that she grew up in a house
with talk of books, ideal societies—
she is gripped by a blue, a foreign air,
a desert absolute: dragged by the roots of her own will
into another scene of choices

(S, 30)

In all these poems it is clear that Rich has paid a steep price for turning her back on the faithful child, the dutiful daughter, she had been. Viewed from her father's perspective, the perspective she uses in *Sources,* however much the product of a "desert absolute," her evolution from dutiful daughter to lesbian poet has also involved her in a lifetime of betrayal. It is no wonder that in "Transit," "For Ethel Rosenberg," "Grandmothers," "Mother-in-Law," "The Spirit of the Place," "In the Wake of Home," and

Sources itself, Rich seems to be writing in the interrogatory mode, questioning over and over again what happened in the past and her relation to it. It is the pieces of herself, not just the lives of other women, that she is now attempting to bring together.

> *With whom do you believe your lot is cast?*
> *From where does your strength come?*
>
> I think somehow, somewhere
> every poem of mine must repeat those questions
>
> which are not the same. There is a *whom*, a *where*
> that is not chosen   that is given   and sometimes falsely given
>
> In the beginning we grasp whatever we can
> to survive

> (S, 12)

For those who wish to see in Rich only the visionary, the prophet, such poetry will have little appeal. It is, indeed, as Vendler asserts, a form of "realist oratory," in which beauty and imagination are often subordinated to more immediate personal ends. But as the poet says, again and again, she is not simple. And writing such poetry has clearly become a vital means for her to keep in touch with herself, not as she wishes to be or as others want her to be, but as she actually is. Insofar as it is more real, it may in the end tell us more about the complicated and conflicting reality of women's lives today and about their true selves than Rich's visionary poetry, with its tendency toward an essentialist definition of womanhood can.

Rich's turn to lesbianism has unquestionably enriched and deepened her poetic voice. But the poetic persona that emerges from a complete study of Adrienne Rich's lesbian-feminist poetry is a far more complex, difficult, and arresting individual than the definition of womanhood controlling such well-known poems as "Transcendental Étude," "Sibling Mysteries," and "Natural Resources" would allow. In these latter poems Rich's need to restore the mother and to reconnect herself to other women leads her to mute, even on occasion to invalidate, what is idiosyncratically powerful in herself. The poet becomes woman as she emphasizes in her own voice those qualities that she views as historically and quintessentially female: silence, nurturance, and bonding.

But these qualities, however necessary to the protection of human life, are not the primary qualities that either now or over the years have distinguished Arnold Rich's poet daughter. Nor is it likely that we would have from Rich the body of poetry we now possess, including the great visionary poems, if they had been. Feminism recharged for Rich poetic energies that seemed in effect to be dying. It gave her a context by which to understand her experience and to know herself as woman. Her commitment to feminism was liberating because it greatly expanded her emotional and thematic repertoire and allowed her to own both her anger and her tenderness in her verse. But when treated as a specific set of political beliefs, promulgating fixed notions of what men and women are, feminism can only narrow the poet's art, and as in Rich's visionary poems—move it back to a definition of female sensibility virtually indistinguishable in many respects from Woolf's Angel in the House.

For all her authentic commitment to feminist vision, Rich has found her own way to resist this narrowing. She remains, as she has always been, her father's daughter, a woman in whom the conflict between what we conventionally think of as male and female qualities continues to be pitched and vivid. It is this conflict that has given Rich's verse its peculiar flavor and shaped its particular destiny and that continues to make her vitally important for us today. For Rich, the achievement of integration through feminism has not meant the elimination of contradictions and differences within the self. It has meant their acceptance. As she says in a poem aptly titled "Integrity" in *A Wild Patience*, wholeness has come through the appreciation of the internal polarities that make us all complete.

In the final poem in *A Wild Patience*, the multisectioned "Turning the Wheel," written in 1981, Rich includes two portraits of a desert witch or "shamaness" belonging to the lost tribe of the Hohokam (a Pima name that, according to Rich's notes, may be translated either as "those who have ceased" or "those who were used up" [WP, 61]). While these poems are unusually powerful in their own right, the fact that they are also self-portraits of the artist gives them special value, the more so since they appear to contain clear warnings on how Rich now wishes to be understood by the community for whom she largely writes. Printed on opposite facing pages in the published text, the two poems function as glosses on each other. The first poem is entitled "Particularity," the second, "Apparition," but finally, they are two sides of a single coin.

> In search of the desert witch, the shamaness
> forget the archetypes, forget the dark
> and lithic profile, do not scan the clouds
> massed on the horizon, violet and green,

for her icon, do not pursue
the ready-made abstraction, do not peer for symbols.
So long as you want her faceless, without smell
or voice, so long as she does not squat
to urinate, or scratch herself, so long
as she does not snore beneath her blanket
or grimace as she grasps the stone-cold
grinding stone at dawn
so long as she does not have her own peculiar
face, slightly wall-eyed or with a streak
of topaz lightning in the blackness
of one eye, so long as she does not limp
so long as you try to simplify her meaning
so long as she merely symbolizes power
she is kept helpless and conventional
her true power routed backward
into the past, we cannot touch or name her
and, barred from participation by those who need her
she stifles in unspeakable loneliness.

If she appear, hands ringed with rings
you have dreamed about, if on her large fingers
jasper and sardonyx and agate smolder
if she is wearing shawls woven in fire
and blood, if she is wearing shawls
of undyed fiber, yellowish
if on her neck are hung
obsidian and silver, silver and turquoise
if she comes skirted like a Christian
her hair combed back by missionary fingers
if she sits offering her treasure by the road
to spare a brother's or an uncle's dignity
or if she sits pretending
to weave or grind or do some other thing
for the appeasement of the ignorant
if she is the famous potter
whose name confers honor on certain vessels
if she is wrist-deep in mud and shawled in dust
and wholly anonymous
look at her closely if you dare
do not assume you know those cheekbones
or those eye-sockets; or that still-bristling hair.

                              (WP, 56–57)

Through obvious parallels in syntactic structure and rhetorical technique, Rich has paired these poems, creating two views of a woman who sounds very much like the poet herself. She is an artist. She is famous. She is viewed as a symbol. She is human. She has betrayed herself. Like her hair, her spirit still bristles. But the perspective in each poem is quite different. In the first poem, as the title "Particularity" indicates, it is the witch's specific being, her existential reality, we are asked to accept. She is not an abstraction nor a symbol. She has her own peculiar face and voice. She scratches and urinates. She smells and snores. She has faults. She limps. Above all, she is not simple. To attempt to simplify her, to reduce her to an abstraction, even an abstract symbol of power, is to route her power back into the past, depriving her of the ability to participate with those who need her now. Thus heroinized, she will be "kept helpless and conventional." Ultimately, her real power will be destroyed.

In "Apparition," on the other hand, it is not the witch's particularity, her *this*ness, we are asked to accept but rather the integrity of the self that lies beneath her many selves. She may be famous or wholly anonymous, all or seemingly nothing that we want. But what matters is that beneath all her masks, her disguises, like the "rockshelf" that lies beneath "everything that grows," a single identity does exist, an identity that will terrify because it is fully aware of its self: its wounds and its power.

The point that Rich is making with these two poems could not, in my opinion, be more clear. Rich herself chose to assume the role of "pioneer, witness, prophet." And in this role she has amassed a tremendous following, becoming the very kind of leader and explorer that Auden, with such unintended irony, claimed our period could not and should not try to produce. She is, or she has seemed to be, as Greenberg writes, the wise woman a generation of women writers "could safely choose to follow." "If we look at the poetry American women have been writing for the last two decades, and want to delineate their discoveries," Alicia Ostriker declares, "it is Rich, over and over again, who says a thing most plainly, most memorably—because she has understood it."[19] Her dreams and visions and her moral passion have unquestionably made her one of the major voices in American poetry today.[20]

But for Adrienne Rich to survive and to continue to grow, she must also be herself: a woman of our time, a woman who has faults, who has failed, who does limp, who carries her wounds as well as her power in hands that are "ringed with rings" both precious and plain.

Whether Rich can do this, given the various pressures on her and her own internal need to be spokeswoman for a community—to be, as she notes in the very recent "North American Time," "politically correct" (FD, 324)—remains to be seen. For now it is enough that, as in the past two decades, Rich stands ready to confront openly and without apology the confusion and conflicting loyalties which are her—and our—lot. There is, as she says, no simple answer to the question of our sources, nor, as Woolf warned, will there be any simple way for us to discover who or what a woman is.

Conclusion:
The Muse as Medusa

. . . .
. . . .
. . . .

Most striking among these differences is the imagery of
violence in the boy's response, depicting a world of dangerous confrontation and explosive connection, where she sees
a world of care and protection, a life lived with others
whom "you may love as much or even more than you love
yourself."
— Carol Gilligan

It helped tremendously that by the time it was born I had
no doubts about being a writer. . . . it was not even a
choice . . . but a necessity. When I didn't write I thought
of making bombs and throwing them. Of shooting racists.
Of doing away . . . with myself. Writing saved me from
the sin and *inconvenience* of violence.
— Alice Walker

I don't want the snakes in my head to turn you to stone. I
do not want the heat of my anger to melt you into a puddle.
. . . And yet I don't think that art can exist unless there is
that power to turn you to stone or to melt you to your
gaseous elements.
— Diane Wakoski

Contemplating what she believed to be the sad state of women's literature in 1949, Simone de Beauvoir remarks with characteristic forthrightness toward the conclusion of *The Second Sex*:

> There are many good reasons for [woman's] timidity [as a writer]. To please is her first care; and often she fears she will be displeasing as a woman from the mere fact that she writes. . . . she lacks, further, the courage to be displeasing as a writer. The writer of originality, unless dead, is always shocking, scandalous; novelty disturbs and repels. Woman is still astonished and flattered at being admitted to the world of thought, of art—a masculine world. She is on her best behavior; she is afraid to disarrange, to investigate, to explode; she feels she should seek pardon for her literary pretensions through her modesty and good taste. . . . she gives literature precisely that personal tone which is expected of her. . . . All this helps her excel in the production of best-sellers; but we must not look to her for adventuring along strange ways.[1]

Like Virginia Woolf before her, de Beauvoir had reason to be dissatisfied. Although there were a small number of women authors prior to the 1950s who had openly rebelled against their lot (among them, she names Austen, the Brontës, and Eliot), the majority had not. Rather, throughout history, most women writers had played the Angel in the House, expressing their anger indirectly at best. At worst they determinedly promoted visions of womanhood that stultified their work and lives.

Sometime in the bitter years between 1963 and 1973, however, American women poets stopped trying to please and began to adventure "along strange ways." Made keenly aware of their anger as well as their oppression by the nationwide disruptions of the civil rights movement and the antiwar movement, the "unheard" women in whose name Adrienne Rich agreed to accept the 1974 National Book Award in Poetry were silent no more.[2] Like Rich herself they picked up their loaded guns; and with a zeal unparalleled in women's history, they did everything Simone de Beauvoir said women lacked the courage to do: they investigated; they disarranged; above all, they exploded.

Nothing is more striking in the feminist poetry written in the first decade of the women's movement than the catholicity of its rage. Where women poets writing prior to 1963 had come largely from the white, well-educated, middle class that had produced Dickinson, Plath, and Rich, by 1973 women poets came from virtually every walk of life and from every heretofore silenced minority: not just women of color, but lesbians, older women, working-class women, country women, prisoners, the poor, and, not without irony, mothers. No longer seeking "pardon for [their] literary pretensions," they saw in poetry a direct means by which to express and change their lives. "At home," the Black poet June Jordan recalls,

> I learned the poetry of the Bible and . . . Paul Laurence Dunbar. As a student, I diligently followed orthodox directions from *The Canterbury Tales* right through *The Waste Land* . . , And I kept waiting. . . . what about Dunbar? When was he coming up again? And where were the Black poets altogether? And who were the women poets I might reasonably emulate? And wasn't there, ever, a great poet who was crazy about Brooklyn or furious about war? . . . And I kept reading apparently underground poetry: poetry kept strictly off campus . . . until I knew, for a fact, that there was . . . an American, a New World, poetry that is as personal, as public, as irresistible . . . as necessary . . . as representative, as exalted, as speakably commonplace, and as musical, as an emergency phone call.[3]

Just as it drove poetry out of the arms of academe where it had been all too comfortably ensconced for the preceding three decades, the desire to have a poetry in which one could express one's love for Brooklyn or one's fury at war drove white women and women of color off campus in the 1960s. Determined to make their writing relevant to their lives, these women banded together to form workshops of their own. They set up collectives in kitchens and storefronts. They took to publishing themselves. By 1973 there were at least a dozen journals on the market devoted exclusively to feminist writing, including *Amazon Quarterly, Aphra, Country Women, Lesbian Tide,* and *Second Wave*. Widely divergent in politics as in literary standards, almost all contained some poetry. By that same year enough poetry of quality had been produced to permit the publication of two first-of-their-kind anthologies: *Rising Tides,* edited by Laura Chester and Sharon Barba, and *No More Masks,* edited by Florence Howe and Ellen Bass. In 1974 feminist poetry received official recognition from the establishment when Alice Walker, Audre Lorde, and Adrienne Rich were simultaneously nominated for the National Book Award. What Maxine Kumin calls "the underground river" of women's poetry, "carrying such diverse cargoes as . . . Bogan, Levertov, Rukeyser, Swenson, Plath, Rich, and Sexton,"[4] had met the "rising tide" of the women's movement, and the woman poet qua woman had come into her own.

In a creative phenomenon that duplicates with uncanny accuracy the experience of Dickinson, Plath, and Rich, for women poets generally in this period it was as if the top had blown off. Emotions, fears, needs that had always been there but that had rarely been admitted into consciousness, let alone expressed, were suddenly recognized and released as the anger generated by the social protest movements of the 1960s pushed women further and further toward confrontation with the truth of their inner feelings, what Woolf called "the depths, the dark places." Alicia Ostriker's marvelously detailed recollection of what it was like to be a beset young mother reading Plath in the mid-1960s typifies the course such reactions took.

> My own response, on first reading *Ariel*, was a thought compounded of something like *Good God, it's real* and *Damn, she did it*—as if having "done it" were a triumph—and a physical sensation like that of being slapped hard: rush of adrenalin, stunned amazement. I was stealing time to read . . . from the demands of family and the demands of freshman classes. Either set of duties was inherently infinite, infinitely guilt-producing. Often it seemed I never slept. . . .
>
> If I ask myself in retrospect precisely what I mean by *Damn, she did it,* the answer is complex. . . . Most obviously: she had dared to kill herself, as in all probability, I never would. . . . Second: she had permitted herself emotions which for me were forbidden, and which I spent a considerable amount of effort attempting to repress. Self-loathing, that drug. Loathing of others, especially my near and dear. Desire to kill as well as die. Fury of the trapped animal. Plenty of TNT in that kitchen cabinet. The authenticity of this poet's hatreds was for me nailed down of course by their rootedness in a feminine body and their location among domestic arrangements.[5]

The adrenalin high that Ostriker experienced reading *Ariel* came obviously from seeing her own repressed emotions in print for the first time located "in a feminine body and . . . among domestic arrangements." Self-loathing, the desire to kill one's "near and dear," and so on, were hardly new emotions to literature. But in such overt, even outrageous, form their expression was new to women writers. As a woman, more than that, as a woman poet using the lyric "I," Plath had finally said what thousands of women in her own and Ostriker's generation felt, but which they could not allow themselves to acknowledge. And in releasing the darkness and malignity that lay at her core like "TNT" in a "kitchen cabinet," or like a loaded but unused gun, Plath had shown such women how to own their anger in their art.

What Plath did for Ostriker in the mid-sixties, by 1970 women generally were doing for each other. Like an avalanche that gathers momentum as it feeds upon itself, the rage generated by feminism's consciousness-raising techniques led women deeper and deeper into themselves and onto paths women writers had never traveled before. Thus Erica Jong writes of a visit by a well-known critic to her undergraduate creative writing class (he told the students that women could never be great writers because they didn't know about "Blood and Guts"):

> It's ironic that Mr Distinguished Critic should have identified Blood and Guts as the thing that women writers supposedly lacked, because in the first years of the women's movement, there was so *much* Blood and Guts in women's writing that one wondered if women writers ever did anything but menstruate and rage. Released from the prison of propriety, blessedly released from having to pretend meekness, gratefully in touch with our own cleansing anger, we raged and mocked and menstruated through whole volumes of prose and poetry.[6]

Filled with precisely the kind of imagery that Carol Gilligan claims women do not use — the imagery of violence and confrontation[7] — the poems these women wrote reflected their compelling need to understand themselves in wholly different terms, not as good girls or dutiful daughters, but as women of power.

Of the images women chose to express their newly discovered sense of self, none is more striking for its ubiquitousness in the early years of the women's movement than the figure of Medusa. In a radical revision of traditional archetypes, Medusa, the angry or unangelic underside of the self, became the muse. In her darkness and rage, as May Sarton writes, these poets now found a source of life. Like Dickinson's gun, but without the gun's intractable masculine associations, Medusa became the passionate symbol for the woman poet's liberated self. In "The Muse as Medusa," Sarton writes:

> I saw you once, Medusa; we were alone.
> I looked you straight in the cold eye, cold.
> I was not punished, was not turned to stone—
> How to believe the legends I am told?
> . . . .
> Forget the image: your silence is my ocean,
> And even now it teems with life. You chose
> To abdicate by total lack of motion,
> But did it work, for nothing really froze?

It is all fluid still, that world of feeling
Where thoughts, those fishes, silent, feed and rove;
And, fluid, it is also full of healing,
For love is healing, even rootless love.

I turn your face around! it is my face.
That frozen rage is what I must explore—
Oh secret, self-enclosed, and ravaged place!
This is the gift I thank Medusa for.[8]

In taking Medusa for their muse, women poets of the past two decades are owning themselves, that is, they are owning those aspects of their being that their families and society have invalidated by treating such qualities as unfeminine and unacceptable. And in repossessing these aspects of themselves they are repossessing the creative as well as the destructive energies to which they give rise. Two poems on Medusa, one by Louise Bogan, written in 1923, the other by Karen Lindsey, published in 1975, will illustrate my point.

With extraordinary brilliance, Louise Bogan's poem on Medusa perfectly captures a vision of the gorgon that both symbolizes and embodies Medusa's traditional horror.

I had come to the house, in a cave of trees,
Facing a sheer sky.
Everything moved,—a bell hung ready to strike,
Sun and reflection wheeled by.

When the bare eyes were before me
And the hissing hair,
Held up at a window, seen through a door.
The stiff bald eyes, the serpents on the forehead
Formed in the air.

This is a dead scene forever now.
Nothing will ever stir.
The end will never brighten it more than this,
Nor the rain blur.

The water will always fall, and will not fall,
And the tipped bell make no sound.

The grass will always be growing for hay
Deep on the ground.

And I shall stand here like a shadow
Under the great balanced day,
My eyes on the yellow dust, that was lifting in the wind,
And does not drift away.[9]

Forced to look upon the gorgon's monstrous visage, the speaker is paralyzed
by the sight. Unable to escape the bald eyes and snake hair, or to embrace
them, she is suspended where she stands and the world she inhabits is
suspended with her. Her eyes are locked forever on the "yellow dust" that,
lifted, "does not drift away." The "tipped bell" will "make no sound."
Both she and everything around her are frozen by this nightmare vision of
the terror latent in female power. In its death-like stasis, "Medusa" is a
poem that, for all its artistic perfection, seems in retrospect tragically
appropriate for a poet of extraordinary gifts who believed only 105 of her
poems worthy of permanent record and who appears to have despised the
very idea that she might be considered a woman poet.[10]

Read against Bogan's "Medusa," Karen Lindsey's brief treatment of the
gorgon could not be more radically different in style, tone, and conclusion.
While not as finished a work of art, Lindsey's "medusa" breathes with the
one quality Bogan's poem deliberately lacks: life. Indeed, it is so alive it
almost seems to writhe on the page.

listen i'm telling you it's
every bit as ugly as you think it is
ive seen it ive stared at it, it
tears your stomach out you
scream you claw the air the pain
holds on, holds on, listen
youre not imagining too much youre
not imagining anything, believe me it
burns your face off with its smile
you scream believe me you
scream you run you cry
but the legends are wrong.

it is those who do not look
who turn to stone.[11]

Where Bogan wrote a metrically subtle poem, complete with rhyme scheme and line ends that make syntactical sense, Lindsey has written a poem whose manners are deliberately, flagrantly bad. Ragged and irregular in construction, its short, broken lines violate sentence grammar and violate the mind. The poem hurts to read. Yet if it hurts, it hurts, as Lindsey asserts in her conclusion, with life not death. Yes, there is ugliness. There is pain. But to the unequivocally feminist poet, it is those who cannot confront these qualities who turn to stone.

Lindsey's inside-out approach to the Medusa myth is based on her implicit acceptance of fundamentally unfeminine, not to mention asocial, qualities within herself. In a considerably longer and more intellectualized version of the Medusa myth, written between 1974 and 1978, Rachel Blau DuPlessis makes this acceptance explicit as she transforms Medusa's story into a tale of female individuation and self-integration.

Even more than Lindsey, DuPlessis employs a tortured irregular form of verse to express Medusa's ugliness and the violence that makes possible her coming to life. At the conclusion of the poem, Medusa must literally give birth to herself out of the darkness (that which Audre Lorde calls the "Black . . . creative . . . female . . . dark . . . rejected . . . [and] messy")[12] within her.

> Tunnel black mouth
> screams in the open
> Propulsive echo-long
> howl from my own tunnel
> Resounding in the round tunnel
> I have unburied
> I wrench the root cord.
>
> With every thick stone split
> a knotty pulp
> root-rattle, stem-snattle
> corona open(r)ing
> in the cave-heavy corridor.
> Roots up! Rouse up!
> It shoots out from inside.
>
> Ten hundred heads blood-rich from mine
> my lava head, my rocky mine.
> The spout the burst the leap
> of sight

The spurt the spoke the ken
of voice

in sight, my netted reach
in voice, my knotted speech.[13]

Like Sarton and Lindsey, DuPlessis is concerned with the way in which
tradition has turned Medusa's legend against her; and the poet firmly
locates the gorgon's rage in her fury or male appropriation of that which she
is. In the first section of the poem, DuPlessis objectifies Medusa, employing
the third person in order to describe the ways in which Medusa's being, the
being of woman, has been faceted or fragmented by men in their "dis-
course." The pun on "balls" emphasizes the sexual nature of the struggle for
linguistic control and the control of myth that is occurring between them.

She is the thing he
flickers with his light.
She sees it
thru his eyes

her days thru his rays
her face thru his orbs
her phase thru his eye-
balls.

Her he can and as he can
he ken and names the
knowing:
breaks her

in
to being ridden.
over the half-spoken,
over the forgotten.[14]

In the poem it is up to Medusa to "unbury" and "re-member" herself.
Instead of beating her "emptied self" against "the rock [her] mother," as
she does at one point in the poem, she must "wrench" her own "root cord"
and "rouse up" the "ten hundred heads blood-rich" that live as volcanic
potentials within her. If language and self, sight and voice, speech and
reach, have been stolen from her, only she can win them back. But to do so

she must be willing to re-enter the long "round tunnel" of her birth canal. She must confront the darkness within herself if she is to recover the source of her power as well as her life and if she is to escape male domination in life and language.

What matters most from my point of view is that in neither Lindsey's nor in DuPlessis's poem is there any attempt to mitigate Medusa's horror. In the feminist poems, far more indeed than in Bogan, Medusa is every bit as hideous as the legends say. In DuPlessis's poem this hideousness is strongly reinforced by the "horrible" English that she speaks. But this is the point in both poems. For Medusa's ugliness—her rage, her violence, her darkness, her sexuality, her mess, her blood, her very physicality (all so antithetical to the good-girl construct to which women in our culture are expected to conform)[15]—is also the source of her life and creative power: her "lava head." Medusa's transforming capabilities, capabilities that are brilliantly symbolized in the original myth by the birth of Pegasus from her headless body and by the reputed healing properties of her blood, cannot be separated from her power to turn the living to stone. Nor, as Karen Lindsey notes in a second poem on the gorgon, can they be separated in women who wish to claim Medusa's powers as their own. Paradoxical though it might seem, the ability to feel rage and to recognize one's destructive power is the necessary precondition for the emergence of a self that is truly capable of creativity and love.

> i will grow snakes in my hair;
> when you touch my face they will leap at you.
> i will grow poison in my breath;
> when you come near me they will suffocate you.
> i will grow a body so ugly
> at the sight of it you will turn to stone, and die.
> and i will flee to the place where the gorgons live,
> and i will touch the snakes in my sisters' hair:
> and the snakes will be rainbows.[16]

Like so many myths, the story of Medusa contains basic psychological and social truths we ignore at our peril. However legion the stories of women's anger and destructive power, these are not qualities that women in our society have been encouraged to own. On the contrary, such stories have traditionally been used to help socialize women out of their feelings of rage. The appearance in women of anger, like darkness, mess, and even the erotic, is the source of tremendous anxiety—both in women and men—

and it has been condemned along with Medusa herself as ugly and unfeminine. What we must recognize, however, is that women themselves have helped make this condemnation possible. Like the Chinese mothers who bound their daughters' feet or the Indian mothers who veiled their daughters' faces, women in our culture have, in Audre Lorde's words, been reared to testify against themselves. That is, they have been taught to distrust and suppress in themselves and in each other the very qualities from which freedom, creativity, and power spring.

> The way you get people to testify against themselves is not to have police tactics and oppressive techniques. What you do is to build it in so people learn to distrust everything in themselves that has not been sanctioned, to reject what is most creative in themselves to begin with, so you don't even need to stamp it out. A Black woman devaluating another Black woman's work. The Black women buying that hot comb and putting it in my locker at the library. It wasn't even Black men; it was Black women testifying against ourselves.[17]

Whatever else the feminist versions of Medusa's story do, they make it clear that for women to become creative, they must accept themselves as they are, not mold themselves to fit the social stereotypes that oppress them. This is true whether they are white women or women of color, lesbian or heterosexual, middle or working class. Each woman must, as Virginia Woolf claims, kill the Angel in the House. For Woolf, born at the end of the Victorian era, this meant rejecting the self-sacrificing obsequiousness of the fully domesticated woman. For the young Black poet Chirlane McCray, who is very much a part of our own era, it means turning her back on the white-identified "pecan dream" that makes it impossible for her to love herself.

> I used to think
> I can't be a poet
> because a poem is being everything you can be
> in one moment,
> speaking with lightning protest
> unveiling a fiery intellect
> or letting the words drift feather-soft
> into the ears of strangers
> who will suddenly understand
> my beautiful and tortured soul.
> But, I've spent my life as a Black girl
> a nappy-headed, no-haired,

fat-lipped,
big-bottomed Black girl
and the poem will surely come out wrong
like me.

And I don't want everyone looking at me.

If I could be cream-colored lovely
with gypsy curls,
someone's pecan dream and sweet sensation,
I'd be poetry in motion
without saying a word
and wouldn't have to make sense if I did.
If I were beautiful, I could be angry and cute
instead of an evil, pouting mammy bitch
a nigger woman. . . .
. . . .
But it's not so bad now.
I can laugh about it,
trade stories and write poems
about all those put-downs,
my rage and hiding.
I'm through waiting for minds to change,
the 60's didn't put *me* on a throne
and as many years as I've been
Black like ebony
Black like the night
I have seen in the mirror
and the eyes of my sisters
that pretty is the woman in darkness
who flowers with loving.[18]

Raised to see herself as "nappy-headed" and "fat-lipped," McCray's speaker
in this lovely and youthful poem must learn to respect the qualities society
has devalued before she can have enough confidence in herself to write.
Otherwise, her negative feelings will draw from her energy and, as Woolf
says, "the heart" will be "plucked . . . out of [her] writing."[19] Indeed, she
will smother in herself the very qualities, including anger and determination, upon which creativity depends.

In what I believe to be one of the clearest statements of the key
assumptions underlying the feminist poetic, Michelle Cliff writes:

The refusal to be anonymous, the decision to separate the self from the expectations and demands of roles, is the choice women must make if we are to survive, if a Women's culture is to survive. To me that is what it means to be a feminist: not to be anonymous, not to deny the self. To be a feminist is to attempt the rescue of other women from the various constraints which culminate in anonymity but the first responsibility is to define the self: To stand separate and alone, saying my woman's self, my matrix, is the source of my identity.[20]

But for the woman poet to "stand . . . alone," and say "my woman's self, my matrix, is the source of my identity," she must first value all she is. If she cannot, then like Denise Levertov in the exquisite but divided "In Mind," written just prior to the women's movement, she will continue to see herself as split in two. For there will be no way for her to reconcile the energies that make her creative—her imagination, her turbulence, her unkindness—with the qualities that she must possess in order to be loved.

There's in my mind a woman
of innocence, unadorned but

fair-featured, and smelling of
apples or grass. She wears

a utopian smock or shift, her hair
is light brown and smooth, and she

is kind and very clean without
ostentation—

    but she has
no imagination.
    And there's a
turbulent moon-ridden girl

or old woman, or both,
dressed in opals and rags, feathers

and torn taffeta,
who knows strange songs—

but she is not kind.[21]

"Fair-featured" and "without / ostentation," Levertov's "utopian" woman, like Woolf's Angel and McCray's pecan dream, is a social construct that permits but half a life. As long as the woman poet commits herself to this construct or to others like it, she cannot help but remain trapped like Levertov's persona within the double bind, her desire for love and social acceptability undermining all that she might otherwise be.

Not surprisingly, then, the most significant task confronting women poets since 1963 has been the validation and integration of the self. No matter to which social group the poet belongs, the great bulk of the poetry that women have written over the past two decades has been poetry of self-definition and self-acceptance.[22] Released from the various myths and social stereotypes that have constrained them, women poets are using their rage to help them explore the disparate elements of their being and to form from these elements a new whole.

Jean Tepperman's 1969 poem, "Witch," which Howe and Bass take as the signature poem for the last third of their anthology, *No More Masks,* is a marvelous example of precisely this kind of self-integration and self-validation. Tepperman's poem is worth quoting at length since it makes so clear how the various assaults upon the self which women endure in the name of being pleasing and good not only lead to rage but to the poet's new identity as witch as she empowers those aspects of her being society has denied.

> They told me
> I smile prettier with my mouth closed.
> They said—
> better cut your hair—
> long, it's all frizzy,
> looks Jewish.
> They hushed me in restaurants
> looking around them
> . . . . . .
> They questioned me
> when I sang in the street.
> They stood taller at tea
> smoothly explaining
> my eyes on the saucers,
> trying to hide the hand grenade
> in my pants pocket,
> or crouched behind the piano.
> They mocked me with magazines

full of breasts and lace,
published their triumph
when the doctor's oldest son
married a nice sweet girl.

  · · · · · · ·

sixteen years old
raw and hopeless
they buttoned me into dresses
covered with pink flowers.
They waited for me to finish
then continued the conversation.
I have been invisible,
weird and supernatural.
I want my black dress.
I want my hair
curling wild around me.
I want my broomstick
from the closet where I hid it.
Tonight I meet my sisters
in the graveyard.
Around midnight
If you stop at a red light
in the wet city traffic,
watch for us against the moon.
We are screaming,
we are flying,
laughing, and won't stop.[23]

With its concluding image of wild, free flight, Tepperman's poem articulates with wonderful clarity the exuberant sense of release that characterizes women's poetry as a result of the feminist movement. The young woman whose parents and society rendered her mute, invisible, and internally divided by their incessant incursions upon her integrity, both physical and behavioral, has finally found her self. The "hand grenade" is no longer hidden "in [her] pants pocket"; she no longer crouches behind the piano. Like her newly discovered sisters, she has become a witch, screaming, laughing, unstoppable. Now firmly rooted in the acceptance of the unacceptable within herself, her identity is intact; her self with all its anger and its power is no longer split in two.

    The sequence of anger followed by the emergence of an integrated and individuated self which Tepperman describes in "Witch," and which lies at the core of the poems by Sarton, Lindsey, DuPlessis, and McCray, is duplicated again and again in the poetry women have written over the past two decades. In these poems witch or Medusa-type figures appear with almost astonishing regularity. In order to re-member themselves, women have, it seems, embarked on a quest for figures of empowerment with whom they could identify. Not just gorgons and witches, but amazons, warriors, mother-goddesses, harpies, furies, maenads, and bacchantes crowd their work, taking their place alongside Dickinson's Queen, Plath's winged lioness, and Rich's visionary androgyne and shamaness, as figures into whom women's rage and their need for healthy self-assertion could be poured.

Thus for the Black poet Audre Lorde, Medusa becomes Seboulisa, the African mother-goddess and amazon-queen, whom the poet encounters at the imaginary crossroads of 125th Street (Harlem, her present life as an American Black woman) and Abomey (inland capital of the ancient kingdom of Dahomey, Lorde's spiritual "home" in Africa). By identifying with Seboulisa here, the poet finds the courage and strength to pursue her art, even though she is still physically severed from the homeland to which her allegiance as a Black and as a lesbian is drawn. Beginning the poem in a state of intense alienation, by its conclusion, Lorde's speaker has fused with the mother goddess to whom she prays. And, like Tepperman at the end of "Witch," she is able in her new state of integration both to laugh and to scream, that is, to write.

> Head bent, walking through snow
> I see you Seboulisa
> printed inside the back of my head
> like marks of the newly wrapped akai
> that kept my sleep fruitful in Dahomey
> and I poured on the red earth in your honor
> those ancient parts of me
> most precious and least needed
> my well-guarded past
> the energy-eating secrets
> I surrender to you as libation
> mother, illuminate my offering
> of old victories
> over men over women over my selves
> who has never before dared
> to whistle into the night
> take my fear of being alone
> like my warrior sisters

who rode in defense of your queendom
disguised and apart
give me the woman strength
of tongue in this cold season.

. . . .

Seboulisa mother goddess with one breast
eaten away by worms of sorrow and loss
see me now
your severed daughter
laughing our name into echo
all the world shall remember.[24]

For Colleen J. McElroy, another Black poet, Medusa becomes Diamonane, the mythic avatar of Black womanhood, "daughter of seven voices," in whom past and present are fused. From the dense richness of her people's history, McElroy is able to draw a poem of startling power as, in effect, she travels from the past to the present inside Diamonane's skin.

I am Diamonane, daughter of seven voices, my language as
old as soft hands across a man's bared chest. Bones
mean nothing. It is the flesh, hot and sweet, it is there
you flower and die. You have seen me walking slowly
at the edge of foreign seas, you have seen me choking
on diesel fumes of cities, eating muskmelons under the
striped tents of incense filled bazaars, quarrelling with
the fishhawkers in the French Quarter, or standing,
head bowed, at the edge of a clearing among Dutch
settlers in those first New England snows. But always,
always, my cape, full and black, billows and flows even
on windless nights.

. . . .

I brought dark songs to piss-stained hallways, aborted un-
named children in cluttered alleys, and loved diseased
men. I have sweated under the smoothness of my sister's flesh, driving her into full heat like the demon I
am, tasted the sweet sperm from my brother's penis,
and rose from both beds refreshed and without guilt. I
have watched hate dance against black skin, turning
and jumping just so, watched it sleep on the sidewalks
of Frisco and wake to the tune of Jim Crow.

Today I walk into hurried streets where exhaust-fumed faces
   of so-called world travelers are as pale as the mountains they have fled. They speak to me with voices like
   stone against stone. I answer in words stolen from the
   dark underside of the brightly plumed touraco. I have
   sold my secrets to survive. I am Diamonane, beloved
   daughter, bird child of obsidian and serpent. I am the
   egg, the sperm.[25]

Finally, on a considerably more playful, if ultimately no less serious
note, "Medusa" for the lesbian poet Judy Grahn becomes "the dyke in the
matter." Determined to redeem the very words by which lesbians have
historically been denigrated, Grahn mingles offensive slang terms with
images connoting strength and determination to suggest that the real
reason lesbians have been vilified—seen as "wicked" or witchlike and
"other"—has been that they refuse to give in or to yield the self.

I am the wall at the lip of the water
I am the rock that refused to be battered
I am the dyke in the matter, the other
I am the wall with the womanly swagger
I am the dragon, the dangerous dagger
I am the bulldyke, the bulldagger

and I have been many a wicked grandmother
and I shall be many a wicked daughter.[26]

Learning to accept the self, whatever that self is, whatever past preceded
it or however it has been denied, is basic to all these poems as it was basic to
the poems cited earlier. But it is emotional liberation, the release of rage,
that is psychologically anterior to the integration of the self and makes
possible the artist's song. Seboulisa with her amputated breast, Diamonane
with her knowledge of the "dark underside of the brightly plumed touraco," Grahn's bulldyke with her swagger and her "dangerous dagger," are
all images of "creative violence," "visionary anger" in the most profound
sense of these terms: "I am the / egg, the sperm."
   In a truly remarkable poem on the process of individuation, the Native
American poet Chrystos declares bluntly that the space in which the "I"
defines itself is a space marked out by knives.

Give Me Back

that anger bone mal mama

that rattle painted red, painted fresh blood, slaughtered enemy
hung with strong feathers, guts of vipers
I'll knock down this old long house this weary war horse
these dry rituals called
how are you
I want that brown thigh bone
carved with eagle beak
that club   dig it out of the dirt

mal mama spirit stole my bones   put them in her burying jug
sealed me up in wax & ashes
I crack out
arrange my bones in their naming places
I take what I want
shaking my sacred hair   dancing out taboo
I mark out the space I am
with knives.[27]

Like Chrystos, too many women poets were deprived by "mal mama,"
however good her intentions, of their "anger bone" and were caught up in
the "dry rituals" of "how are you" and sealed in "burying jug[s]" covered
with "wax & ashes." And in declaring themselves today Medusas, witches,
furies, bulldykes, and amazons, they too are "shaking [their] sacred hair"
and "dancing out taboo," exorcising the Angel in the House, which
repressed their spirit and suppressed their art. Like Adrienne Rich, they are
seeking a new balance between the "energy of relation" and the "energy of
creation" that will allow them to have their lives—and not to duplicate the
self-sacrifice which destroyed their mothers. In "The Mirror in Which Two
Are Seen As One," Rich writes:

Late summer night the insects
fry in the yellowed lightglobe
your skin burns gold in its light
In this mirror, who are you? Dreams of the nunnery
with its discipline, the nursery
with its nurse, the hospital
where all the powerful ones are masked
the graveyard where you sit on the graves
of women who died in childbirth
and women who died at birth
Dreams of your sister's birth
your mother dying in childbirth over and over

not knowing how to stop
bearing you over and over

your mother dead and you unborn
your two hands grasping your head
drawing it down against the blade of life
your nerves the nerves of a midwife
learning her trade

(DW, 15 – 16)

Able finally to separate from the demands of their immediate families and from all that society told them they were supposed to be, women poets are ready at last to have a life, womanhood, and power of their own.

•   •   •

From Audre Lorde to Erica Jong, from Judy Grahn to Diane Wakoski (though Wakoski would deny it), from Chrystos to Jean Tepperman, contemporary women poets have found in feminism a new poetic. Feminist poetry is not limited to a given set of political beliefs nor does it necessarily espouse an eschatological vision[28]—although feminism in poetry often takes both forms. In its broadest sense the feminist poetic merely defines the means by which individual women writers can empower themselves *as women* in their verse.

But for women poets this relatively simple concept of self-empowerment has had revolutionary consequences that have profoundly altered the scope and substance of their work. Like all true poetics, the feminist poetic has radically altered the way in which its practitioners write. Not only has it allowed them to deal with subjects that they never touched before; but it has helped them achieve an authentic speaking voice and it has encouraged them to write with an emotional freedom few women poets, with the exception of Emily Dickinson, enjoyed prior to our own era. As a result of the feminist poetic, women poets are now able to modify existing poetic conventions to express the actual experience of their lives and the true nature of their response to it. As in the Medusa poems, they are reworking the old myths and archetypes in order to re-vision them. As in the poems by the Black writers McCray, Lorde, and McElroy, they are exploring the internalized images of self-hatred in order to fashion themselves anew.

Thus the feminist poetic has allowed women writers not only to recast the old tradition but to find new, woman-centered ways out of it, ways that have transformed their relationship to the culture at large. No longer tied to the love lyric as the staple of women's poetry or compelled to transcend their woman self in order to speak authoritatively to others, women are at last constructing a poetry that is their own and in which they can be themselves. In finding the courage to rest their poetic identity, their voice as poets, on their complete identity as human beings, women poets today have gained access to their power and made it their own. As in Rich's poem, just quoted, they have given birth to themselves.

For women poets this means that after centuries of either silence or subversion, they can at last speak openly and forcefully in their poetry about every aspect of their lives. Freed by the recognition of their oppression, it is, as Wakoski says, in the "heat of [their] anger"[29] that they have found the energy for their art and the means by which to reconcile their poetic gift with the fullness of their woman selves.

But what then does this say of the relationship between anger and creativity in women? In a highly suggestive essay aimed at critics who have scored Virginia Woolf for her polemical writings, Jane Marcus argues that far from being anathema in art, anger is "a primary source of creative energy,"[30] almost a sine qua non. Following Freud, Marcus defines anger in terms of the ego's narcissistic defense against threats to its integrity. Anger originates, she claims, in "the ego's first struggle to maintain itself, to find an identity separate from the mother," and is necessary therefore to the building of a "healthy narcissism" indispensable for self-preservation. In women, however, this narcissism is deflected into "vanity of the body and dress." As a result, Marcus believes, women lack the ego strength, the "fearlessness and ferocity," necessary for great art. It is the rare woman artist, she observes, who can say, with the diarist Marie Bashkirtseff, "'I am my own heroine!'"[31] or, I would add, with the youthful Sylvia Plath, "I am I."

Although Marcus does not develop her ideas into a full-fledged theory, I believe that she is right to stress the importance of anger for self-empowerment in art. Her description of the causal relationship between anger, separation, and self-empowerment not only explains what happened in the careers of Dickinson, Plath, and Rich. Equally important, it illuminates what has happened generally to American women's poetry since 1963—since, that is, women began to use their anger to separate from the stereotypes of the past which oppressed them, and in particular from those stereotypes that derived from and left them bound to their mothers.

If this is true, however, then the generative role anger has played in the creativity of American women poets over the past two decades places a number of current theories on female social and psychological maturation in a difficult and problematic light. In particular, this outburst of creativity raises questions about the value that many feminists, including Jean Baker Miller and Carol Gilligan, have placed on women's tendency to bond at the expense of their development of a secure sense of separate and autonomous self.

As the internal conflicts in Adrienne Rich's recent poetry illustrate, many feminists now view the traditionally sanctioned maturational goals of separation and autonomy in a very mixed light. For if separation is the means to achieve an independent and integrated self, it is also the foundation stone upon which, it appears, male culture and the male moral order have been built. Concerned not just with the salvation of the self but with the redemption of society, some feminists are now arguing, therefore, that women must continue to reject autonomy in favor of bonding as the primary goal of female psychological development if society is to be preserved. In order to protect the values of nurturance and attachment, they are, in effect, prepared to restore the Angel to the House or, at any rate, to dust off her wings.[32]

Nowhere is this current trend more apparent than in the highly popular writings of Carol Gilligan and Jean Baker Miller. For both Gilligan and Miller, woman's greatest asset—and her most important contribution to society—lies simply enough in her ability to relate to, and take responsibility for, others. Dismissing as irrelevant prototypes of maturation based on the male struggle for separation and autonomy, Miller and Gilligan both assert that woman's maturation takes a validly different course, one that prepares her for nurturance, attachment, and care.[33] Within the context of this maturational pattern, a woman's so-called developmental deficits— her failure to achieve strong ego boundaries, her difficulty with separation, her tendency toward empathetic reactions at the expense of self, her need, as Blos said, to be loved as well as to love—may be viewed as positive strengths. For they predispose her, as Nancy Chodorow has argued, albeit from a less sanguine point of view,[34] to her role as mother and they encourage her to work toward maintaining social and familial bonds. Women, Gilligan writes, do not define moral problems in terms of individual "rights" as men do but in terms of the "obligation to exercise care and avoid hurt." "The inflicting of hurt," she observes of her subjects' responses in an abortion study, "is considered selfish and immoral in its reflection of unconcern, while the expression of care is seen as the fulfillment of moral responsibility."[35] Women, Miller opines, "are . . . more thoroughly prepared to move toward more advanced, more affiliative ways of living—and less wedded to the dangerous ways of the present."[36]

Although Miller and Gilligan both recognize that this need for attachment can lead to problems of its own, particularly when it slips into a willingness to please or into a passive refusal to choose, the weight of their argument falls heavily on the healing potential women's connectedness to others represents. Where men, they claim, are prepared to abandon social and familial bonds in their quest for dominance and self-assertion, women's desire for affiliation leads them to place their worth as human beings on their success in maintaining nurturing relationships to others. Miller and Gilligan both write eloquently of women's unique responsibility for weaving the social or communal web that helps human beings live together with relative decency. "Woman's place in man's life cycle," Gilligan declares, is to preserve "the continuing importance of attachment" against "the developmental litany [that] intones the celebration of separation, autonomy, individuation, and natural rights."[37] The fact that "women's embeddedness in lives of relationship, their orientation to interdependence, their subordination of achievement to care, and their conflicts over competitive success leave them personally at risk in mid-life," she concludes, "seems more a commentary on the society than a problem in women's relationships."[38]

Given the trajectory of Western history, this desire on the part of feminists to find an alternative form of maturation to that of male separation and autonomy is understandable enough. According to Nancy Chodorow, it is through the process of separation and individuation that men in our society not only develop a "sense of secure masculine self"[39] but learn to know woman as other, with all the unfortunate consequences that entails for both sexes. But what Gilligan and, to a lesser extent, Miller do not stress is that women's failure to complete separation carries with it serious negative potentials of its own. These potentials are nowhere more apparent than when we look at the struggle of the woman artist to achieve true creativity in her work.

The fact is that one cannot embed one's life in relationships, subordinate "achievement to care," and spend one's primary energy making others happy without paying a price. And if one is an artist, that price comes, as Plath and Rich discovered, from the creative side of the self, from the side that requires solitude in order to function and assertiveness and a sense of autonomy in order to achieve. Although the external impediments to female creativity have been substantial, I believe that the difficulties created by woman's deep-seated need to maintain connectedness to others have made it virtually impossible for her to function unambivalently and with consistent effectiveness in the arts. Unable to separate adequately from those she loves and whose well-being or approval she seeks, the woman artist has been torn between conflicting needs and alienated from her own inner drives. Committed by her womanhood to "the activity of attachment," she has been led to view her personal desires and ambitions as unwomanly. For in their "selfishness" and narcissism, such personal goals are not only in conflict with the stereotype of what a woman is *supposed* to be. They directly contradict what women *feel* is or should be true of themselves.

As Rich said too elliptically in her speech before the Modern Language Association in 1976, it is only "the woman who refuses to obey, who has said 'no'" (OL, 202), who is not a "hack," who is creative.[40] But unlike James Joyce's Stephen Daedalus, whom Gilligan cites as the prototypical male creator, the nascent woman artist cannot simply renounce "relationships in order to protect [her] freedom of self-expression."[41] For to do so she must pay an exorbitant psychological and social price. This price is one most women artists in our culture have not been willing to pay, even though the alternative has meant to suppress in themselves that "healthy narcissism indispensable for self-preservation" and self-expression. As a result, they have found it difficult if not impossible to make those sacrifices upon which the protection of self-expression depends. Constrained by their bonds to others, they have been constrained by their need to please others as well. And in their effort to love and be loved, they have subverted the very power they seek to claim.

For the woman artist to become self-empowered in her creativity and capable of originality, she must have a clear sense of integrated and separate self. This may mean, however, that she will have to limit her commitment to those aspects of her gender identity and role which undermine her integrity and inhibit her ability to function as a self-authorized agent in her profession. If she cannot, then as Plath's life in particular demonstrates, she will remain bound not only by external but by internal constraints that restrict her drive for independence and her need to assert power. Her true deep voice will remain inaccessible to her; and her need to please will consume her energy, creativity, and care.

If, as Chodorow and Gilligan assert, a woman's need for attachment and her sense of gender identity are both rooted in her unresolved pre-oedipal relationship with her mother,[42] then anger's overwhelming importance for female creativity becomes clear. As Marcus observes, anger originates in the child's need to protect itself and to find an identity separate from the mother. But this process of protection and separation—so strategic for male development—is never fully realized in women since, unlike boys, girls do not have to see themselves as separate from the mother in order to develop a secure sense of gendered self. As a result, girls never undergo as thorough a process of differentiation as boys. Instead, they end their oedipal years divided in allegiance. As individuals, they may wish to separate from their mothers but as women they remain bonded to the nurturing figure from whom their sense of gender identity comes. Because they never completely sever this mother-daughter bond, Chodorow believes that women remain susceptible to boundary confusion and regression to pre-oedipal modes of relating in ways that men do not.[43] Girls, she writes, "come to define and experience themselves as continuous with others; their experience of self contains more flexible or permeable ego boundaries. Boys come to define themselves as more separate and distinct, with a greater sense of rigid ego boundaries and differentiation."[44] If these permeable ego boundaries leave women vulnerable to fusion and loss of self, Chodorow believes they also provide women with the psychological basis for empathy that helps them function effectively as mothers. And because they grow up feeling incomplete in themselves, women also want to be mothers—that is, in one way or another they want to perpetuate the attachment that is the essence of the mother-daughter bond.[45]

For women who desire to exercise other forms of creativity besides motherhood, the problem lies, however, precisely here. For the very qualities that the mother-daughter bond fosters and that make women want to be mothers, work against them if they wish to be artists. To the degree that the mother-daughter bond inclines women to be nurturant and empathetic, it makes it more difficult for them to access the anger necessary for differentiation. And, therefore, it makes it all but impossible for them to develop the ego strength needed for the arts. Indeed, as the lives of Aurelia and Sylvia Plath demonstrate, when taken to extremes, the inability to access anger can even make it impossible for women to develop the selfhood necessary for mothering or survival, let alone art.

For women to have selves and to be creative they must be able to be angry because, as Marcus observes, anger is the principal means by which the ego keeps its boundaries intact. "'No,'" Emily Dickinson wrote in 1878, when rejecting Judge Otis P. Lord's offer of marriage, "is the wildest word we consign to Language" (L, 617). For the woman artist it is also the most important. Just as the child learns to differentiate himself or herself from the mother by saying no, so the woman artist must use her no to draw the necessary limits around herself and her life that will protect her integrity and allow her to reconcile herself with her gift. Otherwise, like Plath, she will be torn apart by her need to be loved on the one hand and her need for self-assertion on the other.

While autonomy carries with it the dangers of isolation and coldness, too much attachment leads to disempowerment and the sacrifice of the self. Taken to extremes, both maturational goals carry with them the potential for abuse. As we saw in the lives of Dickinson, Plath, and Rich, aggression and self-centeredness are no more or less destructive to truly empathetic and nurturant relationships than fusion and the passive aggressiveness so often employed by those who lack access to real power. The Black women who placed a hot comb among Audre Lorde's things were in this act as destructive toward her as those who devaluate her because of her gender, race, or sexual orientation. For all of them, the Other represents a threat to the self. The father or mother who overidentifies with his or her children and in the name of good parenting seeks to invade and control their children's lives is no more nurturant or truly empathetic than the parent who ignores or deserts them. Both fusion and withdrawal are forms of abuse. As in all forms of oppression, they require that the child learn to use her anger to empower and protect herself.[46]

Ironically, it is probably because the feminist movement, like the Black movement, provided its adherents with a safe context of bonding within which to express their rage that so many women poets have been able to undergo the process of separation and self-empowerment since the mid-sixties.[47] Participation in this movement has eased these women's fears of isolation and social opprobrium and encouraged them to take pride in the discovery of their selves. It has allowed them to have it both ways by giving them the attachment they need as women to support the process of separation and individuation which as artists and complete human beings they cannot live without.

Traditionally, women poets either converted their anger into depression, giving us a literature of pain and victimization such as Gilbert and Gubar describe in *The Madwoman in the Attic*,[48] or they sought to transcend the reasons for anger by neutralizing their speaking voice, producing the literature of the generic *he*. In encouraging women writers to own their rage, feminism has for the first time allowed women poets to achieve real separation, making the full expression of their creative gifts potentially possible. The emergence of the feminist poetic does not guarantee that we will now be inundated with great women poets—what poetic can make that claim? But it does explain the extraordinary outpouring of poetry now being written by women, the many poems on separation and individuation, and the tremendous sense of newly discovered power in their work. It also explains why so many women poets feel an insistent need to take Medusa, a figure symbolizing the separated or empowered self, as their muse. In adopting Medusa, women poets are unquestionably adopting the imagery of "confrontation and explosive connection" that Dickinson first discovered when she picked up her loaded gun. And as both Gilligan and Rich admonish, there is danger in this. But, as Rich also recognizes, the only way to avoid such danger is to avoid life itself. This women poets are no longer prepared to do.

Notes

Introduction

1. Virginia Woolf, "Professions for Women," in *The Death of the Moth* (London: The Hogarth Press, 1942), p. 151.
2. Woolf, "Professions," p. 151.
3. Woolf, "Professions," p. 153.
4. Woolf, "Professions," p. 152.
5. Woolf, "Professions," p. 153.
6. *Shakespeare's Sisters: Feminist Essays on Women Poets*, ed. Sandra M. Gilbert and Susan Gubar (Bloomington: University of Indiana Press, 1979), p. xxii. See also p. xvii, where Gilbert and Gubar elaborate on Suzanne Juhasz's theory of the "double bind of the woman poet" in *Naked and Fiery Forms: Modern American Poetry by Women, A New Tradition* (New York: Harper and Row, 1976), pp. 1–6. Juhasz was the first feminist critic to clearly label this conundrum.
7. Albert Gelpi, "Emily Dickinson and the Deerslayer: The Dilemma of the Woman Poet in America," in *Shakespeare's Sisters*, p. 134.
8. Interpretations of "My Life had stood—a Loaded Gun" are legion. Those of special relevance to feminists begin with John Cody's psychoanalytical reading of the poem in *After Great Pain: The Inner Life of Emily Dickinson* (Cambridge, Mass.: The Belknap Press of Harvard University Press, 1971), pp. 397–415. Since Cody, the poem has been subject to extensive, sometimes tortured analysis by many writers including Robert Weisbuch, *Emily Dickinson's Poetry* (Chicago: University of Chicago Press, 1975), pp. 25–39; Adrienne Rich, "Vesuvius at Home: The Power of Emily Dickinson," (OL, 157–83); Albert Gelpi, "Emily Dickinson and the Deerslayer," in *Shakespeare's Sisters*, pp. 122–31; Sharon Cameron, *Lyric Time: Dickinson and the Limits of Genre* (Baltimore: Johns Hopkins University Press, 1979), pp. 65–74; and Vivian Pollak, *Dickinson: The Anxiety of Gender* (Ithaca: Cornell University Press, 1984), pp. 150–55.
9. In associating these two words so closely I am following Gelpi, "Emily Dickinson and the Deerslayer," in *Shakespeare's Sisters*, p. 130.
10. Robert Lowell, foreword to *Ariel*, by Sylvia Plath (New York: Harper and Row, 1966), p. vii.
11. Gelpi, "Emily Dickinson and the Deerslayer" in *Shakespeare's Sisters*, p. 129. Since the eider duck was known for pulling feathers from its breast to line its nest, Gelpi suggests that the duck connotes masochism as well as softness in the poem. I would agree.
12. See Carroll Smith-Rosenberg, "The Female World of Love and Ritual: Relations between Women in Nineteenth-Century America," in *Signs: Journal of Women in Culture and Society*, 1 (Autumn 1975): 1–29. In *An American Triptych: Anne Bradstreet, Emily Dickinson, Adrienne Rich* (Chapel Hill: University of North Carolina Press, 1984), pp. 148–64, Wendy Martin argues that Dickinson's relationships with other women, "the female sphere," were

positive and nurturant. Within limits I would agree. But it is also important to recognize that although Dickinson did correspond with women and loved many individual women deeply, she had nothing but contempt for the life most women in her period lived and appears to have intensely disliked women in groups. See, for example, her comments on women do-gooders, L, 82, 500, and Karl Keller's entirely negative interpretation of Dickinson's feelings for women in *The Only Kangaroo Among the Beauty: Emily Dickinson and America* (Baltimore: Johns Hopkins University Press, 1979), pp. 222–50. The fact that two such able critics as Keller and Martin could write at such totally opposite extremes on this subject underscores the complexity and ambivalence of Dickinson's attitude.

13. "Emily Dickinson" in *Emily Dickinson: A Collection of Critical Essays,* ed. Richard B. Sewall (Englewood Cliffs, N.J.: Prentice-Hall, 1963), p. 20.

14. For my purposes the two most important attempts by feminist critics to apply or adjust Bloom's theories to women writers are Sandra M. Gilbert and Susan Gubar, *The Madwoman in the Attic: The Woman Writer and the Nineteenth-Century Literary Imagination* (New Haven: Yale University Press, 1979), pp. 46–53 and throughout; and Joanne Feit Diehl, *Dickinson and the Romantic Imagination* (Princeton: Princeton University Press, 1981), p. 13–33 and throughout. I consider both attempts wayward.

Chapter 1

1. Among the writers who have treated the best-selling literature poured forth by America's nineteenth-century "literary domestics" are Emily Stipes Watts, *The Poetry of American Women from 1632 to 1943* (Austin: University of Texas Press, 1977); Cheryl Walker, *The Nightingale's Burden, Women Poets and American Culture before 1900* (Bloomington: Indiana University Press, 1982); and Mary Kelley, *Private Women, Public Stage: Literary Domesticity in Nineteenth-Century America* (New York: Oxford University Press, 1984). In "Sentimental Power: *Uncle Tom's Cabin* and the Politics of Literary History," reprinted in *The New Feminist Criticism: Essays on Women, Literature, and Theory,* ed. Elaine Showalter (New York: Pantheon Books, 1985), pp. 81–104, Jane P. Tompkins has launched a passionate defense of this literature's power and quality; but Dickinson had little use for its sentimental pieties in her life or her art and never seems consciously, at any rate, to have aligned herself with these writers. Stories of "pure little lives, loving God, and their parents, and obeying the laws of the land," she told Susan Gilbert in 1852, didn't *"bewitch* [her] any" (L, 195), and as her poem on Elizabeth Barrett Browning makes clear, bewitched was what she wanted to be. (See No. 593; P, 494–95.)

2. Mary Lyon as quoted in *The Power of Christian Benevolence Illustrated in the Life and Labors of Mary Lyon,* ed. Edward Hitchcock (Northampton, Mass.: Hopkins, Bridgman, and Company, 1852), p. 303.

Recent feminist critics have tended to stress the importance of Dickinson's rebellion against her mother in understanding the direction her vocation took. See, for example, Barbara Antonina Clarke Mossberg, *Emily Dickinson: When a Writer Is a Daughter* (Bloomington: Indiana University Press, 1982), pp. 37–96, along with Cody, *After Great Pain,* pp. 39–103, and Pollak, *The Anxiety of Gender,* pp. 35–58.

While I would not ordinarily dispute the overriding importance of the mother-daughter relationship for women writers, I believe that the particular nature of Dickinson's rebellion was shaped more by the limitations of the society in which she lived than by her quarrel with her mother, from whom after adolescence she appears to have achieved a real degree of separation. In the end she saw both her mother and her father more as victims than as conduits of the society she despised. However much she disagreed with them, by the time they died she had made peace with their flaws. (See L, 526–31, 745–55, 759–60.)

3. *The Mother's Journal*, ed. Mrs. Mary G. Clarke (Philadelphia, 1852), vol. 17, p. 218.
4. As quoted by Jay Leyda, *The Years and Hours of Emily Dickinson* (New Haven: Yale University Press, 1960), vol. 1, pp. 17–18.
   A thorough discussion of Dickinson's education is available in Richard B. Sewall's *The Life of Emily Dickinson* (New York: Farrar, Straus and Giroux, 1974), vol. 2, pp. 335–67.
5. *The Mother's Journal*, vol. 17, pp. 138, 139.
6. *The Mother's Journal*, vol. 17, p. 25.
7. Hitchcock, *The Power of Christian Benevolence*, p. 127.
8. Leyda, *Years and Hours*, vol. 1, p. 163.
9. As quoted in Sewall, *Life*, vol. 2, p. 361.
10. Hitchcock, *The Power of Christian Benevolence*, p. 311.
11. Hitchcock, *The Power of Christian Benevolence*, p. 301.
12. Hitchcock, *The Power of Christian Benevolence*, p. 191.
13. As quoted by Sarah D. (Locke) Stow in *History of Mount Holyoke Seminary, South Hadley, Mass. During its First Half Century 1837–1887* (South Hadley, Mass.: Mount Holyoke Seminary, 1887), p. 121.
14. See David Higgins, *Portrait of Emily Dickinson: The Poet and Her Prose* (New Brunswick, N.J.: Rutgers University Press, 1967), p. 53. Higgins's statement is based on a remembrance of Emily Fowler Ford's. According to Mrs. Ford, Higgins writes, Dickinson

> was one of the two wits of the school, and a humorist of the "comic column" [in the school newspaper *Forest Leaves*]. She often wrote comic sermons in a standard pattern, "the art of which consisted in bringing most incongruous things together. . . . ending always with the same refrain, 'He played on a harp of a thousand strings, sperrets of just men made perfec' Emily's combinations were irresistible. . . ."

Unfortunately no copies of *Forest Leaves* have survived so the remembrance cannot be verified. However, Mrs. Ford's memory meshes well with the one example of parody we do have from Dickinson's hand, her "sermon" Valentine "'sic transit gloria mundi'" (no. 3, P, 3–5) and I would very much like to believe it is true.
15. Hitchcock, *The Power of Christian Benevolence*, p. 304.
16. In Bianchi, *Emily Dickinson Face to Face: Unpublished Letters with Notes and Reminiscences* (Boston and New York: Houghton Mifflin Co., 1932), p. 6. In contrast to the portrait of Dickinson drawn by many feminist critics—from Gilbert and Gubar to Mossberg—as a painfully wounded woman, obsessed with her own deprivation, the image that emerges from Bianchi's memoir is that of a woman very much in possession of herself, who loved children, loved play, had a brilliant but sharp tongue, and did not tolerate fools gladly.
17. In *Signs* 1: 15.
18. This idea was first advanced by the psychoanalyst John Cody in *After Great Pain*. It has since been elaborated by Barbara Mossberg and Vivian Pollak, and seems to form the basis for much of the feminist "re-vision" of Dickinson's life.
19. As quoted in *Emily Dickinson's Home: Letters of Edward Dickinson and His Family*, ed. Millicent Todd Bingham (New York: Harper and Brothers, 1955), p. 414. In *Face to Face*, Martha Dickinson Bianchi writes of her grandmother:

> She was gentle of nature, but never second in actual control until . . . a fall . . . left her . . . a helpless invalid. Up to this accident she kept a firm hand on her household, always anxious for untoward events that might bear down on those she loved. . . .
> . . . She shrank from sin or wrongdoing, was timid of mistakes, of displeasing husband or conscience; but she never flinched before any exacting duty of hospitality . . . nor did

she quail before . . . rearing . . . three of the most exigent children a mild New England mother of the early nineteenth century was ever called upon to produce. (p. 88.)

See also Sewall's largely positive portrait of Mrs. Dickinson, *Life,* vol. 1, pp. 74–90.

20. See Barbara Gelpi, "Introduction," *Victorian Women: A Documentary Account of Women's Lives in Nineteenth-Century England, France, and The United States,* ed. Erna Olafson Hellerstein, Leslie Parker Hume, and Karen M. Offen (Stanford: Stanford University Press, 1981), p. 15.

21. John Cody (*After Great Pain*) was the first critic to explore the implications of the poet's romantic attachment to Susan Gilbert, her sister-in-law. Cody's Freudian bias dictated, however, that he view the poet's bisexuality in terms of what he conceived to be its pathological etiology: the poet's dysfunctional response to an inadequate, non-nurturing mother with whom she could not identify. "With a different mother," he concludes, "Emily Dickinson may well have married and had children and in all ways have pursued a conventional life" (p. 499). Sewall (*Life,* vol. 1, pp. 161–69, 197–214) tries to offer a more balanced approach to the relationship between Dickinson and Gilbert; but his intense dislike for Dickinson's "saccharine" letter-writing style leads him to undervalue the importance of the adolescent letters for Dickinson's development as a poet.

Since Carroll Smith-Rosenberg's pioneering work in woman-to-woman relationships of the nineteenth century, other critics have tried to modify Cody's assertions. See, in particular, Lillian Faderman, "Emily Dickinson's Letters to Sue Gilbert," *Massachusetts Review* 18 (Summer 1977): 197–225, and *Surpassing the Love of Men: Romantic Friendship and Love Between Women from the Renaissance to the Present* (New York: William Morrow, 1981), part II, section A, chapters 1–5; Paula Bennett, "The Language of Love: Emily Dickinson's Homoerotic Poetry," *Gai Saber* 1 (Spring 1977): 13–17; Jean McClure Mudge, "Emily Dickinson and 'Sister Sue,'" *Prairie Schooner* 52 (1978): 90–107; Adalaide Morris, "'The Love of Thee—a Prism Be,'" in *Feminist Critics Read Emily Dickinson,* ed. Suzanne Juhasz (Bloomington: Indiana University Press, 1983), pp. 98–113; and Pollak, *The Anxiety of Gender,* pp. 59–82.

Dickinson's relationship with Susan unquestionably fits the pattern of romantic attachments described by Smith-Rosenberg and Faderman and therefore in itself is not necessarily a symptom of pathology since such relationships were considered normal during the period. But as with so many things, Dickinson brought to her love for Susan an exclusivity and an intensity that, particularly under the circumstances, were problematic independent of any pathology that might have been involved. And it is with these issues, rather than the question of bisexuality or lesbianism per se, that I believe we should be concerned. See Chapter 2, pp. 58–61.

22. Faderman makes the same observation in "Emily Dickinson's Letters," pp. 201–5.

23. Sewall gathered together these terms from Lyman's various letters and notations on both Dickinson and a woman named Mintie Wharton whom, Sewall claims, Lyman saw in much the same way. See *The Lyman Letters: New Light on Emily Dickinson and her Family* (Amherst: University of Massachusetts Press, 1965), p. 67.

24. Sewall, *Lyman Letters,* p. 35. Lyman is quoting from Tennyson's *Maud.*

25. Bianchi, *Face to Face,* p. 54.

26. Only two of Susan's letters to Emily Dickinson survive but they suggest that she did try to meet the poet on as equal a footing as possible, linguistically speaking. (See L, 379–80, and Sewall, *Life,* vol. 1, p. 203.)

27. Donald G. Mitchell, *Reveries of a Bachelor or A Book of the Heart* (New York: Charles Scribner's Sons, 1890), p. 8.

28. Sewall, *Life,* vol. 1, p. 118.

Chapter 2

1. Cody, *After Great Pain*, pp. 259–60. Since Dickinson left no writing of any kind for the crucial year and a half between August 1856 and January 1858, this period has been subject to a good deal of speculation. See Pollak, *The Anxiety of Gender*, pp. 76–79, for a review of recent theories.

2. The general accuracy of Johnson's dating, particularly of the early poems (before 1865), has been supported by R. W. Franklin (MS, xv). Where the two authorities differ, I have followed Franklin.

From my point of view the dating of Dickinson's poems is of extreme importance since I believe that the poet underwent a period of intense artistic and psychological growth between 1858 and 1862 (the "annus mirabilis"). This is not the conventional view of Dickinson's development, which has on the whole been treated as relatively static from the beginning. Pollak reviews the arguments in favor of an achronological reading of the poems in a lengthy note on pp. 22–23 of *The Anxiety of Gender*. She concludes that Dickinson's poetry "exhibits no clear-cut psychological development" and has "no early, middle, and late manner." I could not disagree more strongly.

3. "Elizabeth Barrett Browning," *Atlantic Monthly* 8 (September 1861): 368–76 and "George Sand," *Atlantic Monthly* 8 (November 1861): 513–34. In light of the avidity with which Dickinson read the *Atlantic*, the joining of names in the Norcross letter hardly seems accidental.

4. Gilbert and Gubar, *Madwoman*, p. 584 and throughout. Gilbert and Gubar's failure to make a clear distinction between Dickinson's art and life leads them to view her poetic voice as far more unstable than I believe it actually was. Dickinson seems to have confined most of her highly manipulative posing to life; in her art there was a gradual growth towards greater and greater coherence and integration as she learned to accept the choices she had made. Her late style—for yes, there is one—is terse, gnomic, brilliant, and, on the whole, quite self-satisfied, the style, I am tempted to say, of a "Queen."

5. As quoted by Leyda, *Years and Hours*, vol. 2, p. 77.

6. Gilbert and Gubar, *Madwoman*, p. 582.

7. Dickinson's statement to Higginson on her poetic persona or "supposed person" must be read against Austin's statement that she "definitely posed in those letters" to Higginson. See Millicent Todd Bingham, *Ancestor's Brocades* (New York and London: Harper and Brothers, 1955), p. 167. In the cat and mouse game Dickinson was playing with her preceptor, this effort to appear innocent and confiding was part of the strategy. Whether she meant what she said is another matter.

8. Bianchi, *Face to Face*, p. 57.

9. Yvor Winters, "Emily Dickinson and the Limits of Judgment," in Sewall, *Emily Dickinson*, p. 28.

10. George Whicher, *This Was a Poet: A Critical Biography of Emily Dickinson* (New York: Scribners, 1938), p. 92.

11. Rebecca Patterson, *The Riddle of Emily Dickinson* (Boston: Houghton Mifflin, 1951).

12. From a letter by Kate Scott Anthon to Martha Dickinson Bianchi, October 8, 1917, as quoted by Leyda, *Years and Hours*, vol. 1, p. 367. As with Dickinson's contributions to *Forest Leaves*, the loss of her piano compositions, which were, apparently, quite wild and brilliant, is incalculable for any study of the poet's creativity.

13. Patterson, *Riddle*, pp. 88–89, 139–41, Cody, *After Great Pain*, p. 127. In light of the research done by Smith-Rosenberg and Faderman, Cody's statement is particularly unfortunate and misleading: "Emily Dickinson," he declares, "possessed a puritan super-ego derived from the very moralistic culture in which she lived and from her church-going and conventionally high-principled parents. It would be remarkable if she had not therefore

regarded homosexuality as depraved and reacted to the mere thought of it with abhorrence." Remarkable though it might be, at no time prior to the early twentieth century did this kind of abhorrence apply to romantic friendships between women. (Women who cross-dressed or used dildoes for sexual penetration were another matter. See Faderman, *Surpassing the Love of Men,* pp. 47–61, 239–94.)

14. The women referred to by Dickinson in this letter are, according to Johnson, probably Susan Gilbert Dickinson, Susan Phelps, Eliza Coleman and Martha Gilbert Dickinson. Sarah Tracy and Harriet Merrill were two members of the "circle of five" who seem to have dropped out early.

15. Hitchcock, *The Power of Christian Benevolence,* pp. 58–59.

16. Hitchcock, *The Power of Christian Benevolence,* p. 258.

17. Dickinson's passionate identification with Antony is one of the most striking uses she makes of Shakespeare. See L, 533, 754, 791, 870, 894, 920. Not only was *Antony and Cleopatra* the first work she read upon recovering the use of her eyes in 1865, but throughout her life the Roman tragedy appears to have served as a touchstone for the New England poet, a way to test the presence of both poetry and love. See her comments on the play to Joseph Lyman in Sewall, *Lyman Letters,* p. 76.

18. Patterson, *Riddle,* pp. 151–55. Patterson, however, does not believe the relationship was consummated.

19. Faderman "Emily Dickinson's Homoerotic Poetry," *Higginson Journal* 18 (1978): 19–20.

20. Faderman cites letter no. 74: "The wind blows and it rains. . . . Oh Susie, I would nestle close to your warm heart, and never hear the wind blow, or the storm beat, again" (L, 177).

21. In *The Riddle of Emily Dickinson,* Patterson becomes so entranced with her find that she continues to track Kate in her wanderings long after the putative subject of the book, Dickinson, has died. Despite Patterson's enthusiasm, however, the picture of Anthon that emerges is not particularly flattering, although it does make clear that she maintained romantic involvements with women throughout her life. See in particular pp. 291–344, which describe her passionate eight-year attachment to a woman named Florence Eliot.

22. "Emily Dickinson," in Sewall, *Emily Dickinson,* p. 40.

Chapter 3

1. Gilbert and Gubar, *Madwoman,* p. 555. According to Gilbert and Gubar, Dickinson's sense of herself as an isolated and unpublishable "Nobody," had "far-reaching" and deleterious "literary consequences" for her, "ranging from a sometimes grotesquely child-like self-image to a painfully distorted sense of size, a perpetual gnawing hunger, and even, finally, a deep confusion about identity." What the critics do not note is that the poems they specifically use to substantiate their case for Dickinson's low self-esteem were largely written before 1862. (See pp. 591–606.) Like so many Dickinson critics, they assume no growth anywhere on the poet's part.

2. On the basis of handwriting, Johnson places these poems in 1861; Franklin dates them as 1862. I see them as probably transition poems.

3. While most critics relate the terror to Dickinson's relationship with the Master, other explanations for this event, as for the blank period that preceded it are possible. In his standard biography of the poet, Sewall calls the five year period from 1858 to 1862, "the most crucial—certainly the most discussed—five years in Emily Dickinson's life." He reviews the various theories (from psychosis to eye problems) that critics, including himself, have advanced to explain it. See Sewall, *Life* vol. 2, pp. 605–7.

The identity of the Master is the single most vexed question in Dickinson criticism. Of the various contenders, male and female, those who appear to have the best case are Samuel

Bowles, editor of the *Springfield Republican*, and Charles Wadsworth ("My Philadelphia"), minister of the Arch Street Presbyterian Church, Philadelphia. See Sewall, *Life*, vol. 2, pp. 444–531. Sewall favors Bowles. Most recently, Wadsworth's claims have been championed by Vivian Pollak, *The Anxiety of Gender*, pp. 95–102, and William H. Schurr in *The Marriage of Emily Dickinson: A Study of the Fascicles* (Lexington, Ky.: The University of Kentucky, 1983), pp. 142–70. Schurr not only believes that Wadsworth consummated the passion but that he may actually have impregnated the poet.

4. Wadsworth's one extant letter to Dickinson, reprinted by Johnson immediately after the third and last Master letter, indicates that he had indeed encouraged her to do precisely that:

I am distressed beyond measure at your note, received this moment,—I can only imagine the affliction which has befallen you, or is now befalling you . . .

I am very, very anxious to learn more definitely of your trial—and though I know no right to intrude upon your sorrow yet I beg you to write me, though it be but a word. (L, 392)

The letter is undated but appears to have come early in their relationship since he misspells her name in addressing her.

5. Pollak, *The Anxiety of Gender*, p. 101.

6. When first meeting Higginson, Dickinson similarly insisted on her silence. "I never see strangers," she claimed "& hardly know what I say—but," he adds, "she talked soon & thenceforward continuously. . . . I never was with anyone who drained my nerve power so much. Without touching her, she drew from me. I am glad not to live near her" (L, 473, 476). One suspects the Master, whoever he was, felt much the same way. See also Bianchi's descriptions of her aunt's verbal abilities in *Face to Face*. Contemplating Dickinson's acuity, one can truly sympathize with her nephew Ned Dickinson's desire to have "a quiet, pleasant little house somewhere. . . . No fame, no brains, no family, no scholarship, *No anything* amounts to anything beside that. . . ." As quoted by Leyda, *Years and Hours*, vol. 2, p. 143.

7. Gilbert and Gubar cite a letter by Charlotte Brontë, presumably to Constantin Huger, in which the English novelist appears to take something of the same attitude of self-abasement toward the "larger-than-life male Other": "Believe me, *mon maitre*, in writing to me it is a good deed that you will do. So long as I believe you are pleased with me, so long as I have hope of receiving news from you, I can be at rest and not too sad. But when a prolonged and gloomy silence seems to threaten me with the estrangement of my master . . . then fever claims me—I lose appetite and sleep—I pine away." As the feminist critics observe, when compared to Dickinson, Brontë's style in her own words is "unromantic as Monday morning" but the posture of dependence remains the same. *Madwoman*, pp. 604–5.

8. With differing emphases and quite different results, the marriage or bridal poems have been treated as a group by Charles R. Anderson, *Emily Dickinson's Poetry: Stairway of Surprise* (New York: Holt, Rinehart and Winston, 1960), pp. 178–90, Schurr, *Marriage*, pp. 10–42, and Pollak, *The Anxiety of Gender*, pp. 157–59, among others. Although she does not develop her argument in depth, Wendy Martin (*American Triptych*, pp. 103–4) comes closest to my own hypothesis when she suggests that the poems deal less with Dickinson's feelings for men and marriage than they do with her "commitment to poetry" and her "increasing autonomy." If the pre-1862 bridal poems are treated together with those she wrote from 1862 on, then the clarity of this interpretation is lost.

9. Gilbert and Gubar, *Madwoman*, p. 589.

10. In "Given in Marriage unto Thee," Dickinson describes herself as "Bride of the Father and the Son / Bride of the Holy Ghost" (no. 817; P, 618). This is also her most conventional, as well as religious, use of the bride figure. However, in the two poems in which she actually refers to herself as a nun ("Sweet Mountains—Yet tell Me no lie" [no. 722; P, 553] and

"Only a Shrine, but Mine")—it is, interestingly enough, to a maternal deity, the Madonna, that this "wayward nun" of Presbyterian Amherst prays.

Only a Shrine, but Mine—
I made the Taper shine—
Madonna dim, to whom all Feet may come,
Regard a Nun—

(no. 918; P, 672)

11. Franklin (MS, 199) places this poem in Fascicle 11 (1861), which would make it a little early for the bridal group I am discussing. However, it seems to look two ways: on the one hand, the Master is seen as the prime mover behind the poet's experience of transcendence and as the ultimate reward of her martyrdom; on the other hand, the poet's own status within the poem is entirely autonomous ("Seven years of troth have taught thee / More than Wifehood ever may!"). It may, therefore, be a transition poem.

12. See Peter Blos, *On Adolescence: A Psychoanalytic Interpretation* (New York: The Free Press of Glencoe, 1962): ". . . conflicts are only partially resolved at the close of adolescence; but nonetheless a synthesis is achieved which proves to be highly individualistic and stable. One might say that certain conflictual complexes attain the rank of a leitmotiv by being rendered ego-syntonic. At any rate, it is my contention that this definitive ego synthesis at the close of adolescence incorporates unresolved (traumatic) remnants of early childhood, and that these dynamically active remnants in turn furnish an urgent and determined driving force (repetition compulsion) which becomes apparent in the conduct of life. These ego processes are subjectively felt as an awareness of a purposeful and meaningful existence" (p. 189). Succinctly, I am arguing that Dickinson was able to incorporate the unresolved conflicts of her childhood and adolescence into her new identity as "Queen of Calvary" or woman poet and thus achieve "an awareness of a purposeful and meaningful existence" and control over the "conduct of [her] life."

13. Pollak (*The Anxiety of Gender*, p. 133) has recently made the same point: "Relatively few of Dickinson's love poems are unmistakably inspired by a woman, but once the presence of even a small body of such poems is noted, we also note how many of her poems are addressed to a sexually indeterminate 'thee.'" Most critics, when treating her poems to women, have confined themselves to those in which the poet is explicit in her address. See Faderman, "Emily Dickinson's Homoerotic Poetry," pp. 19–27; Adalaide Morris, "'The Love of Thee—A Prism Be': Men and Women in the Love Poetry of Emily Dickinson," in Juhasz, *Feminist Critics*, pp. 98–113; and Margaret Homans, "'Oh, Vision of Language!': Dickinson's Poems of Love and Death," in *Feminist Critics*, pp. 114–33.

14. Both Faderman and Morris argue on stylistic grounds that there is a clear distinction between the poems Dickinson addressed to women and those she addressed to her male lover. While I would also recognize clear differences among Dickinson's early poems to women and men, by 1862 the differences between the poems had become, in my opinion, far less significant than the similarities. Whether Dickinson was deserted by a "Bird" or by a male-sun-God, the fact was she had been deserted, she was in pain, and from her pain came both her art and her identity.

15. The actual date of Susan's wedding was July 1, 1856, sufficient evidence unto itself that Dickinson, like other poets, used her life freely in her poetry when she chose.

16. As I have discussed in "The Language of Love," Dickinson employs this same imagery with extraordinary consistency from adolescence on whenever she describes herself in the posture of a forsaken lover. See her 1850 letter to Abiah Root: "Save me a *little* sheaf" (L, 99); and to Susan Gilbert in 1852: ". . . Susie, promise me again, and I will smile faintly—and take up my little cross again of sad—*sad* separation." (L, 176) Whether with a man or a

woman, whether at nineteen or thirty-one, love for Dickinson meant crucifixion. It was the cross she had to carry as well as the banquet on which she longed to dine.

17. Compare Dickinson's comment on Susan: "What depths of Domingo in that torrid Spirit!" (L, 791). Apparently Dickinson's feelings for Susan did not change much in nineteen years—if, that is, the poem is also about Sue.

18. Antony's "new heaven, new earth" itself represents a play on Revelation (Rev. 21:1: "I saw a new heaven and a new earth"). Compare Dickinson's comment to Susan: "Oh Matchless Earth—We underrate the chance to dwell in Thee" (L, 478), a line that sounds like it could come from Antony's mouth.

19. Volcanoes appear in seven poems: 175, 601, 754, 1146, 1677, 1705, 1748, as well as in the second Master letter.

20. Like a number of other Dickinson critics, Cody (*After Great Pain*) argues that after 1864 Dickinson's creative energies went into a sharp decline. Certainly it is true that her production rate went down (one is tempted to say, returned to a normal level); but the quality remained firm and much of her surplus energy appears to have gone into her letters which became increasingly "public." For example, she wrote to Mrs. James S. Cooper in 1885: "Nothing inclusive of a human Heart could be 'trivial.' That appalling Boon makes all things paltry but itself" (L, 863). Unhappily, Dickinson's late letters have yet to be treated as the prose masterpieces they are and, therefore, the trajectory of her career has yet to be fully appreciated.

21. This poem is among Dickinson's more cryptic efforts. In analyzing it, I make a sharp distinction between the two "Summers" of the first two stanzas and the two "Seasons" of the last two stanzas. The two summers are 1) the "real" summer, 2) marriage. The two seasons are 1) marriage ("the Summer of the Just"), 2) the poet's frosty "North." Whether I am right I do not know. Certainly the poem is susceptible to a wide variety of interpretations; but mine does fit both with the poem's internal logic and with what Dickinson has to say elsewhere using these same image patterns. I apologize to the reader for ending on so crabbed a note; but whatever the poem is saying, it is marvelous.

Chapter 4

1. "Notes on the Chronological Order of Sylvia Plath's Poems," in *The Art of Sylvia Plath: A Symposium,* ed. Charles Newman (Bloomington: University of Indiana Press, 1971), p. 188.

2. Box 2, MSS II; September 16, 1951; as quoted by Lynda K. Bundtzen, *Plath's Incarnations: Woman and the Creative Process* (Ann Arbor: The University of Michigan Press, 1983), pp. 66–67.

3. Judith Kroll has examined the influence of Graves on the poet's writing in *Chapters in a Mythology: The Poetry of Sylvia Plath* (New York: Harper and Row, 1976). To my knowledge, Lawrence's influence on Plath has yet to receive the attention it deserves.

4. Suzanne Juhasz, *Naked and Fiery Forms: Modern American Poetry by Women, A New Tradition* (New York: Harper and Row, 1976), p. 114.

5. Juhasz, *Naked and Fiery Forms,* p. 114.

6. This observation has been made by a number of different critics including Adrienne Rich (OWB, 230), and the editors of Plath's *Journals,* Ted Hughes and Frances McCullough (J, 265–66). Lynda Bundtzen has subjected the relationship to a lengthy Freudian discussion in *Plath's Incarnations,* pp. 57–65, 85–108; and Marjorie Perloff has analyzed its effect on the poet's writing style(s) in "Sylvia Plath's 'Sivvy' Poems: A Portrait of the Poet as Daughter," in *Sylvia Plath: New Views on the Poetry,* ed. Gary Lane (Baltimore: Johns Hopkins University press, 1979), pp. 155–78.

7. Betty Friedan, *The Feminine Mystique* (New York: Dell Publishing Co., 1970), p. 38.

8. Friedan, *The Feminine Mystique,* p. 37.

9. Peter Blos, *On Adolescence: A Psychoanalytic Interpretation* (New York: The Free Press of Glencoe, 1962), p. 167.

10. Friedan, *The Feminine Mystique,* p. 148.

11. Matina Horner, "Femininity and Successful Achievement: A Basic Inconsistency," in *Feminine Personality and Conflict* by Judith Bardwick et al. (Belmont, California: Brooks/Cole Publishing Co., 1970), p. 55. Since the original publication of her "fear of success" theory, Horner's material has been subject to massive criticism, most recently by Carol Gilligan in *In a Different Voice: Psychological Theory and Women's Development* (Cambridge, Mass.: Harvard University Press, 1982), pp. 14–15 and throughout. However, once Horner's observations have been qualified to indicate that it is the *consequences* of success that women fear when entering male-identified fields of endeavor, her conclusions maintain their validity. That is, fear of success remains a valid issue for women like Plath who "are" Ann and who, therefore, must pay the price society exacts from those who seek success in sexually deviant roles. See Michael Lewis and Marsha Weinraub, "Origins of Early Sex-Role Development," *Sex Roles* 5 (April 1979): 135–53. A further discussion of this issue will be found in the conclusion of this book.

12. Nancy Chodorow, *The Reproduction of Mothering: Psychoanalysis and the Sociology of Gender* (Berkeley: University of California Press, 1978), p. 178. Chodorow's contention is supported by Gilligan's research as well. See *In a Different Voice,* pp. 35–45. Where men are engaged by stories of competition and threatened by images of connectedness, women exhibit the reverse pathology in their response to TAT images. "The contrast between a self defined through separation and a self delineated through connection, between a self measured against an abstract ideal of perfection and a self assessed through particular activities of care" is fundamental not only to the way in which men and women perceive moral issues (Gilligan's subject) but also to the way in which they conduct their lives (*In a Different Voice,* p. 35). The result is a perpetuation of traditional familial roles.

13. Perloff, "Sylvia Plath's 'Sivvy' Poems," p. 157.

14. In her most recent and presumably final statement on her daughter, Aurelia Plath notes that Plath reorganizes biographical material in the final four stanzas of this poem, claiming her mother's childhood ballet lessons for herself and implying that she was forced to take piano lessons when, in fact, it was her own idea. See "Letter Written in the Actuality of Spring," *Ariel Ascending: Writings about Sylvia Plath,* ed. Paul Alexander (New York: Harper and Row, 1985), pp. 215–16. Such factual discrepancies in Plath's works do not, however, invalidate the affective truth of the poem any more than they invalidate the truths disclosed in her fictionalized account of her childhood and adolescence in *The Bell Jar.* Whether Mrs. Plath imposed on her daughter in a particular instance or not, all the evidence of Plath's writing supports the basic contention which "The Disquieting Muses" makes that in order to satisfy her mother's needs and to satisfy her own need to please her mother, Plath split herself in two.

15. Alice Miller, *For Your Own Good: Hidden Cruelty in Child-Rearing and the Roots of Violence,* tr. Hildegarde and Hunter Hannum (New York: Farrar, Straus, Giroux, 1983), pp. 257–58.

16. Perloff, "Sylvia Plath's 'Sivvy' Poems," p. 159.

17. In late 1958, Plath returned to therapy with Dr. Ruth Beuscher, her old therapist. The effect, according to her journal editors, was "extraordinary," allowing the poet to vent her hostility toward her mother and releasing Plath from the writer's block that had stymied her creativity for years. The pages containing material connected to these therapy sessions (J, 266–313) are the richest in the published journals and the most important for anyone wishing to study the convolutions of Plath's struggle to achieve authenticity in her writing. To Aurelia Plath's credit, she recognized their importance and gave permission for them to be published.

18. Nancy Hunter Steiner, *A Closer Look at Ariel: A Memory of Sylvia Plath* (New York: Popular Library, 1973), p. 112.

19. In "Letter" (p. 215) Aurelia Plath claims that the biographical material in "Ocean-1212-W" was also rearranged "for the sake of art" but she does not specify how, nor does it ultimately matter. Once again it is affective truth with which we are concerned.

20. Erik Erikson, *Identity: Youth and Crisis* (New York: W. W. Norton & Co., 1968), p. 283. In *The Reproduction of Mothering*, Nancy Chodorow argues that it is through motherhood and the reestablishment of a fusion relationship with their children that most women actually achieve this sense of wholeness. Marriage is less satisfactory as a means of completing adult identity for women because the husband's male need to affirm separation makes him ambivalent at best in intimate relationships and rarely satisfactory as a partner in fusion.

21. This is Edward Butscher's sobriquet for Plath in *Sylvia Plath: Method and Madness* (New York: Seabury Press, 1976), p. xi and throughout.

22. In one of those uncanny moments when art comes too close to life, John Greenleaf Whittier, in the poem "In School Days," attributes the following lines to a young girl who has just beaten out a boy in a spelling match:

> "I'm sorry that I spelt the word:
> I hate to go above you,
> Because,"—the brown eyes lower fell,—
> "Because, you see, I love you!"

The girl dies, presumably rejected, in the end. (*The Poetical Works of John Greenleaf Whittier* [Boston: Houghton Mifflin, 1892], p. 350).

Horner quotes these lines at the conclusion of "Femininity and Successful Achievement: a Basic Inconsistency," *Feminine Personality*, p. 72. Their applicability to Plath's situation hardly needs stressing.

Chapter 5

1. Butscher, *Method and Madness*, p. 342.
2. Steiner, *A Closer Look*, pp. 56–57.
3. Steiner, *A Closer Look*, p. 64.
4. Steiner, *A Closer Look*, p. 58.
5. Steiner, *A Closer Look*, p. 59.
6. Steiner, *A Closer Look*, p. 59.
7. Butscher, *Method and Madness*, p. 74.
8. Alice Miller, *The Drama of the Gifted Child (Prisoners of Childhood: How Narcissistic Parents Form and Deform the Emotional Lives of Their Talented Children)*, trans. Ruth Ward (New York: Basic Books, 1981), p. 14. The original title for Miller's book could stand for a succinct, one-sentence encapsulation of Sylvia Plath's life.
9. An individual who has developed an "as-if personality" or "false self," Miller writes, "fuses so completely with what he reveals that—until he comes to analysis—one could scarcely have guessed how much more there is to him. . . . He cannot develop and differentiate his 'true self,' because he is unable to live it. It remains in a 'state of noncommunication.' . . . Understandably, these patients complain of a sense of emptiness, futility, or homelessness, for the emptiness is real" (*Drama*, p. 12). It is precisely this kind of emptiness that Plath appears to be describing in the Smith journal entries.

Miller goes on to warn against viewing this conception of the "true self" (originally described by D. W. Winnicott) as "a fully developed self hidden behind the false self" (p.

21). The feelings that are suppressed are both inchoate and archaic—hence the patient's state of emptiness and depression. It is only through analysis that these deeply buried feelings can be released, precisely, one may note, as happened to Plath. (See, in particular, the comments made by Hughes and McCullough at the beginning of the section of Plath's *Journals* that treats her return to therapy with Dr. Ruth Beuscher in 1958 and the material that follows, J, 265–333.)

10. Plath saw her false self as her image and in part it was a conscious creation; but other aspects of her false self were not the result of deliberate construction. They were developed in response to her mother's needs. The image was, in effect, the social mask, corresponding to what a woman was supposed to be; the false self was a psychological mask. It meshed so well with the image because Aurelia Plath's notions of what her daughter should be meshed all too well with social definitions of what women were supposed to be. Both image and false self covered the vacuum within. What remains to be explored and cannot be discussed here is the extent to which women—and men—generally in our culture end up developing false selves in order to meet their parents' expectations that they will conform to the social image.

11. In *Plath's Incarnations*, Lynda Bundtzen treats the novel from somewhat the same perspective but gives most of her emphasis to a Freudian interpretation. See pp. 109–56.

12. Sandra Gilbert, "A Fine, White Flying Myth: The Life/Work of Sylvia Plath," in Gilbert and Gubar, *Shakespeare's Sisters*, p. 246.

13. Steiner, *A Closer Look*, p. 109.

14. Bundtzen, *Incarnations*, pp. 114–15. As Bundtzen observes, "the real sources for [Esther's] feelings of inadequacy remain submerged and inaccessible to [her] conscious mind." By the same token, I believe they were also still largely submerged and inaccessible to Plath when she wrote *The Bell Jar*, which makes a psychoanalytic reading of the novel treacherous at best.

15. Butscher, *Method and Madness*, p. 342.

16. Butscher, *Method and Madness*, p. 136.

17. Gilligan, *In a Different Voice*, p. 159. It is important to note that Gilligan, like Chodorow in *Reproduction*, makes no allowance for the atypical woman, the woman who, to quote Chodorow, does "*not* mother or want to mother," who, like Dickinson, is "not 'maternal' or nurturant" (p. 215). Equally disturbing, Gilligan also ignores the women who, like Plath, are torn between their competitive and nurturant needs and would like to have both. It is with the fate of these women that this book is largely concerned for it is from their ranks that the majority of our women artists come.

18. Given Plath's enormous need to satisfy parental expectations, and the "sensitivity," as Miller would say, of her "antennae," it is likely that she would have responded to the slightest sign of approval from Beuscher by creating the personality she believed her therapist considered healthy. This is not an unusual situation for analysands suffering from "as-if personality" disturbances. See Miller, *Drama*, pp. 22–24.

19. The same year in which Plath wrote this poem, 1956, she was reading D. H. Lawrence's *The Man Who Died* with Dorothea Krook at Cambridge. Her identification with Lawrence's depiction of female sexuality was complete: "Lawrence died in Vence, where I had my mystic vision with Sassoon; I was the woman who died, and I came in touch through Sassoon that spring [with] that flaming of life, that resolute fury of existence. All seemed shudderingly relevant; I read in a good deal; I have lived much of this" (J, 128). Compare also Plath's comments on Lawrence, in particular on *Lady Chatterly's Lover*, J, 196.

20. A. Alvarez, *The Savage God: A Study of Suicide* (New York: Pocket Books, 1972), p. 6.

21. "Introduction," *Ariel*, p. ix.

22. See LH, 198, 219; J, 125.

23. Margaret Dickie Uroff, *Sylvia Plath and Ted Hughes* (Urbana: University of Illinois Press, 1979), p. 169.

Chapter 6

1. Hughes, "Notes on the Chronological Order," *The Art of Sylvia Plath*, p. 193. Actually, Hughes and others following him use two dates: one marked by "Poem for a Birthday," written in 1959, her "first major poem" and the immediate result of her return to therapy in late 1958 (see J, 266); the other marked by "Tulips" and "In Plaster," written immediately after her miscarriage in March 1961.

2. Hughes, "Chronological Order," p. 193.

3. George Stade, "Introduction," to Steiner's *A Closer Look at Ariel*, p. 12.

4. Hughes, "Chronological Order," p. 194.

5. "The moon in Plath's poetry functions, more particularly, as her emblematic muse — her Moon-muse — which symbolizes the deepest source and inspiration of the poetic vision, the poet's vocation, her female biology, and her role and fate as protagonist in a tragic drama; and through the use of a lunar iconography, it gives concrete form to the particular spirit of the mythicized biography." Kroll, *Chapters in a Mythology*, p. 21.
Both Eileen Aird and Judith Kroll have discussed Plath's moon symbolism at length. See Eileen Aird, *Sylvia Plath: Her Life and Work* (New York: Harper and Row, 1973), pp. 101–11 and Kroll, *Chapters in a Mythology*, pp. 21–79 and throughout.

6. No reason is given, either by Hughes or Frances McCullough, for the exclusion of this material from their edition of the *Journals*. It must simply be noted as one of the many irritants present in Plath scholarship at this time. Hopefully someday all of Plath's writing that is still extant will be presented to the public in a rational and coherent manner.

7. Bundtzen, *Incarnations*, pp. 198–99.

8. "She is defiantly female like Godiva, but she assumes the masculine power of her horse. She is both the female 'furrow' of earth, ready to be sown with male seed, that 'splits and passes' and also 'the brown arc / Of the neck I cannot catch.'" Bundtzen, *Incarnations*, p. 255. I am indebted to Bundtzen for her reading of this very fine poem.

9. Gilbert, "A Fine, White Flying Myth" in *Shakespeare's Sisters*, p. 259.

10. Butscher, *Method and Madness*, p. 424, n. 4.

11. Plath's dilemma was of course exacerbated enormously by the fact that her mother had delivered a double message. To satisfy what appear to have been Aurelia Plath's highly conflicted demands, Sylvia on the one hand had to be a good girl, committed to attachment; on the other, she also had to be a writer. The good girl image was supported by society; but the writer was not. Indeed, to become a writer was a dangerous business for, as Dickinson found, it meant leading a selfish life and putting one's work before others. As Plath states specifically in her *Journals*, she was able to write seriously only when she stopped writing for her mother and started writing for herself. But in thus insisting on her autonomy, she was also cutting herself off from the safety mechanisms that allowed her to survive. There was, in effect, no way out for her, at least not in that time and place.

Chapter 7

1. Elly Bulkin, "An Interview with Adrienne Rich," *Conditions: One* (April 1977): 50.

2. Bulkin, "Interview," *Conditions: One*, p. 52.

3. Preface, *Contemporary Poetry in America*, ed. Robert Boyers (New York: Schocken Books, 1974), p. vii.

4. In the essay "Beginning Again," Jane Vanderbosch provides a brilliant analysis of the fundamental importance of the mother-daughter relationship to *Dream of a Common Language*. "In reversing Freud's Oedipal theory, Rich distinguishes between the known and the learned. The daughter 'knows' the mother's body as she knows her own. Yet, says the poet, she is trained to deny that knowledge; she learns to teach men lessons about what she is supposed to have forgotten." Much of *Dream*, Vanderbosch argues, is devoted to the recovery

or "re-vision" of the "forgotten" knowledge of the mother. See "Beginning Again," in *Reading Adrienne Rich: Reviews and Re-Visions, 1951–81,* ed. Jane Roberta Cooper (Ann Arbor: University of Michigan Press, 1984), p. 126.

5. *New York Times,* Friday, April 19, 1968, p. 47.

6. "Interview," *Island,* 3 (May 1966): 2.

7. In her *Journals,* Plath records a meeting with Rich at Harvard University in 1958: "Adrienne Cecile Rich: little, round and stumpy, all vibrant short black hair, great sparking black eyes and a tulip-red umbrella: honest, frank, forthright and even opinionated." Given that she viewed Rich as an "arch-rival" at this time, the description is unusually generous on Plath's part, and therefore one suspects unusually accurate as well (J, 217).

8. See Marianne Whelchel, "Mining the 'Earth-Deposits': Women's History in Adrienne Rich's Poetry," for an excellent discussion of the poem *in situ.* In Cooper, *Reading Adrienne Rich,* pp. 51–71.

9. Among Rich's establishment critics, Helen Vendler has articulated the case against the poet most effectively. See *Part of Nature, Part of Us: Modern American Poets* (Cambridge: Harvard University Press, 1980), pp. 237–62 and her review of *A Wild Patience Has Taken Me This Far,* "All too Real," *New York Review of Books* (December 17, 1981): 32–36. Vendler's dissatisfaction with the direction Rich's poetry has taken in recent years seems particularly painful because, as a brilliant young woman working in a virtually all-male field, Vendler originally identified with the poet so closely. See *Part of Nature,* p. 237.

10. Rich talks about her influences in the essay "When We Dead Awaken: Writing as Re-Vision" (OL, 39), and elsewhere. One of the principal goals of Rich's critical writing (which ranges from Ann Bradstreet to Judy Grahn) is clearly the establishment of a women's tradition in literature which will obviate the need for male models for young women poets in the future. For an invaluable bibliography of Rich's views and articles up to 1983 see Cooper, *Reading Adrienne Rich,* pp. 330–39.

11. William H. Pritchard, "Poetry Matters," *Hudson Review* 26 (Autumn 1973): 588. This review is a classic example of "masculinist" criticism.

12. See Tillie Olsen, "One Out of Twelve: Writers Who Are Women In Our Century," *Silences* (New York: Delta/Seymour Lawrence, 1978), pp. 22–46. Olsen arrived at her figure by counting the ratio of women to male writers in "twentieth-century literature courses, required reading lists, textbooks, quality anthologies, the year's best, the decade's best, the fifty years' best, consideration by critics or in current reviews" (*Silences,* p. 24).

13. David Kalstone, "Talking with Adrienne Rich," *Saturday Review: The Arts* (April 22, 1972): 57.

14. In "Split at the Root" Rich says that she married as a way of disconnecting from her family (NJG, 78). Probably both explanations are true.

15. Rich says of this poem, it "is a poem of reconnection with a part of myself I had felt I was losing—the active principle, the energetic imagination, the 'half-brother' whom I projected, as I had for many years, into the constellation Orion. It's no accident that the words 'cold and egotistical' appear in the poem and are applied to myself. . . . The choice" she concludes, "seemed to be between 'love' . . . and egotism" ("When We Dead Awaken," OL, 45–46).

It is worth noting that even as late as 1975, when she wrote her brilliantly suggestive essay on Dickinson, "Vesuvius at Home: The Power of Emily Dickinson," still the best piece of feminist criticism on Dickinson available (OL, 157–84), Rich identified the "active principle, the energetic imagination" of the woman artist with the male side of herself: her "animus." The alienation of the woman artist from her own power is nowhere more evident than in the need of both these superbly talented women to see their poetic gift as a form of masculine energy.

Chapter 8

1. "Poetry and Experience: Statement at a Poetry Reading (1964)," in *Adrienne Rich's Poetry: Texts of the Poems, The Poet On Her Work, Reviews and Criticism*, ed. Barbara Charlesworth Gelpi and Albert Gelpi (New York: W. W. Norton, 1975), p. 89.

2. Rich, "Poetry and Experience," p. 89.

3. *Island*, p. 4.

4. Rich, "Poetry and Experience," p. 89.

5. Adrienne Rich; The Poetics of Change," in Gelpi and Gelpi, *Adrienne Rich's Poetry*, pp. 130–48. Albert Gelpi calls Rich's statement at the 1964 poetry reading "one of the remarkable statements about contemporary poetry; it describes not just the direction she would increasingly explore but also the controlling impulse of most of the poetry now being written" (p. 138).

Of this same change in the direction of Rich's poetry occurring after her marriage, David Kalstone writes: "With *Snapshots*, Rich began dating each of her poems by year, a way of limiting their claims, of signalling they spoke only for their moment. The poems were seen as instruments of passage, of self-scrutiny, and resolve in the present." David Kalstone, *Five Temperaments: Elizabeth Bishop, Robert Lowell, James Merrill, Adrienne Rich, and John Ashberry* (New York: Oxford University Press, 1977), p. 148.

6. In a gloss to this poem provided in *Adrienne Rich's Poetry*, Rich notes that "I let the young man speak for me" (p. 16).

7. See Rich's comment in "When We Dead Awaken" (OL, 45): "I hadn't found the courage yet to do without authorities, or even to use the pronoun 'I' —the woman in the poem is always 'she.'"

8. Plath makes this same point in "Lesbos" (CP, 227–29), her most biting comment on woman-to-woman relationships in our society. Confined within their island-kitchen, a perverted Leslion, neither woman in the poem is able to meet the other's needs. Instead, like "whores" they have sold themselves to men. The result is not love and support in mutual difficulties, but hatred, jealousy, and the inability to "communicate" (CP, 227–29).

9. Glossed by Rich in the 1967 edition of *Snapshots of a Daughter-in-Law*: "c'est un helicoptère et c'est un oiseau" (*Le Deuxième Sexe*, vol. 2, p. 574).

10. *Island*, p. 5.

11. "Interview," *Conditions: One*, pp. 50–51.

12. "Interview," *Conditions: One*, p. 51.

13. See Robert Boyers, "On Adrienne Rich: Intelligence and Will," in Gelpi and Gelpi, *Adrienne Rich's Poetry*, pp. 148–60. Boyers mourns Rich's loss to "propaganda" and to such "parochial" concerns as "what it means to be a man, what it means to be a woman" (Rich's phrasing, p. 154).

14. This same point is made by Kalstone, *Five Temperaments*, p. 160. Kalstone sees the poem as a "turning point." After "Shooting Script," he argues, there is "a remarkable shift of emphasis in the sequence. Rich turns away from . . . 'the temptations of the projector' with its images of pain from the past. . . . She begins to look at the historical misunderstandings behind battered sexual relationships, the long record of conflicts between men and women." I would agree; but I would also emphasize that the poem itself led nowhere. Rich had to make a radical and unrelated shift in direction to be able to write again.

15. "I know that I could not have gone on writing without a feminist movement, a community to support what I felt were my own intuitions" ("Interview," *Conditions: One*, p. 52). It's tempting to wonder how many women writers could now say that.

16. *New York Times*, October 20, 1970, p. 48.

Chapter 9

1. "Planetarium" appeared in *Aphra*, vol. 1, no. 4 (Autumn 1970), a feminist literary magazine of the early seventies.

2. Vendler, "All too Real," p. 35.

3. "Two Sisters in Poetry," *New York Times*, August 25, 1973, p. 21.

4. *Christopher Street* (January 1977): 14.

5. The phrase is Joyce Greenberg's. See "By Woman Taught," *Parnassus: Poetry in Review* 7 (Spring/Summer 1979): 91. Greenberg studied under Rich at Douglass College in 1976 and this article deals with her feelings about Rich as a teacher as well as a poet. It throws an interesting and unusual light on Rich, particularly on her need for privacy, which Greenberg clearly found frustrating and confusing in light of the increasingly self-revelatory elements in Rich's poetry. Rich does not and never has viewed herself as a confessional poet. However, she does use her poetry, as she explained in a 1971 interview, for self-exploration. See Stanley Plumly, Wayne Dodd, and Walter Tevis, "Talking with Adrienne Rich," *Ohio Review* 13 (1971): 30.

6. Karen Whitehill, "'A Whole New Poetry'"; review of *Dream of a Common Language*, *Virginia Quarterly Review* 55 (Summer 1979): 563.

7. In the *Conditions* interview, Rich strenuously attacks the concept of androgyny, calling it a "useless term." She says that it is "associated with the idea of 'liberating' men, giving males the desirable attributes that females have had without having to pay the dues" (*Conditions: One*, p. 62). Carolyn Heilbrun launches a spirited defense of the concept, if not the term, in "Androgyny and the Psychology of Sex Differences," in *The Future of Difference*, ed. Hester Eisenstein and Alice Jardine (New Brunswick, N.J.: Rutgers University Press, 1985), pp. 258–66. Although I appreciate Rich's concern, my sympathies are with Heilbrun. Rich is discarding one of her most impressive poems. It's not words themselves but how they are used and for what purpose that matters.

8. As quoted in Martin, *An American Triptych*, pp. 170–71.

9. "An Interview with Adrienne Rich," *Conditions: Two* (October 1977): 58. This is actually the second part of the interview that begins in *Conditions: One*. The material was split in two.

10. I am indebted to Gertrude Reif Hughes's excellent reading of this poem in "'Imagining the Existence of Something Uncreated': Elements of Emerson in Adrienne Rich's *Dream of a Common Language*," in Cooper, *Reading Adrienne Rich*, pp. 155–59.

11. "Interview," *Conditions: Two*, pp. 53–54. Rich recounts the same scene in her introduction to Grahn's poetry, "Power and Danger: Works of a Common Woman," reprinted in *Of Lies*, pp. 247–58. Three months later she published "From an Old House in America" in *Amazon Quarterly*, thus announcing publicly, as it were, the change in her sexual orientation. See *Amazon Quarterly* 2 (March 1974): pp. 38–48.

12. *The Work of a Common Woman: The Collected Poetry of Judy Grahn, 1964–1977* (New York: St. Martin's Press, 1978), pp. 130–31.

13. The phrase is the Gelpis', "Introduction," *Adrienne Rich's Poetry*, p. xi.

14. In *Of Woman Born* (p. 223) Rich notes that she has been permanently disabled by arthritis since she was twenty-two. In recent years she has used her debilitating condition as a symbol for her cultural and personal situation. See, for example, "Transit" and "Particularity" in *A Wild Patience*.

15. Vendler, "All too Real," p. 35.

16. Greenberg, "By Woman Taught," p. 99: "Adrienne's emphasis on an unedited female voice also troubles me. Last week, she said sarcastically, when we were discussing Gertrude Stein and Amy Lowell, 'Male critics expect women to be lapidary.' Before this course, I had always thought of poetry as distillation. She is encouraging me to include all the complexities, the imperfections, the confusions; she wants me to write in long loose lines as she is

doing in her newest poems. I find it difficult" (pp. 88–89).

17. Greenberg, "By Woman Taught," p. 103.

18. Perhaps most interesting, in one of her very recent poems, "North American Time" (1983), published in *Fact of a Doorframe*, Rich examines the whole question of political correctness and the effect it is having on her work:

> When my dreams showed signs
> of becoming
> politically correct
> no annily images
> escaping beyond borders
> when walking in the street I found my
> themes cut out for me
> knew what I would not report
> for fear of enemies usage
> then I began to wonder
>
> (FD, 324)

While as poetry these lines seem weak, one can only admire the poet's courage and honesty in posing the question at all. Poetry clearly remains Rich's principal means of working through the personal and cultural issues that confront her.

19. Alicia Ostrika, "Her Cargo: Adrienne Rich and the *Common Language*," *American Poetry Review* 8 (July/August 1979): 7.

20. My phrasing is drawn from Nancy Milford's "Messages From No Man's Land"; review of *A Wild Patience*, *New York Times Book Review*, December 20, 1981, p. 7.

Conclusion

1. Simone De Beauvoir, *The Second Sex*, tr. and ed. H. M. Parshley (New York: Vintage Books, 1974), p. 787.

2. Rich actually rejected the award as an individual. Her statement, which was written with Alice Walker and Audre Lorde, together with two other nominees, reads in part: "We . . . accept this award in the name of all the women whose voices have gone and still go unheard in a patriarchal world, and in the name of those who, like us, have been tolerated as token women in this culture, often at great cost and in great pain." See *Adrienne Rich's Poetry*, ed. Barbara Charlesworth Gelpi and Albert Gelpi, p. 204.

3. June Jordan, "Preface: For the Sake of the People's Poetry: Walt Whitman and the Rest of Us," *Passion: New Poems, 1977–1980* (Boston: Beacon Press, 1980), pp. x–xi.

4. Maxine Kumin, "How It Was: Maxine Kumin on Anne Sexton," in Anne Sexton, *The Complete Poems* (Boston: Houghton Mifflin, 1981), p. xxxiii.

5. Alicia Ostriker, *Writing Like a Woman* (Ann Arbor: The University of Michigan Press, 1983), pp. 43–44. The great popularity of Plath's poetry is often attributed to the fact that "she did it," but had the poetry itself not been so forceful, it is doubtful that Plath's suicide alone would have been enough to carry it.

Plath's continuing appeal to undergraduate women readers is discussed by Susan Lanser in "Beyond *The Bell Jar*: Women Students of the 1970s," *The Radical Teacher: Special Issue on Women's Studies in the 70s, Moving Forward* (December 1977): pp. 41–44. This appeal is in my opinion one of the most important aspects of the Plath phenomenon.

6. Erica Jong, "Blood and Guts: The Tricky Problem of Being a Woman Writer in the Late Twentieth Century," in *The Writer on Her Work*, pp. 171–72.

7. Gilligan, *In a Different Voice*, p. 38.

8. May Sarton, "The Muse as Medusa," *Collected Poems 1930–1973* (New York: W. W. Norton, 1974), p. 332. See Annis Pratt, "Aunt Jennifer's Tigers: Notes Toward a Preliterary History of Women's Archetypes," *Feminist Studies* 4 (February 1978): pp. 164–71. Although my emphasis is very different, I am indebted to Pratt's discussion of the Medusa archetype in this essay and in her unpublished paper on the origins of the Medusa myth, "'The Other Side of a Mirror': The Medusa Image as Feminist Heritage," for bringing feminists' special interest in the gorgon to my attention.

The use of Medusa by women poets has also been studied fruitfully within the context of the mother-daughter relationship by Karen Elias-Button, "The Muse as Medusa," in *The Lost Tradition: Mothers and Daughters in Literature*, ed. Cathy N. Davidson and E. M. Broner, (New York: Frederick Ungar Publishing Co., 1980), pp. 193–206.

9. Louise Bogan, *The Blue Estuaries: Poems 1923–1968* (New York: The Ecco Press, 1977), p. 4.

10. See Gilbert and Gubar, *Shakespeare's Sisters*, pp. xxii–xxiii. The strength of Bogan's distaste for "female songbirds," so evident in the letter to John Hall Wheelock, her editor, which Gilbert and Gubar quote here, suggests a reaction formation against her own womanhood.

Bogan's small production is discussed by Gloria Bowles in "Louise Bogan: To Be (or not to Be?) a Woman Poet," *Women's Studies: An Interdisciplinary Journal* 5, no. 2 (1977), pp. 131–35. Mary DeShazer takes a more positive view of Bogan's silence, describing it as a female poetic strategy in "'My Scourge, My Sister': Louise Bogan's Muse," in *Coming to Light: American Women Poets in the Twentieth Century*, ed. Diane Wood Middlebrook and Marilyn Yalom (Ann Arbor: University of Michigan Press, 1985), pp. 92–104. As Marilyn Hacker noted to me in private correspondence, Bogan's later poem on a gorgonesque figure, "The Sleeping Fury," presents her relationship to the muse in a more active and positive light; but the fact that the fury is *asleep* at the end of this poem—that is, locked inside the poet's unconscious—suggests to me that the poet was still not ready to come fully to terms with her.

11. Karen Lindsey, *Falling Off the Roof* (Cambridge, Mass.: Alice James Books, 1975), p. 22. Apropos Jong's comment, the cover of Lindsey's book depicts a woman menstruating—with "witch" images (black cats, etc.) emanating from her vagina along with her menstrual flow.

12. Audre Lorde, *Sister Outsider: Essays and Speeches* (Trumansburg, N.Y.: The Crossing Press, 1984), p. 101.

13. Rachel Blau DuPlessis, "Medusa," in *Wells* (New York: The Montemora Foundation, Inc., 1980), unpaginated.

14. DuPlessis, "Medusa," in *Wells*. In personal correspondence, DuPlessis communicated to me that her primary concern in this poem was with language. Regarding the problem of male ownership of Medusa's being, Jane Harrison in *Prolegomena to the Study of the Greek Religion* noted as early as 1912 that we know Medusa largely as a head, that is, as the victim of male appropriation.

15. In "'Nice Girl': Social Control of Women through a Value Construct," *Signs* 2 (Summer 1977): 805–17, Greer Litton Fox examines this phenomenon while analyzing the social and psychological consequences for women of what she calls the "'nice girl' construct."

In "Who is Sylvia? On the Loss of Sexual Paradigms," in *Women: Sex and Sexuality*, ed. Catharine R. Stimpson and Ethel Spector Person (Chicago: University of Chicago Press, 1980), pp. 4–20, Elizabeth Janeway comes at the same point in a different way when she notes that "female a priori knowledge . . . cannot be taken as valid by the female self who is required by the laws of otherness to live as a displaced person not only in man's world but also within herself" (p. 6).

The point both authors are making is that women are alienated from their own intuitions by the social constructs that help define them. While this point tends to gloss over the extent to which the stereotype *does fit* women's intuitive apprehension of themselves—a subject I treat at the end of this section—it still needs to be made again and again since it is the principal reason women require the support of movements like the women's movement (i.e., outside validation) to make basic changes in themselves.

16. Lindsey, "visions i-Gorgon," *Falling*, p. 25.

17. Lorde, *Sister*, p. 102.

18. Chirlane McCray, "I Used to Think," in *Home Girls: A Black Feminist Anthology*, ed. Barbara Smith (New York: Kitchen Table: Women of Color Press, 1983), pp. 57, 58–59.

19. Woolf, "Professions for Women," in *The Death of the Moth*, (London: The Hogarth Press, 1942), p. 151.

20. Michelle Cliff, "Anonymity and the Denial of the Self," *Sinister Wisdom* 9 (Spring 1979): 70.

21. Denise Levertov, "In Mind," *Poems: 1960–1967* (New York: New Directions, 1967), p. 143.

22. I have tried to provide a fairly wide sample of this kind of poem here, but to prove my point it would be necessary to take the reader through what might seem like an endless series of volumes from anthologies such as *No More Masks* (1973) to single volumes such as Robin Morgan's *Monster* (1972) to more recent work, particularly by ethnic writers, such as Nelly Wong, Cheryl Clarke, Joy Harjo, Paula Gunn Allen, and Toi Derricotte. The title of Michelle Cliff's prose-poem on her Jamaican heritage, *Claiming an Identity They Taught Me to Despise* (1980), encapsulates the themes of this poetry and applies to all these poets whether they are Black, Asian, Native American, lesbian, working class, or, like Morgan, in *Monster*, simply mothers.

23. Jean Tepperman, "Witch," in *No More Masks: An Anthology of Poems by Women*, ed. Florence Howe and Ellen Bass (New York: The Anchor Press, 1973), pp. 333–34. In the introduction to *No More Masks*, Howe writes about this poem: "Young poets today have transformed the Medusa or the storm heads of Plath into 'witches.' . . . They are not frightened by their own impulses, to poetry, to the mountains and forests to sensuality, perhaps because these impulses no longer place them in hidden, painful, and self-destructive conflicts with a male world. Instead, the 'wild and holy' witches of the seventies are part of a social movement that validates their existence, even their art" (p. 32). Although written in 1972, Howe's essay remains one of the most stimulating short descriptions of the recent development of twentieth-century American women's poetry to date. Both her essay and the organization of *No More Masks* have had a substantial influence on my thinking.

24. Audre Lorde, "125th Street and Abomey," in *The Black Unicorn* (New York: W. W. Norton, 1978), pp. 12–13.

25. Colleen McElroy, "Woman's Song," in *Black Sister: Poetry by Black American Women, 1746–1980*, edited with an introduction by Erlene Stetson (Bloomington: Indiana University Press, 1981), pp. 291, 293.

26. Judy Grahn, "I am the wall at the lip of the water," in *The Work of a Common Woman*, p. 98.

27. Chrystos, "Give Me Back," in *This Bridge Called My Back: Writings by Radical Women of Color*, ed. Cherríe Moraga and Gloria Anzaldúa (Watertown, Mass.: Persephone Press, 1981), p. 197.

28. Mary J. Carruthers makes this interesting point in an article on four major lesbian-feminist poets: "The Re-Vision of the Muse: Adrienne Rich, Audre Lorde, Judy Grahn, Olga Broumas," *Hudson Review* 36 (Summer 1983): 293–322.

29. Diane Wakoski, *Toward a New Poetry* (Ann Arbor: University of Michigan, 1980), p. 320. During the interview with Diane Wakoski from which this quotation comes, Andrea Musher refers to a poster of Wakoski holding a revolver pointed at the camera which

the poet used to advertise a reading she gave at Cornell in 1968. Musher was so frightened by the poster she did not attend the reading; but she goes on to admit that what she was really frightened of was the anger she was suppressing in herself (pp. 318–21).

30. Jane Marcus, "Art and Anger," *Feminist Studies* 4 (February 1978): 94.

31. Marcus, "Art and Anger," p. 71.

32. A profound and on occasion acrimonious split has developed in the field of women's studies over this issue. In the United States this split has crystalized over the issue of "women's culture"; in France, over the issue of "féminité." Advocates of women's culture and *féminité* tend toward essentialist definitions of womanhood based on women's past performance in culture. In her well-known essay "The Laugh of the Medusa," in *Signs* (Summer 1976), Hélène Cixous declares, for example, that "in women there is always more or less of the mother who makes everything all right, who nourishes, and who stands up against separation" (p. 882), a passage that can only remind one of that marvelous moment in "Professions for Women," when Woolf's Angel takes the chicken leg and sits in the draught. Those opposing the restoration of the Angel argue, on the other hand, that "there is nothing liberatory . . . in women's claiming as virtues qualities that men have always found convenient. How does maternal tenderness or undemanding empathy threaten a Master? The liberating stance is, rather, the determination to analyze and put an end to the patriarchal structures that have produced those qualities without reference to the needs of women." See Ann Rosalind Jones, "Writing the Body: Toward an Understanding of *l'Écriture féminine*," in *The New Feminist Criticism*, ed. Showalter, p. 371.

Prominently featuring the writing of Monique Wittig, the classic locus for French criticism of the French position is available in *Feminist Issues* 1, no. 1 (Summer 1980). Americans work out their issues most recently in *The (M)other Tongue: Essays in Feminist Psychoanalytic Interpretation*, ed. Shirley Nelson Garner, Claire Kahane, and Madelon Sprengnether (Ithaca: Cornell University Press, 1985), and in the essays reprinted in the Showalter volume.

33. Gilligan, *In a Different Voice*, pp. 151–74, and Jean Baker Miller, *Toward a New Psychology of Women* (Boston: Beacon Press, 1976), pp. 83–97. In attempting to rectify what she sees as an imbalance in the direction of "separation" rather than "attachment" as the basis for maturation, Gilligan, in particular, leans too far in the other direction. Dismissing "the concept of the separate self and of moral principles uncompromised by the constraints of reality" as an "adolescent ideal" (p. 98), she equates the concept of separation with the imagery of violence and confrontation which permeates male adolescent responses to intimacy in the thematic apperception tests. At the same time, she underplays the negative side of the adolescent girl's corresponding terror of isolation and achievement (pp. 40–41). Like Jean Baker Miller, Gilligan tends to depict both women and men in stereotypical black and white terms: men are incapable of intimacy, women are healing and nurturing; men bring war, women peace. Not only do such one-sided presentations ignore the importance of separation and a drive for achievement if women are indeed to change the world as Miller and Gilligan want; but they also ignore the way in which suppressed anger in women tends to be channeled into less overt forms of destructive behavior. Since women are afraid to—or are unable to— use the energy that anger generates in the service of self-assertion, they tend to use it manipulatively instead, particularly in their domain: intimacy. This is good for neither sex. For more balanced views of this issue, see Dorothy Dinnerstein, *The Mermaid and The Minotaur: Sexual Arrangements and Human Malaise* (New York: Harper Colophon Books, 1976); Luise Eichenbaum and Susie Orbach, *Understanding Women: A Feminist Psychoanalytic Approach* (New York: Basic Books, 1982); and Chodorow, *The Reproduction of Mothering*. The dangers of suppressing anger are discussed at great length by Alice Miller in *For Your Own Good*. I find Miller's treatment of the parental issues involved particularly impressive.

34. Chodorow, *The Reproduction of Mothering*, pp. 211–19. The warnings and recommenda-

tions contained in this extraordinary afterword have generally been ignored by those theorists who have attempted to use Chodorow to support their own positions on the value of permeable ego boundaries for the development of empathy.

35. Gilligan, *In a Different Voice*, p. 73.

36. Miller, *Toward a New Psychology*, p. 86.

37. Gilligan, *In a Different Voice*, p. 23.

38. Gilligan, *In a Different Voice*, p. 171.

39. Chodorow, *The Reproduction of Mothering*, p. 165. See also pp. 173–90 for Chodorow's discussion of the social consequences of this form of gender identity development.

40. In reprinting this open le ("It is the Lesbian in Us . . . ") in *Of Lies*, Rich felt moved to include a long explanatory note describing the reaction from the floor to her statement that it was "the Lesbian in us who is creative, for the dutiful daughter of the fathers in us is only a hack" (OL, 201–2). I am quoting out of context from that note. Rich would have us say no to the fathers, I would have us say no to the mothers as well. Indeed, I think Rich spoke here far more accurately than she herself appreciates both about her own situation as a creative artist and about the situation of creative women generally. Insofar as the lesbian stands figuratively for the self-authorized woman, the woman who is autonomous, and not identified with the mother, she stands for the creative side of the self. I would also add however that there is to my knowledge no evidence yet that lesbians in real life are less prone to problems with attachment and mother-bonding than other women even though their sexual orientation clearly sets them apart and may make it easier for them to function as artists, i.e., endure isolation, the sense of opprobrium, and so forth.

41. Gilligan, *In a Different Voice*, p. 157. Gilligan's discussion of the differences between Joyce's and Mary McCarthy's orientations as writers is particularly interesting since it highlights so well her avoidance of the difficulties that the "ethic of caring" creates for the would-be woman writer (see pp. 156–58) as well as the negative consequences involved in women's failure to establish the kind of separation that, in Gilligan's own phrasing, "defines and empowers the self" (p. 156). Disempowered women are rendered ineffective as creators and, ironically, ineffective as moral agents as well, however "caring" they might be.

42. See Chodorow, *The Reproduction of Mothering*, pp. 108–10, 125–29, 164–70, and Gilligan, *In a Different Voice*, pp. 7–17.

43. Chodorow, *The Reproduction of Mothering*, p. 167.

44. Chodorow, *The Reproduction of Mothering*, p. 169.

45. Chodorow, *The Reproduction of Mothering*, pp. 204–15.

46. This is the essential theme of Miller's two books, *The Drama of the Gifted Child* and *For Your Own Good*. I want to thank Donna O'Connell Blatt and Michael DeSisto for helping me work these ideas through.

47. I would like to credit Kate Dunn of Crossing Press with this observation made to me in conversation.

48. This is also the theme of Cheryl Walker's *The Nightingale's Burden* (see Chapter 1, note 1). Perhaps the shift in women's poetry can be best summarized by the fact that where women poets traditionally saw their grief figured in the story of Philomela, the victim-nightingale, they are now taking Medusa as their muse.

Index

* MY— writing always follows the visual
arts it is behind because it takes longer
to write then it does to paint

    Joyce — Ulysses

    Benett — picasso

Benett disagrees with previous
    1) reveal avant previous research
    2) present new thesis
    3) look to convey self other dialectic
    writing another persons autobiography

Benett
    — theme of brother (overt) —rage (overt)

* my— like Einstein/hawking is secure in her
    intellect and does not need to prove herself
    with high diction

— subtext in footnotes to avoid targets
    footnotes are more speculative, allow to
    question some of decisions
        (278 — 12,14)   280 ((0)

—her theses could also be applied to men
but she purposely leaves out relevant material

* my — should have realized that women have such a part of culture that is already been hardwired into ALL of us

* my — relate to rollo may's search for a more accurate thesis

— her thesis most of introduction
— our opinion forms her voice
— also to familiarize reader with writings
— Barnett (10) - "people not angels create art" "only what their lives enable them to say"

├ is there revelation of deeper in music
├ this is (just biography (less deep)
   create (reality / feeling of time to give
      historical perspective   mansion
— reluctant / afraid to question persona

THESIS — was a god, music about life, looked only for material

up to pg 165
father (6)   (22) brother absent, mother nag
(34) asked him to move out   (136) mother — concert
reflect his persona, rejection of parents

the usefulness of rage
what does it tell us
   itself as a text

all (non-white, non-male, etc.) had something
to do with the body
      female — menstruation — lactation

our culture mind/body split

Rollo May   poet writes out of rage (28-29)

Bennett — rage to do with silencing, don't
     fear death   cannot speak (live)

Rollo May   (6) — need physical carnage
             (11) — two different fears, of life and death

Bennett — society wants you to go counter clockwise

rage
   counter- ——→ independence ⤸
   dependency   interdependence
   (NO) ⬅ dependency ⤸ danger of returning